EVERYDAY FASHIONS, 1909-1920

As Pictured in Sears Catalogs

Edited and with an Introduction by

JOANNE OLIAN

Curator Emeritus, Costume Collection
Museum of the City of New York

Dover Publications, Inc.
New York

Copyright

Published in Canada by General Publishing Company, Ltd., 30 Lesmill Road, Don Mills, Toronto, Ontario.
Published in the United Kingdom by Constable and Company, Ltd., 3 The Lanchesters, 162–164 Fulham Palace Road, London W6 9ER.

Bibliographical Note

Everyday Fashions, 1909–1920, as Pictured in Sears Catalogs is a new work, first published by Dover Publications, Inc., in 1995.

Library of Congress Cataloging-in-Publication Data

Everyday fashions, 1909–1920, as pictured in Sears catalogs / edited and with an introduction by JoAnne Olian.
p. cm.
ISBN 0-486-28628-2 (pbk.)
1. Costume—United States—History—20th century. 2. Fashion—United States—History—20th century. 3. Sears, Roebuck and Company—Catalogs. I. Olian, JoAnne.
GT615.E89 1995
391′.00973′09041—dc20 95-10568
CIP

Manufactured in the United States of America
Dover Publications, Inc., 31 East 2nd Street, Mineola, N.Y. 11501

Introduction

"Goods suitable for the millionaire, at prices in reach of the millions." This 1887 advertising slogan summarizes the philosophy of American merchandising and explains why Americans, as a people, are the best-dressed in the world. Class differences in clothing are so subtle as to be perceptible only to the professional eye, for mass-production techniques have made it possible to create reasonable facsimiles of high-priced garments. In addition, nationwide distribution has tended to minimize regional differences. This lack of class and national distinction in American apparel has long been apparent to foreigners. In the 1840s the British consul in Boston complained that servant girls "when walking the streets, [were] scarcely to be distinguished from their employers." Sometime afterward, a Hungarian visitor, lamenting the absence of colorful peasant garb, noted that "no characteristical costumes mark here the different grades of society, which, in Eastern Europe, impress the foreigner at once with the varied occupations and habits of an old country."

Implicit in this homogeneity is the security afforded by protective coloration. Daniel Boorstin describes "consumption communities" connected by the similarity of what they consumed, instead of by common beliefs. Instead of prizing an object for its uniqueness, "If an object of the same design and brand was widely used by many others, this seemed an assurance of its value." He concludes, "Never before had so many men been united by so many things."

Small-town America, the model for the Main Street of Sinclair Lewis' 1920 novel, exemplified Boorstin's thesis, which Lewis termed the "philosophy of dull safety." Describing the fictional town of Gopher Prairie, Lewis wrote,

> Nine-tenths of the American towns are so alike that it is the completest boredom to wander from one to another. . . . The shops show the same standardized, nationally advertised wares; the newspapers of sections three thousand miles apart have the same "syndicated features"; the boy in Arkansas displays such a flamboyant ready-made suit as is found on just such a boy in Delaware, both of them iterate the same slang phrases from the same sporting-pages, and if one of them is in college and the other is a barber, no one may surmise which is which.

The wide distribution of the Sears, Roebuck catalog was largely responsible for the similarity of goods available nationwide. Helped by the establishment of Rural Free Delivery in 1902 and Parcel Post in 1913, mail-order volume increased dramatically. Opposition to a government parcel-post system by small-town merchants and private express companies such as Wells Fargo and American Express was countered by farsighted merchant John Wanamaker, Postmaster General from 1889 to 1893, who continued to press Congress for postal reform after he left office, testifying that it would "compel construction of roads for mail deliveries," encourage settlement of sparsely populated areas and lead to the "vaster circulation of goods" necessary for economic growth. Wanamaker's predictions were justified within a year of the introduction of Parcel Post, when 300 million packages were mailed. Mail order was also aided immeasurably by a fast-growing network of railroads crisscrossing the country, which accounted for one third of the total rail mileage of the world by 1910.

In the early years of the century nearly half of America's towns and cities, like Lewis' Gopher Prairie, had fewer than 10,000 inhabitants. Sixty percent of the population was rural, and as late as 1920 the farm population was about 32 million, the rural population even higher. Thanks to the mail-order houses, no farm was too isolated to be aware of the latest clothing, furniture, farm equipment, music and literature. The 1916 Sears catalog even offered complete plumbing kits, diagrams and instructions to enable "Mr. American Husband" to install running water by himself in his own home, also available in its entirety from Sears.

One of Wanamaker's arguments in favor of Rural Free Delivery was that the regular arrival of papers and magazines would keep the young from fleeing to the city and "add to their ambition and determination to make the old farm pay." His sentiments were corroborated by a congressman who maintained that R.F.D. would "destroy the isolation and loneliness of the country life and stop the constant and deplorable drift from country to town." So widespread was this disaffection that in 1908 President Roosevelt appointed a Commission on Country Life to find ways to retain the advantages of farm life while relieving its isolation.

While the mail-order catalog was the arbiter of fashion to small-town America, it provided welcome relief from the utter isolation that was the lot of immigrant farmers living on homesteads separated from each other by miles of unsettled areas on the Great Plains. The Homestead Law awarded land in quarter-sections, meaning that farms would be at most four to a square mile, and could be even farther apart if homesteads were larger or intervening tracts remained unoccupied. "These people came from cheery little farm villages. Life in the fatherland was hard and toilsome, but it was not lonesome," editorialized *Northwest Illustrated Monthly Magazine* in 1893. After discussing the depressing effect of the harsh climate, it added, "Neighborly calls are infrequent because of the long distances which separate the farmhouses, and because, too, of the lack of homogeneity of the people. They have no common past to talk about." Sears brought the world to these people. Edna Ferber, in her novel *Fanny Herself*, sent her heroine to work for Haynes-Cooper, a large Chicago mail-order house clearly based on Sears, noting the place of honor given the catalog in every farmhouse. "The Bible's in the parlor, but they keep the H. C. book in the kitchen where they live." The cheerful women on Sears's pages, garbed in calico housedresses, and their strong helpmates in sheepskin-lined mackinaws were as close as many farmers came to outside contacts during the long winter months.

For immigrants desirous of becoming Americans, the catalog was a primer. Here they learned how to dress, how to furnish their parlors and, when the bimonthly Sears grocery supplement arrived, replete with recipes and special menus for holiday dinners, how to cook American fare. Even frontier women tried to dress fashionably. In 1854 a feminist publication, the *Lily*, deplored the fact that women of all classes and in every part of the country, including the West, trimmed their clothing with "furbelows and flounces." There is a poignancy in such efforts, when virtually the only occasion to wear their Sunday best would have been for attending church or funerals, weather permitting.

Women continued to sew a large part of their wardrobes long after men were purchasing all their clothing ready-made. The greatest factor in the formation of the menswear industry was the Civil War, which created an unprecedented demand for uniforms. At its close, the call for civilian clothing to outfit returning soldiers was no less great. The need to outfit an army prompted the government to specify measurements to the manufacturers, which led to the standardization of sizes; and manufacturers, with the aid of constantly improving sewing machines, were able to produce garments to fit most of the male population. From 1860 to 1870 the value of manufactured men's clothing doubled but, as late as 1880, ready-to-wear still accounted for only half of the men's apparel purchased. However, by the turn of the century it would have been the exception not to be completely clothed in mass-produced garments. While women could buy little else besides undergarments in 1870, by 1910 every article of women's clothing could be purchased, ready-made, from catalogs as well as department stores in major cities catering to female shoppers. One of the earliest mass-produced garments for women was the shirtwaist, popularized by Charles Dana Gibson in the 1890s. Suitable for every occasion, depending on the material, and worn under a suit or with a skirt, it provided variety and possessed the added virtue of making wardrobes seem larger than they actually were, allowing women on tight budgets to have the thrill of something new to wear. A mainstay of the Sears catalog for nearly 25 years and an important factor in the democratization of fashion, the shirtwaist sold from 49 cents to $6.95 in 1914. So ubiquitous was this article of clothing that in 1910 production in New York City alone amounted to $60 million. Made in every fabric from cotton to silk, and often trimmed with laces and embroidery imported from Europe, the shirtwaist is a hallmark of American style. The infamous Triangle Shirtwaist Company fire of 1911, in which 146 garment workers lost their lives, attests to both the popularity of the shirtwaist and the abysmal conditions under which such garments were produced.

The years from 1909 to 1920 were marked by radical changes in American life. A complex decade, it began with the ebullient optimism of Theodore Roosevelt and ended with the somber introspection of Woodrow Wilson. While technology was rapidly improving the quality of life, labor unrest was prevalent and strikes of long duration hindered production. Nonetheless, the gross national product, $30.4 billion in 1910, more than doubled to $71.6 billion in 1920. The chief factor for change was World War I. The economy boomed during the war, and at its end America emerged as the predominant economic power in the world. While the United States did not enter the war until 1917, farm prices more than doubled between 1914 and 1918. In 1919 farmers received more than $14 million for agricultural products, which had risen in value faster and higher than all other commodities. Europe needed American farm and factory products, and this demand, coupled with several years of good harvests, led to new-found prosperity and created a consumer with such strong buying power that Sears had difficulty in satisfying its customers' demands. Even prior to the war, farmers were becoming more comfortable. By 1910, while "occasional sod houses were still to be seen on the prairies of Nebraska or the Dakotas, the typical farm now had its frame house and commodious barns, and the agricultural West, which for three decades had seethed with unrest, showed by its well-kept buildings, its new equipment and improved roads that a new era had come" (Emmet and Jeuck, *Catalogues & Counters,* 1965).

As farmers moved west of the Mississippi and prospered, growing crops for consumption in the East and abroad, additional markets were created for manufactured goods. Farms increased in size, leaving their occupants little time to make clothing and other necessities. With the onset of war, time for such activities was curtailed even further, as men entered the armed forces and women replaced them in the fields. In urban areas, women served as auto mechanics, telegraph messengers, elevator operators, streetcar conductors, traffic policemen and assembly-line workers. Eleven thousand women joined the Navy as yeoman clerks and stenos. The realization that it was not necessary to sew many of the articles they were accustomed to making at home created more customers for ready-made goods. Directly attributable to this change in buying habits was the demotion of piece goods for home sewing from its place of importance at the front of the Sears catalog, and its replacement with ready-made dresses. The appearance of sportswear, from riding and cycling outfits, gym bloomers and bathing suits for girls and women to golf and motorcycle costumes for men, reflected the growing prosperity.

During the war, the cities swelled with transplanted farm families working in factories, many of them European immigrants eager to become Americans. Advertising and installment buying, available to Sears customers, encouraged "keeping up with the Joneses." In the decade following Henry Ford's introduction of his Model T in 1908, ten million passenger cars were sold, changing American life and consumer patterns irrevocably. To capitalize on its customers' increased mobility, Sears augmented its catalog sales by opening retail stores, competing with such chains as J. C. Penney.

Sears had no pretensions to fashion leadership, attempting only to provide what its customers wanted, but its buyers realized that prosperity, better communication and mobility had changed clothing. Women wanted to dress more fashionably, and welcomed new styles. While fashion changed less drastically at lower price levels, it was still necessary to offer new apparel. Starting in mid-decade, higher-priced suits and dresses were featured in layouts reminiscent of *Vogue*, with little copy, chic accessories, bobbed hair and few outfits on a page, while less expensive, modified versions of the same styles were presented in the traditional Sears format. The Sears catalog of 1920 is infinitely more worldly than its predecessor of 1909. Not quite sophisticated enough, however, to command the $20 to $45 it wanted for a dress designed by Lady Duff-Gordon, who, as Lucile, was a household name and whose made-to-order recherché, custom-made creations for society women and celebrities were as familiar to the American public as the immensely popular dance team of Vernon and Irene Castle. In 1916, *Printer's Ink*, predicting a great success for this venture, wrote, "Romance and a sense of smartness are thus brought into the remotest homes that the Sears, Roebuck catalog reaches." Their optimism was greatly exaggerated, for Lucile's two collections for Sears—fall 1916 and spring 1917—in spite of the Lady Duff-Gordon label and models called "I'll Come Back to You" and "Miss Naïve," proved too understated for its customers, and resulted in a net loss of over $250,000 to the company.

The trendsetter of the era, Irene Castle, was employed with better results by Philipsborn's, a Chicago-based mail-order house, founded in 1890 and specializing in apparel similar in style and price to Sears. As their "style authority," her imprimatur was used successfully to sell dresses. Exhorting her readers to wear "better things," Mrs. Castle explained, "Good dressing gives grace, and poise and confidence. Good dressing attracts admiration. The well-dressed woman just naturally radiates happiness, and happiness, after all, is the one great thing that makes our lives worth while." Philipsborn's also claimed the honor of being the first mail-order house to receive the newest Paris styles by Wells Fargo Express Company aeroplane.

The Sears catalog, "America's Wish Book," is a social history of the nation, providing a pictorial view of attitudes and manners of ordinary Americans from 1895 to 1993 when the company, to the dismay of the entire country, ceased publication of the catalog. For almost 100 years the Big Book had furnished the panorama of American life. In 1911, having toured the Chicago headquarters of Sears, Roebuck & Company, Arnold Bennett noted in his journal,

> [The] most interesting thing was glimpses of real life of these outlying communities everywhere, as seen in ugly common simple stuff they ordered. Thousands of cheap violins. In one basket, ready for packing, all sorts of little cooking utensils and two mugs (fearfully ugly) labelled "father" and "mother." 4 cents curling iron. All the life (cheap music, chairs, etc.) of these communities could be deduced from this establishment.

Julius Rosenwald, who headed Sears during the war years, accompanied Secretary of War Newton D. Baker on a visit to Army hospitals in France. Taking with him wooden crates filled with Sears catalogs, he explained what they meant to a boy,

> thousands of miles from home . . . both sick and homesick. . . . He turns the pages. He sees the shotgun that right now is standing in his room back home in Illinois. He recalls the day when he killed a rabbit in the pasture or shot a lot of crows in the corn. A few pages farther on the boy runs into fishing tackle. From that second it is no longer cold, rainy weather in France, but warm springtime at home. He digs worms behind the barn, puts them in a can, and pretty soon he is pulling fish out of the creek as fast as he drops his line. In other words, the catalog helps our soldier boys to escape the miseries of war and live happily again, if only for a little while, amid the scenes of their childhood at home.

Perusing the pages of the catalog, we learn which pastimes were popular in farm parlors. Pillows with mottoes such as "The Dear Old Home I Can't Forget" and "Thoughts of You, Sweet and True" could be embroidered while listening to favorites like "There's a Long, Long Trail A-Winding," played on musical instruments from Sears or its own line of Silvertone phonographs, The perennial best-seller, excluding the Bible, was *Ben-Hur*, first published in 1880, and offered in 1915 for 68 cents in a "read the book—see the movie" edition. *Pollyanna*, *Seventeen*, *The Four Horsemen of the Apocalypse* and the novels of Zane Grey, Gene Stratton Porter and H. G. Wells were to be found in millions of American homes. Self-help books included *How to Obtain Citizenship*, *Ease in Conversation*, *Everyman's Lawyer* and *The Art of Taxidermy*, as well as Sears's own four-volume manual, *Farm Knowledge*, which had 2000 pages and 3000 illustrations. Sears also encouraged sending books "to help dispel the 'blues' from some lonesome and neglected soldier boy in camp or in the trenches." In 1920 a volume of official pictures of the World War, taken by the United States Signal Corps, was offered.

In many respects, what we think of as the twentieth century actually began about 1910. The movies, the automobile and the extension of the railroad accelerated the pace of change, as millions of Americans, utilizing new technology, began to experience the joys of leisure. The differences from the beginning of the decade to its end are astonishing. In 1919 a United States Navy seaplane crossed the Atlantic via the Azores, jazz bands were playing such favorites as "I'm Always Chasing Rainbows" for tea dancing; Charlie Chaplin, Theda Bara, Mary Pickford and Pearl White were the names most often on marquees; and, on November 2, 1920, radio station KDKA in East Pittsburgh broadcast the Harding–Cox election returns.

Nowhere is the contrast between 1909 and 1920 more marked than in fashion. The tall, stately, statuesque and generously proportioned Gibson Girl, in her shirtwaist or ballgown which showed off her magnificent bosom and shoulders, was supplanted by the lithe, slender young thing personified by Irene Castle, who bobbed her hair and tied a strip of velvet across her brow, inventing the "headache band." She exchanged corsets and petticoats for silk bloomers and a little slip to wear under her filmy "Castle frocks," and wore shiny black patent-leather pumps with ribbons crisscrossed over her ankles.

In 1909 women were still wearing the shirtwaist, Suits outnumbered dresses in the 1909 catalog. The suit had been a mainstay of daytime fashion since the latter years of the nineteenth century. In 1893 it was hailed by *Harper's Weekly*, which observed that the "evolution of sensible dress had kept pace with women's expanded participation in colleges, in the professions and in the work force." In 1898 *Vogue*, rather snobbishly taking credit for its role in "improving taste," remarked that "fitness has perhaps been the most noticeable effect on dress . . . the jacket and skirt model has attained a popularity never before accorded it and its general adoption has wrought an amazing transformation in the women and girls of the middle and lower classes with whom fitness and neatness have replaced ill-made tawdryness." In 1900 the *Ladies' Home Journal* recommended that the "business girl," who had to be prepared to go out in all kinds of weather, should make her first wardrobe consideration "the business suit."

Throughout the decade, suits remained an important part of fashion, following the prevailing silhouette. Since its customers were not in the forefront of fashion and less likely to accept radical change than their city counterparts, Sears introduced new styles slowly and cautiously. In addition, drastic changes would have rendered women's clothing obsolete, which they could not afford. *Vogue*'s description of the fashionable figure in May 1908, was still in advance of Sears in 1909: "The fashionable figure is growing straighter and straighter, less bust, less hips, more waist, and a wonderfully long, slender suppleness about the limbs . . . the long skirt reveals plainly every line and curve of the leg from hip to ankle. The leg has suddenly become fashionable!" Not in Gopher Prairie for another couple of years! In Sears, the corset was still short, molding the body into a mature S-shaped monobosom, the upper torso thrust out in front and the hips in back, separated by a well-defined waistline. Suit jackets ended at mid-calf, and skirts, often pleated, flared at the hem, which was floor-length for women and slightly shorter for misses. By 1912 the silhouette in Sears had become vertical, with no emphasis on the waist. Strictly tailored suits were relieved by shirtwaists, which, even when simple, were often of delicate materials such as lace or silk. Softness and draping appeared in 1913 in dressy clothes while the figure remained tubular, mature and solidly encased in corsets ending well below the hips.

Nineteen fourteen showed the marked influence of Irene Castle, Lucile and the reigning French couturier, Paul Poiret. Tunics, hobble skirts, harem-effect draping and lace standing collars were shown even for day. Jackets (some of which were short) and coats had raglan sleeves and cutaway hems. Shoes, usually high-topped, were now varied with the "Tango" pump making its debut in Sears (p. 48). In 1915 double or triple-tiered skirts widened at the hem and were shorter. The waistline was becoming more defined and blouses, no longer true shirtwaists, sometimes sported deep V-necks. Corsets remained long, rising barely above the waist, necessitating brassieres and bust confiners. Clothing continued to relax and loosen, creating an appearance of youth that was replacing the matronly rigidity of the earlier style. In 1917, the year of America's entry into the war, peg-topped skirts belted at the natural waist were high fashion and the vogue for bobbed hair à la Irene Castle spread across the United States and Great Britain.

The following year the waistline was more pronounced, low shoes, worn with black stockings, were visible under shorter skirts and a uniform-like sobriety governed suits and coats. In 1919 skirts tapered and lengthened. The silhouette was narrow and the general effect was one of slenderness and ease. The waistline was demarcated by soft belts and low-necked over-blouses, often collarless, were worn. The styles of 1920 were even more attenuated and willowy than those of 1919, and prints, pleated edgings, ruffles and fichus were the height of fashion.

Throughout the decade several trends prevailed, such as real or fake-fur coats and accessories for men, women and girls. The perennially popular nautical motif appeared in sailor dresses for girls, women and little boys, whose sailor suits shared equal billing with Russian, Norfolk and military styles. Women also opted for middies on informal occasions. Another favorite was the lingerie dress of cotton with elaborate broderie anglaise, tucks and lace. Petticoats and corset covers, also lavishly trimmed at the beginning of the decade, gave way to simple brassieres and chemises by its close. The military motif made its first appearance in 1915 in suits (p. 57), and even women's housedresses sometimes bore a strong resemblance to uniforms. Knitted sweater coats for men, women and children appeared in the catalog throughout the decade. Men's shirts relaxed, just as women's clothing had. The shirt with detached stiff collar yielded to a softer shirt with attached collar, formerly worn by laborers, now deemed appropriate for "negligee" and "outings." In summer men topped their lightweight two-piece Palm Beach suits with caps or straw hats. Working men, complained a merchant, were "no longer content with substantial low-priced goods, but demanded 'nifty' suits that looked like those everyone else buys and like they see in the movies." Women's hats, at the beginning of the decade so elaborate that they recalled the extravagance of eighteenth-century French court coiffures, became smaller and somewhat simpler until 1920, when their deep crowns presaged the flapper cloche of the new decade. During the entire period extreme headwear, with striking shapes and feathers protruding at perilous angles, was a hallmark of high fashion.

Sears dressed the entire family, from baby's layette to dignified millinery for elderly ladies. Dresses for mourning, weddings, maternity and large women appeared in every issue. Sunbonnets and sturdy housedresses shared space with party frocks. Boys, whose graduation from knickers to long trousers was heralded in an ad entitled "When Willie Becomes William," wore Sears's own Ucanttear brand clothing of sturdy blue serge or corduroy. Warm pajamas with booties and hats were available for the hardy who believed in the salutary effect of sleeping in the open air no matter what the mercury read. Sears literally provided all a family's material needs from cradle to grave, even selling tombstones and cenotaphs to honor the "soldier whose remains still rest in foreign lands."

The Big Book and its reputation for dependability were part of a time-honored American tradition reaching back to Benjamin Franklin, who published his first catalog in 1744, selling books with a guarantee that "those persons who live remote, by sending their orders and money to said B. Franklin may depend on the same justice as if present." It also played a vital role in maintaining the reputation of the American woman for her blend of simplicity and style, celebrated since the time of Abigail Adams, who wrote from London, "The American ladies are much admired here by the gentlemen, I am told, and I wonder not at it. O, my country, my country! preserve, preserve the little purity and simplicity of manners you yet possess."

Carrying on the tradition a hundred and fifty years later was Sears, the quintessential American institution, whose reputation was reaffirmed incontrovertibly by a popular Georgia governor when he told rural voters that they had only three true friends: "God Almighty, Eugene Talmadge and Sears, Roebuck."

JoAnne Olian

THE ARLINGTON.

$5.88

No. 18R32555 **Rich looking hand made velvet hat on a buckram frame 17 inches wide,** the frame being completely covered with black mirrored silk velvet. The trimming consists of a single 17-in. ostrich plume in black, applied from the left side of crown, drooping across the front to the right brim. Draped around the crown in loose folds appears a very wide band of heavy black satin, which is caught gracefully in front by two jet trimming pins. **A most serviceable style, not too extreme.** Very pretty as described in all black. Comes also in medium brown, medium navy blue, very dark green, or taupe gray, all with plumes to match, or with black or white plumes, if desired. **State color desired.** Price........**$5.88**

THE DOWAGER.

$2.98

No. 18R32560 **Our very best quality ladies' bonnet with good head size.** Made of splendid materials. The facing is of shirred black mirrored silk velvet, while the crown is of silk finished braid laid in folds. **The trimming consists of a cluster of two good quality ostrich tips, used together with sweeping vulture aigrettes.** A dash of color sets off the hat by the use of a small drape of old rose mirrored silk velvet set off by jet ornament, applied directly beneath the tips. The ties, which are caught in the back with jet ornaments, are of best quality soft finished 18-inch chiffon, beautifully shirred, each being 45 inches long. Very pretty as described in black with a touch of old rose. May also be ordered with a touch of light blue, a touch of white, a touch of lavender, or in all black. **State color desired.** A real $5.00 value. Price..**$2.98**

THE SHERETON.

$2.49

No. 18R32565 **Splendid moderately priced bonnet, very rich in effect.** The facing is a wide band of openwork jet spangled braid, laid over heavy black silk, the crown and upper brim being made of silk finished braid. The trimming consists of a bunch of three pretty black ostrich tips set off with a touch of Copenhagen blue satin taffeta ribbon applied directly below the tips. The ties are of 2-inch black taffeta ribbon, one yard long on each side, the ribbon extending over the back of the crown. May be ordered as described in black with a touch of Copenhagen blue. Comes also in black with a touch of light blue, white, lavender or in all black. **State color desired.** Extra good value. Price **$2.49**

THE RAVINIA.

$6.25

No. 18R32570 **Most becoming dress hat, literally loaded with ostrich plumes.** The brim, which is 15¾ inches wide, is of black mirrored silk velvet, while the large Tam o'Shanter crown is made entirely of spangled jet braid. Completely encircling this large crown are nine medium size black demi plumes, while on the left side are three half plumes, each about 13 inches long. A fold of black satin taffeta ribbon is laid around the base of the crown beneath the ostrich tips, ending in a knot on the left side. At the price asked this hat is a tremendous value, being particularly dressy. Comes in black only. Price **$6.25**

THE SUPERBA.

$13.50

No. 18R32575 **Our very finest ostrich trimmed hat.** Made up of most elegant materials, with two beautiful black plumes, each 17 inches long and very wide. The shape is rather large, with graceful sweeping brim 17½ inches wide, slightly turned on each side and drooping in the back. The edge of brim and large French crown are covered with finest quality black mirrored silk velvet, while the facing is of pure white grosgrain silk. An elegant imported band of appliqued silk braid studded with jet ornaments is laid on a wide drape of black silk maline, daintily applied around the crown. Guaranteed equal to any $25.00 imported pattern obtainable in any store. Very pretty as described in all black with white facing. **Comes also in all black with black plumes; or in black with one white and one black plume, with white facing. State color desired.** Price..............................**$13.50**

THE KENMORE.

$7.95

No. 18R32580 **One of our newest ostrich trimmed hats in beautiful style and of splendid materials.** The novelty shape, which is 17 inches wide, is faced with black mirrored silk velvet, having a wide folded binding on edge of brim; the upper brim and crown being of white silk pyroxylin braid. The trimming consists of one black and one white ostrich plume, each about 16 inches long, which extend from a large knot of black satin taffeta ribbon, caught with jet trimming pin. The ribbon is laid in folds around the base of the crown. Charmingly pretty hat in black and white combination as described. Comes also in all black; in dark green and black; all brown, or all navy blue. **State color desired.** Price..**$7.95**

THE CLARENDON.

$2.99

No. 18R32360 **Stunning dress hat, made of best quality black mohair felt with very wide binding of black silk velvet.** The shape is 16½ inches wide. The trimming consists of six white single layer uncurled ostrich feathers about 16 inches long (not full plumes), being caught at the crown with large crush rosette of black silk velvet, centered by a large jet ornament, the velvet being laid in folds around the crown. Very pretty as described in all black with white uncurled ostrich feathers. Comes also in all black; in medium brown with natural shaded feathers and light blue velvet; in navy blue with Copenhagen blue feathers and velvet; in all navy blue, or all brown. **State color wanted.** One of the greatest values ever offered. Price **$2.99**

THE BRAMFORD.

$2.63

No. 18R32365 **Dainty mushroom style in one of the very newest and most becoming shapes.** The hat, which is 16 inches wide, is made of long nap mohair felt, in navy blue, with large rounded crown. The trimming consists of a pair of very handsome navy blue wings, applied against the side of the crown, pointing to the side, while a huge rosette of light blue mirrored silk velvet, centered with large jet cabochon, is applied directly in front of the wings, folds of velvet being laid around the entire base of crown. Very pretty as described in navy blue with a touch of light blue. Comes also in medium brown with dark Copenhagen blue velvet; in all brown; in dark cardinal red with black wings and black velvet; in black with black wings and dark green velvet; in black with black wings and violet shaded velvet, or in all black. **State color wanted.** Fine $4.00 value. Our price..**$2.63**

THE CRANSTON.

$2.38

No. 18R32370 **Splendid value medium size turban in strictly hand made style** the frame being covered with rows of black novelty braid, the edge of brim being bound with black silk velvet. The trimming consists of three medium quality black ostrich tips applied on the left side and drooping gracefully over the brim; a fold of black, heavy Jap silk being laid around the inner brim and crown, ending directly under the tips, caught with a jet ornament. Very pretty and serviceable as described in all black. Comes also in shades of medium brown; all navy blue with tips to match; in taupe gray with black tips; Copenhagen blue with navy blue tips, or in all black with light blue silk. **State color wanted.** A hat sold at $3.50 by all milliners. Our price........................**$2.38**

BETTER VALUES NEWER STYLES

CORSETS

QUALITY CONSIDERED YOU MAKE A BIG SAVING

DON'T HESITATE ABOUT SENDING US YOUR ORDER. WE TAKE ALL THE RISK.

WANDA.

Splendid Value at a Very Low Price - 47c

No. 18R101 Designed to improve the slender figure. Medium high bust, rather short over hips. Made of good quality coutil, well boned throughout with non-rusting tipped steels, 12¾ in. long in front and 11 in. long in back. Has front hose supporters. Top is trimmed with dainty lace drawn with baby ribbon. Color, white only. Sizes, 18 to 30. **Be sure to give us size wanted.** Price.... 47c
Postage extra, 9 to 11 cents.

MARION.

Habit Hip Corset. Comfortable and Shapely. 57c

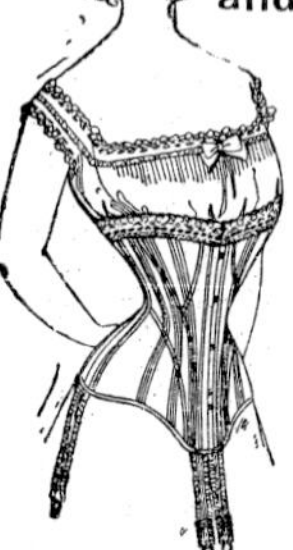

No. 18R108 Suitable for the average figure. Made of good quality coutil, fully gored, boned throughout with non-rusting tipped steels. Has 11-inch front steel and is 13 inches long in back. Has hose supporters on front and sides. The top is trimmed with a pretty Valenciennes lace, drawn with satin baby ribbon. Regular $1.00 value. Color, white only. Sizes, 18 to 30. **Be sure to give size wanted when ordering.** Our price..... 57c
If mail shipment, postage extra, 11 to 13c.

GRACIA.

Girdle Top, Rather Long Over Hips. 50c

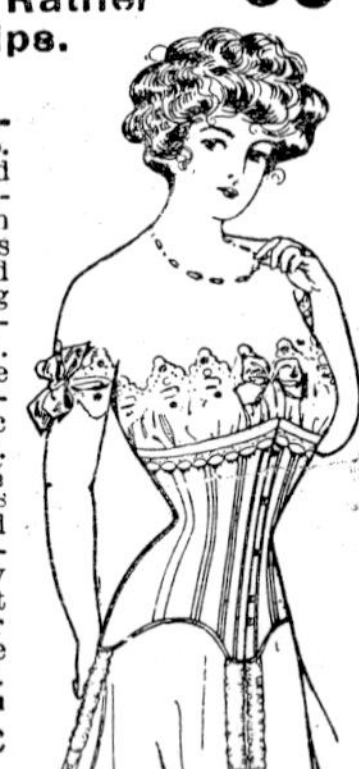

No. 18R112 The tremendous popularity of our No. 18R151 has induced us to offer our customers a similar style in a cheaper corset. This corset is made of good American twill (strong white material, heavier than batiste). Trimmed with lace and has hose supporters of frilled elastic both front and sides. The front clasp is 11½ inches long. All steels are non-rusting and all eyelets are aluminum. Strictly straight front effect and great value at our price. Comes in white only. Sizes, 18 to 26. **Be sure to mention size.** Price........ 50c
Postage extra, 11c.

EXTRA SPECIAL OFFER 95c

GUARANTEED FINE $1.50 VALUE.

WE SPECIALLY RECOMMEND THIS CORSET AS ONE TO GIVE ABSOLUTE SATISFACTION, BOTH IN FIT AND QUALITY.

OUR RADIA MODEL

No. 18R143 **This Corset is made in the very popular long hip medium high bust effect and will fit the average figure.** Made of the best quality of French coutil, acknowledged by all to be the best wearing corset material. It is fitted with non-rusting stays and aluminum eyelets. The front clasp of the corset is 11½ inches long and fitted with nickel plated skirt fastener 14¾ inches long in back. Four extra heavy 9-inch hose supporters of fine frilled edge elastic are attached to the front and sides. Corset is finished with 2-inch wide Valenciennes lace drawn with satin ribbon. **We absolutely guarantee this corset to be equal to any $1.50 garment on the market.** When we tell you without exaggerating that we are selling more than 20,000 pairs of this corset per annum, you can best appreciate what value we offer. Color, white only. Sizes, 18 to 30. **Be sure to give size.** Price......................... 95c
If mail shipment, postage extra, 12 to 15c.

FRANCIS.

STYLISH AND POPULAR MODEL

Our Newest Hip Confining Corset. Regular $2.00 Value. Price - - - $1.38

No. 18R147 The very newest and tremendously popular Long Skirted Corset, deep over the back and hips, giving a straight slender figure, which is so much desired. As the basis for a perfect fitting gown we can highly recommend this corset. It is constructed on scientific lines, which insure comfort and style. Made of highest grade English coutil, stayed with non-rusting stays, each stay stitched into the casing to prevent slipping and adding a wearing feature to the corset. The trimming consists of 1½-inch corded taffeta ribbon, edged with Valenciennes lace, finished with a large bow of the ribbon in front. Corset is fitted with extra wide, strong hose supporters, and has skirt hook attached. Has 13-inch front clasp, back is 15¼ inches long.
Altogether, this is one of the best corsets we have ever offered to our trade. Guaranteed $2.00 value. Color, white only. Sizes, 18 to 30. **State size.**
Our price............. $1.38
If mail shipment, postage extra, 15 cents to 17 cents.

MARIETTA.

HIGHEST QUALITY

Finest Style. Unequaled $5.00 Value. Price - - $3.45

No. 18R148 Every woman recognizes the importance of having a perfect corset as the foundation for a perfect fitting gown, and the corsetieres' art is surely illustrated in this elegant model. Every new feature is brought out strongly. Medium high bust, long supple waist effect, slender sloping hips and finest workmanship and materials. Made of beautiful, firm, white, imported coutil, elegantly trimmed with silk embroidery. The stays are of the best quality and the corset is silk stitched throughout. Back steel, 16 inches long; front clasp, 12 inches long. Four extra heavy hose supporters on front and sides. Comes in white only. Sizes, 18 to 26. Please state size wanted. **Guaranteed $5.00 value.**
Our price.................................. $3.45
If mail shipment, postage extra, 19 cents.

RUTH.

Fine Girdle Top Corset, 93c

No. 18R151 Our most popular Girdle Top Corset, with lengthened hips, close fitting and very stylish. Designed to insure great comfort and perfect freedom of arm and shoulder movement. Fits the average figure perfectly. Made of best quality imported coutil, straight seamed, with non-rusting stays. Trimmed with pretty lace, drawn with satin baby ribbon. Fitted with four hose supporters on front and sides, all made of 1-inch wide lisle elastic. Comes in white only. Sizes, 18 to 30 inches. $1.35 value. **Give size when ordering.** Our price...... 93c
If mail shipment, postage extra, 18 cents.

PRINCESS.

Popular Priced Corset in Medium Length - 85c

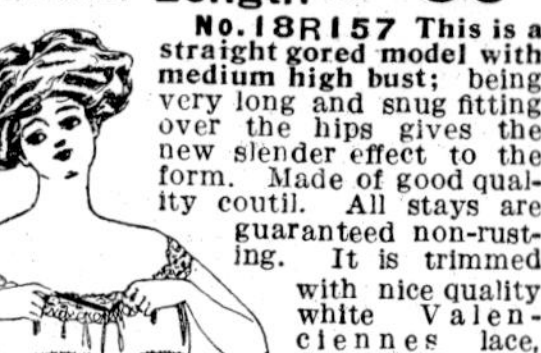

No. 18R157 This is a straight gored model with medium high bust; being very long and snug fitting over the hips gives the new slender effect to the form. Made of good quality coutil. All stays are guaranteed non-rusting. It is trimmed with nice quality white Valenciennes lace, drawn with satin baby ribbon and finished with taffeta ribbon bow. Fitted with 1-inch wide hose supporters on both front and sides, all of good quality elastic. Length of front clasp, 12 inches; 15 inches long in back. Comes in white only. Sizes, 18 to 30. **State size.** Price........... 85c
If mail shipment, postage extra, 12 to 15 cents.

JANICE.

Will Surely Fit Well - 88c

No. 18R160 This Corset is a copy of a fine fitting French model sold at $5.00. Made of fine quality French sateen boned with non-rusting tipped steels, straight seamed medium high bust and tapering waist, long sloping dip hip and back. This gives a graceful, slender figure. Lisle elastic patent catch hose supporters on front and sides. Trimmed with delicate Valenciennes lace, drawn with satin baby ribbon insertion. Full length in front, 14½ inches; back, 11½ inches. Color, white only. Sizes, 18 to 30. **Be sure to give size wanted.** Price. 88c
If mail shipment, postage extra, 13 to 16 cents.

DOROTHEA.

Splendid Value Corset at a Very Low Price - 49c

DESIGNED FOR THE AVERAGE FIGURE. No. 18R153 This Corset is made of medium quality coutil, full bias gored and boned with patent "Kant Rust" stays. Is medium high in the bust and rather long and narrow over the hips, giving the popular slender figure. fitted with hose supporters on both front and sides, all of 1-inch elastic. The top is neatly trimmed with lace. Many stores ask **$1.00** for no better style or value. Comes in white only. Sizes, 18 to 30. **Be sure to give size wanted.** Price........ 49c
If mail shipment, postage extra, 10c to 12c.

SYLVIA.

Fine Quality, Mercerized Tape Girdle. 48c

No. 18R130 This is a very dainty Girdle, made of fancy mercerized cotton tape, with stripes running through the center. Boning set in sections covered with batiste. Boned with non-rusting steels and has aluminum eyelets. Ribbon bow on top and fitted with front hose supporters. Equal in style, looks and fit to the 75-cent girdles sold elsewhere. Made in all white only. Sizes, 18 to 26. **Be sure to give size wanted.** Our price.................. 48c
If mail shipment, postage extra, 6c.

FLORENCE.

Extra Well Made. Batiste Girdle - - - 47c

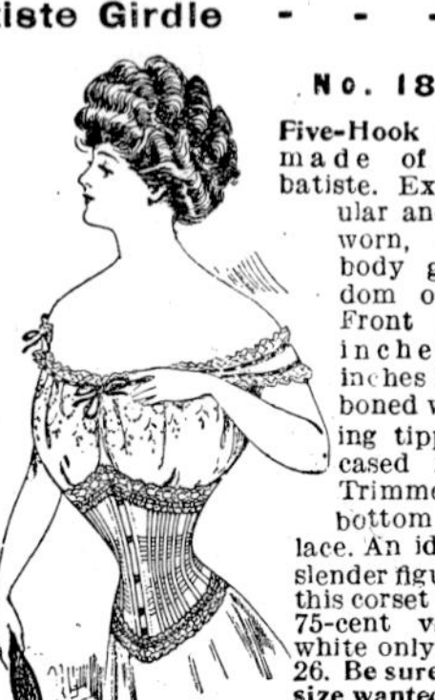

No. 18R135 Five-Hook Girdle Corset, made of fine quality batiste. Extremely popular and extensively worn, allowing the body greatest freedom of movement. Front steel, 10¾ inches long, 11 inches long in back; boned with non-rusting tipped steel, encased in batiste. Trimmed top and bottom with dainty lace. An ideal corset for slender figures. We offer this corset as a regular 75-cent value. Color, white only. Sizes, 18 to 26. **Be sure to give size wanted.** Price. 47c
Postage extra, 7 cents.

HELENE.

Popular Style for Average Figures - - 90c

No. 18R169 Bias Gored Corset designed in a very popular long hip style with medium high bust. Made of superior quality firm coutil, trimmed with beautiful 3-inch wide Valencienes lace and dainty satin taffeta ribbon bow. Has good quality hose supporters on front and sides and strong non-rusting stays, 13¼ inches long in front and 12½ inches long in back. Comes in white only. Sizes, 18 to 30. **State size wanted.** Price... 90c
If mail shipment, postage extra, 13c to 15c.

LADIES' WHITE LAWN WAISTS

Lawn and Lingerie Waists, smart, dainty and up to the minute. Your money back if they fail to please you.

Sizes, 32 to 42 inches bust measure. No larger or smaller sizes can be furnished. See page 191 for instructions on measuring, how to order, etc.

Mail shipments. If you want any waist shipped by mail, send postage extra, 1 cent an ounce, according to shipping weight given.

No. 27R500 SMART LAWN WAIST with allover embroidered front alternating with tucks. Short sleeves; tucked cuffs and collar finished with lace edging; buttons in back. Very neat and an unusually great value. **State bust measure.** Shipping wt., 12 oz.
No. 27R500 Color, white only. Price....................49c

No. 27R501 AN IMPRESSING CREATION IN A LAWN WAIST. Embroidered front in beautifully assorted designs. Long sleeves with tucked cuffs and collar; buttons in back. A garment worth at least one-third more. A regular 98-cent value. **State bust measure.** Shipping wt., 13 oz.
No. 27R501 Color, white only. Price....................63c

No. 27R502 A WAIST THAT DESERVES MORE THAN ORDINARY MENTION. Made of fine lawn. Long sleeves, buttons in back, tucked front in panel effect alternating with embroidered front in pretty assorted designs; tucked collar and cuffs; collar finished with lace edging. Very smart and a splendid value. **State bust measure.** Shipping wt., 13 oz.
No. 27R502 Color, white only. Price....................78c

No. 27R503 A LAWN WAIST with embroidered front in floral pattern. Front panel of waist is embroidered in dainty raised circle and button effect; long sleeves; tucked collar and cuffs finished with lace edging; waist buttons in front. **State bust measure.** Shipping wt., 13 oz.
No. 27R503 Color, white only. Price....................89c

No. 27R504 WHITE LAWN WAIST with five artistically embroidered bands in front. Long sleeves with tucked cuffs, tucked collar, buttons in front under panel, tucked in back and front. Something very pretty and stylish. **State bust measure.** Shipping wt., 13 oz.
No. 27R504 Color, white only. Price....................89c

No. 27R505 A DAINTY DESIGN IN A LAWN WAIST with a beautifully embroidered front. Yoke and collar of Valenciennes lace, three-quarter length sleeves with lace insertion, tucked cuffs. waist buttons in back. A garment that you would be asked to pay much more for elsewhere. **State bust measure.** Shipping wt., 13 oz.
No. 27R505 Color, white only. Price....................98c

No. 27R506 ALLOVER EMBROIDERED WAIST. Made of lawn. Tucked front and back, long sleeves, with embroidery and tucked cuffs and collar finished with lace edging; waist buttons in back. Very neat and dressy. **State bust measure.** Shipping wt., 14 oz.
No. 27R506 Color, white only. Price....................98c

No. 27R507 GIBSON WAIST. Made of lawn. Embroidered front in charming diamond and button effect; waist buttons in front; long tucked mousquetaire sleeves finished with lace edging; tucked collar. A garment that is popular. **State bust measure.** Shipping wt., 13 oz.
No. 27R507 Color, white only. Price....................98c

No. 27R508 LINGERIE WAIST in a pleasing design. Yoke of tucks and lace, lace insertion in front, long mousquetaire tucked sleeves with lace edging and trimmed with buttons, lace collar; waist buttons in back. A garment sometimes sold at twice what we ask. Guaranteed to be satisfactory. **State bust measure.** Shipping wt., 13 oz.
No. 27R508 Color, white only. Price....................98c

No. 27R509 LAWN WAIST with front of dainty flower pattern allover embroidery and tucks. Tucked in back, long sleeves; tucked collar and cuffs finished with lace edging; waist buttons in back. A garment that is pretty and stylish. **State bust measure.** Shipping wt., 13 oz.
No. 27R509 Color, white only. Price....................$1.19

No. 27R510 ALLOVER EMBROIDERED WAIST. Front and back of lawn. A waist that cannot fail to meet your every want. Tucked front, long mousquetaire sleeves, tucked collar; collar and sleeves finished with lace edging; waist buttons in back. **State bust measure.** Shipping wt., 14 oz.
No. 27R510 Color, white only. Price....................$1.35

No. 27R511 LINGERIE WAIST, the front being a charming combination of lace insertion, embroidered medallions and pin tucks. Long mousquetaire sleeves with lace insertion and edging, giving the desired dressy effect; collar of Valenciennes lace; waist buttons in back; back also trimmed with lace inserti[illegible] **measure.** Shipping wt., 13 oz.
[illegible]o. 2[illegible] Price....................[illegible]1.55

This is One of the Fashion Plates of Our Ladies' Made to Order Suits From Our Beautiful Special Catalog of Ladies', Misses' and Children's Wearing Apparel.

THIS FASHION PLATE shows only three out of more than fifty New York and Paris styles in ladies' made to order tailored suits, but they will give you some idea of the beautiful styles from which we give you the opportunity to select. You may have your suit made to your individual measure in any of the styles on the above fashion plate or in any of the styles on the fashion plates in the special catalog above mentioned, and in your choice of over 100 different fabrics which are shown in our free Sample Book No. 79. Prices range from $12.00 to $35.00. Highest grade man tailoring guaranteed.

LENGTHS OF COATS. The coats illustrated on this fashion plate are all made in the longer lengths which are correct according to the dictates of fashion. However, in our ladies', misses' and children's wearing apparel style book you will find fashion plates illustrating coats in lengths ranging from 34 to 45 inches. You can have any style shown made in the length you prefer.

COLLAR AND LAPELS. Our fashion plates of ladies' tailor made to order suits show all the latest effects in plain tailored collars and lapels, shawl collars, Dutch collars, military or standing collars, all in different shapes, some trimmed in various manners and some untrimmed. We will, without any extra charge, trim a collar or lapel with corded silk satin, velvet or with plain or fancy braid, whichever the customer may wish.

BUTTONS. Although jet buttons are very popular this season, yet some people do not care for them, preferring rather the self covered or silk, satin or velvet covered buttons, a combination of the three, or ivory buttons. Jet buttons are not suitable for every kind of cloth or color; in fact, the kind of buttons to use all depends on the style, cloth and color that the customer chooses, and for this reason it is advisable to always leave the matter of buttons to us. We always use the buttons best adapted to the style, cloth and color. However, if you wish, you can have any kind of buttons you prefer, as we always carry a large variety of jet and ivory buttons in stock and have the machinery for making every kind of combination or covered buttons.

SKIRTS. Our fashion plates illustrate all of the prevailing styles in skirts, both flared, plaited and kilted. You may select any style of skirt shown on our fashion plates with any style of coat. The style of coats worn this reason require a nine or eleven-gored skirt, and plaited skirts are also very popular. When having a coat made in an extremely long style it is always advisable to have the skirt made in a plain flared style on account of the weight.

WE WANT EVERY LADY who is interested in finely tailored made to order suits to write and ask for our free Sample Book No. 79, and our special Catalog of Ladies', Misses' and Children's Wearing Apparel. Both these books will be mailed to you free and postpaid on request. Be sure to ask for both books. See page 149.

STYLE 110

A chic military effect style, in a ladies' made to order tailored suit, that meets with every requirement of fashion and good taste. Single breasted cutaway coat with lap over front, standing collar and fancy patch pockets. Effectively trimmed with buttons, as pictured. You can have suit made in this style from any one of the one hundred or more different fabrics shown in our free Sample Book No. 79 at prices from $12.00 to $35.00. This sample book is FREE. Write for it.

STYLE 111

An elegantly tailored model, exhibiting refined distinctiveness in every line. Single breasted coat with round cutaway corners, pretty shawl collar, and tasteful trimmings, as illustrated. We will make a suit in this style for you from any one of the one hundred or more fabrics shown in our free Sample Book No. 79 at prices from $12.00 to $35.00. Write for it, it's FREE.

STYLE 112

A jaunty four-button single breasted tailored model with a touch of individuality that will appeal to most every woman. Corners of coats show just a small opening when coat is buttoned. Effectively trimmed, as illustrated. We will make a suit to order for you in this style from any one of the one hundred or more fabrics shown in our free Sample Book No. 79, at prices from $12.00 to $35.00.

$9.75 BEAUTIFUL ONE-PIECE PARTY OR WEDDING DRESS.

Very dainty net dress, richly trimmed with embroidery, as illustrated; yoke inlaid with lace, attached lace collar, long sleeves; beautifully trimmed with embroidery in button effect and inlaid with lace, belt of Venise lace, trimmed in front with two pretty rosettes. **Skirt**—Made very full with a wide flounce and two rows of self tucks around bottom, handsomely embroidered and inlaid with lace to match waist; 3¼-yard wide sweep; drop skirt of lingerie. **Give bust measure, waist measure and front length of skirt.** Shipping wt., 35 oz.

No. 31R4539 Color, white only. Price **$9.75**

$7.75 STUNNING CHIFFON TAFFETA JUMPER STYLE ONE-PIECE DRESS.

Very pretty panel front extending from yoke to bottom of skirt, neat square cut yoke; yoke, panel and belt edged with silk taffeta in contrasting color, trimmed with neat Oriental buttons; sleeves inlaid, as illustrated, with lace; waist closes in back with hooks and eyes. **Skirt**—Cut very full in gored style, trimmed with tabs of self material, piped with silk taffeta in contrasting color around bottom; 3¼-yard sweep. **Give bust measure, waist measure and front length of skirt.** Shipping wt., 28 oz.

No. 31R4543 Color, black. Price......**$7.75**
No. 31R4544 Color, blue. Price......**$7.75**
No. 31R4545 Color, brown. Price....**$7.75**

$8.95 VERY FINE QUALITY SILK TAFFETA ONE-PIECE DRESS

Neat panel front extending from yoke to bottom of skirt. **Waist**—Tucked on each side, pretty round yoke inlaid with lace and net, soft attached collar to match, finished with tie of self material; waist closes in back with hooks and eyes; prettily trimmed with self covered buttons; long mousquetaire sleeves. **Skirt**—Made very full in gored style with three tucks around bottom and self covered button trimming, as illustrated; 3¼-yard wide sweep. **Give bust measure, waist measure and front length of skirt.** Shipping wt., 30 oz.

No. 31R4546 Color, black. Price.....**$8.95**
No. 31R4547 Color, navy blue. Price.**$8.95**
No. 31R4548 Color, brown. Price.....**$8.95**

$10.00 CHARMING CHIFFON TAFFETA ONE-PIECE DRESS.

Notice the rich hand made yoke of silk corded lace; has panel front extending from yoke to bottom of skirt. **Waist**—Plaited on each side and in back, trimmed with jet buttons; long tucked mousquetaire sleeves; waist made to button in back. **Skirt**--Made very full with fold of self material around bottom; panel, belt sleeves and fold on skirt trimmed with silk braid; 3¼-yard wide sweep. The style and trimming of this dress speaks for elegance and refinement. **State bust measure, waist measure and front length of skirt.** Shipping wt., 30 oz.

No. 31R4549 Color, black only. Price **$10.00**

$10.75 HANDSOME ALL WOOL CHIFFON PANAMA ONE-PIECE DRESS.

Has a pretty round yoke inlaid with fine white net and trimmed with small satin covered buttons, as illustrated; soft attached collar to match. **Waist**—Tucked on each side in front and in back, beautifully trimmed with satin straps, satin ornaments and satin covered buttons; long tucked mousquetaire sleeves trimmed with satin straps, crushed satin belt; waist closes in back with hooks and eyes. **Skirt**—Made very full in gored style with welt seams, neatly trimmed in front with two satin straps, as illustrated; 3¼-yard wide sweep. **State bust measure, waist measure and front length of skirt.** Shipping wt., 43 oz.

No. 31R4550 Color, black. Price **$10.75**
No. 31R4551 Color, navy blue. Price.............**$10.75**
No. 31R4552 Color, reseda green. Price............**$10.75**

$9.98 JAUNTY COLLARLESS EFFECT ONE-PIECE DRESS.

A very rich, lustrous Brilliantine. Colors, black, navy blue or gray. Tailor made waist with pretty tucked front, plait on each side and in back; pointed yoke, as illustrated; trimmed with two rows of silk soutache, self straps and satin covered buttons; long sleeves finished with box plaits and trimmed with small satin covered buttons. **Skirt**—Full gored style, 3¼-yard sweep, inverted plaited panel front. **Give bust measure, waist measure and front length of skirt.**

No. 31R4553 Color, black. Price......**$9.98**
No. 31R4554 Color, blue. Price......**$9.98**
No. 31R4555 Color, gray. Price......**$9.98**

$12.50 HANDSOMELY EMBROIDERED ALL WOOL CHIFFON PANAMA ONE-PIECE DRESS.

A very pretty yoke, as illustrated, inlaid with very fine net, trimmed with six small satin covered buttons; soft attached collar to match. **Waist**—Tucked on each side and made in plaited Gibson effect, richly embroidered around yoke and belt with silk; long tucked mousquetaire sleeves embroidered to match waist; waist closes in back with hooks and eyes. **Skirt**—Full gored style with wide box plait panel front, well tailored; 3¼-yard wide sweep. **Give bust measure, waist measure and front length of skirt.** Shipping wt., 42 oz.

No. 31R4556 Color, navy blue. Price.**$12.50**
No. 31R4557 Color, gray. Price.....**$12.50**
No. 31R4558 Color, old rose. Price.**$12.50**

SIZES. **The Ladies' Ready Made Dresses illustrated and described on this page are furnished in sizes from 32 to 42 inches bust measure, 23 to 29 inches waist measure and 37 to 43 inches front length of skirt. We will make dresses in larger sizes to special order for 20 per cent extra, or one-fifth more than our regular catalog price. Give measurements as explained on page 136.**

MAIL SHIPMENTS. **If you desire any dress shipped by mail, send postage extra, 1 cent an ounce, according to shipping weight given.**

AUTO, STREET OR RAIN COATS

These coats are smart in tone, up to date in style and workmanship. They are certainly a credit to the designer's art.

17R5701 17R5699 17R5714 17R5702 17R5706 17R5705

YOUNG GIRLS' AND CHILDREN'S COATS

READY TO WEAR TUXEDO, PRINCE ALBERT AND FULL DRESS SUITS

$20.00 FOR TUXEDO OR PRINCE ALBERT SUIT

DON'T PAY

FROM $35.00 TO $45.00

FOR READY TO WEAR DRESS SUITS.

FOR JUST ABOUT ONE-HALF of these prices **we offer you thoroughly up to date, high grade ready to wear dress suits,** and guarantee them to be as finely tailored and to have just as high class linings and trimmings. Suits of this kind are intended for very fine dress wear, so it is absolutely necessary that the finest finish and workmanship be put into them, and in ordering one of these suits from us you may rest assured that they will lack nothing of either, and at the same time, you are paying only about one-third of what you would pay if you had this suit made to order by home tailors. **The cloth** is an unfinished black worsted of medium weight, having a very rich finish. If you wish to see a sample of it, write and ask for our free Sample Card No. 291. This sample card will be sent to any address, free and postpaid, upon request.

SIZES. From 34 inches up to and including 44 inches breast measure and from 30 inches up to and including 42 inches waist measure. No larger. See page 353 for simple measuring plan.

If you want the double breasted Prince Albert suit, as above illustrated, faced with silk, ask for **Goods No. 45R6090**

PRICES

Suit **$20.00**
Coat and vest **15.00**
Pants **6.00**

If you want Tuxedo suit, as above illustrated, with silk facing, ask for **Goods No. 45R6092**

PRICES

Suit **$20.00**
Coat and vest **15.00**
Pants **6.00**

If you want the full dress style suit, as above illustrated, with silk faced lapels, ask for **Goods No. 45R6094**

PRICES

Suit **$22.00**
Coat and vest **17.00**
Pants **6.00**

FULL DRESS SUIT $22.00

THE PRINCE ALBERT SUIT is made in double breasted style, as shown in illustration. **Coat** cut in at the waist line and having a flare at the bottom. Lapels are faced with silk to buttonholes; has two rows of three buttons each, hand made buttonholes; one inside breast pocket, one inside change pocket and two skirt pockets. Venetian lining in body and striped sateen lining in sleeves. **Vest,** five-button, single breasted, with notched collar and the usual pockets; lining to match coat. **Pants** in prevailing style.

THE TUXEDO SUIT is made exactly as illustrated. Coat has peak lapels, which is the very latest fashion; lapels are faced with silk. Has two inside breast pockets. Venetian lining in body and striped sateen in sleeves. **Vest,** three-button, low cut, full dress style, with two outside lower pockets and one inside pocket. **Pants** cut in the usual fashion.

THE FULL DRESS SUIT is made as shown in illustration. Coat, lapels being silk faced. Has two inside breast pockets, two skirt pockets; lined with Venetian in body and striped sateen in the sleeves. **Vest,** low cut, full dress style, with three buttons; two outside lower pockets; lining to match coat. **Pants** made in the prevailing style. All coat fronts are interlined with genuine haircloth, so that they will not wrinkle and lose their shape. All seams are sewed with pure silk. Finely tailored and finished in every detail.

EVENING, RECEPTION AND OPERA COATS

17R5002 17R5001
17R5000 17R5010 17R5006

LADIES' STYLISH THOROUGHLY TAILORED SKIRTS

27R147 27R129 27R138

27R141 27R144 27R153

27R132 27R135

LADIES' RIDING SUITS AND SKIRTS.

These are Combination Riding and Walking Suits or Skirts. For riding the skirt is made divided by simply unbuttoning the front panel and arranging it as shown in the smaller illustration. Semi-fitted coat with straps and belt furnished in different materials and colors as stated. Sizes, 32 to 42 inches bust measure, 22 to 30 inches waist measure and 37 to 44 inches front length of skirt. For all information regarding measurements see page 181.

No. 27R400 SUIT, made of tan khaki or soldier's cloth. Shipping wt., 5½ lbs. Price ....**$8.75** Unmailable.

No. 27R401 SUIT, made of all wool broadcloth. Color, black only. Shipping wt., 5½ lbs. Price ....**$15.00** Unmailable.

No. 27R402 SUIT, made of high grade covert cloth. Color, castor only. Shipping wt., 6 lbs. Price...**$13.75** Unmailable.

No. 27R403 SKIRT, made of khaki or soldier's cloth. Color, tan. Shipping wt., 58 oz. Price **$3.98**

No. 27R404 SKIRT, made of cotton covert cloth. Color, castor. Price **$2.98**

No. 27R405 SKIRT, made of cotton covert cloth. Color, gray. Price ....**$2.98** Shipping wt., on above two, 36 oz.

No. 27R406 SKIRT, made of all wool covert cloth. Color, black. Price.**$6.75**

No. 27R407 SKIRT, made of all wool covert cloth. Color, oxford gray. Price **6.75**

No. 27R408 SKIRT, same as above. Color, castor. Price .... **6.75** Shipping wt. on any of above three, 40 oz.

No. 27R409 SKIRT, made of all wool broadcloth. Color, black only. Shipping wt., 45 oz. Price...**$6.75**

No. 27R410 SKIRT, made of good quality corduroy. Color, castor only. Shipping wt., 60 oz. Price...**$5.75**

No. 27R411 SKIRT, made of good quality repellant cloth. Color, olive brown. Shipping wt., 40 oz. Price...**$3.75**

No. 27R412 SKIRT, made of melton. Color, black only. Shipping wt., 45 oz. Price **$4.75**

JUVENILE SKIRTS.

Juvenile skirts are in more demand this season than heretofore. The skirts we have shown above are the latest in these juvenile styles, are made of good materials and are furnished in sizes from 22 to 28 inches waist measure and 24 to 34 inches front length of skirt. We guarantee these skirts to be exceptional values at the price, and if in your opinion you do not think that they are worth even more than the prices quoted, **we will gladly take them back and refund every cent** you have paid. While these **skirts are** shown with **suspenders** if you so desire the suspenders can be taken off and the skirt worn in the ordinary way.

No. 27R418 PRETTY GARMENT IN A JUVENILE SKIRT of chiffon Panama. Double box plait in front, side plaited style, front trimmed with combination covered buttons; suspenders as shown; inverted plait in the back. **State waist measure and front length of skirt.** Average sweep, 102 inches. Shipping wt., 26 oz.

No. 27R418 Color, navy blue. Price..**$1.98**
No. 27R419 Color, brown. Price....**$1.98**
No. 27R420 Color, wine. Price.....**$1.98**

No. 27R421 A NOBBY LITTLE GARMENT IN A JUVENILE SKIRT of worsted Panama. Side plaited style with box plait in front, trimmed around bottom with alternating self tucks and bands of taffeta silk; suspenders to match; inverted plait in back. Average sweep, 88 inches. **State waist measure and front length of skirt.** Shipping wt., 27 oz.

No. 27R421 Color, navy blue. Price..**$2.75**
No. 27R422 Color, brown. Price....**$2.75**
No. 27R423 Color, wine. Price.....**$2.75**

No. 27R424 TASTY JUVENILE SKIRT of worsted Panama. Side plaited style with front of inverted and box plaits as shown; trimmed in front with combination covered buttons and straps of taffeta silk; trimmed around bottom with one wide and two narrow folds of taffeta silk; suspenders trimmed to match; inverted plait in back. Average sweep, 100 inches. **Give waist measure and front length of skirt.** Shipping wt., 25 oz.

No. 27R424 Color, navy blue. Price..**$2.98**
No. 27R425 Color, brown. Price....**$2.98**
No. 27R426 Color, wine. Price.....**$2.98**

UCANTTEAR BRAND BOYS' KNEE PANTS SUITS

All the latest styles and patterns. Ucanttear Brand Boys' Suits are manufactured and sold only by us. They are made with such features as double stitched and taped seams, pocket bar tacks, bottom facings, padded shoulders, interlined fronts, reinforced seat and reinforced fronts. It is through these features that our **Ucanttear** brand has gained the reputation of being the strongest and best wearing boys' clothing on the market. **SIZES,** to fit boys from 8 to 16 years of age. **When ordering give age of boy. If he is extra large or small for his age mention this and the size of suit which he is now wearing.**

$2.98 No. 40R659 STYLISH DOUBLE BREASTED SUIT WITH KNICKERBOCKER PANTS, IN SOFT FINISHED MATERIAL.

Pattern, dark stone gray with stripes in black and light gray. As illustrated, with three outside pockets, cuff effect on sleeves. Derby back with false plaits and buttons at end of side seams. Perfectly tailored, interlined, padded, and well stayed. Bar tacks on all pockets, bottom facings, and good button stands on coats. Knickerbocker pants, double stitched and taped seams, suspender buttons, and strap and buckle at knee. Extra buttons and patch piece free. **SIZES, 8 to 16 years. Mention age of boy.**

$3.65 No. 40R661 SPECIAL VALUE IN A KNICKERBOCKER SUIT WITH EXTRA PAIR STRAIGHT PANTS.

Material, soft finish Union cassimere. Pattern, dark navy blue with a faint stripe effect in black, green and dark maroon. Suits in this material and style always sell extremely well and we have endeavored to give the greatest possible value. Our **Ucanttear** brand has no equal for quality of material or workmanship. Buy it once and you won't buy any other brand. This is proven by the enormous increase in our sales of boys' clothing. **SIZES, 8 to 16 years. Give age of boy.**

$3.45 No. 40R663 DRESSY WORSTED FINISH SUIT IN ONE OF THE SEASON'S NEWEST EFFECTS.

Material, worsted front with a cotton chain in the back. Pattern, black with neat stripes formed by alternating gray, red, and black threads. Notice the beautiful shape of lapels, the stylish flap on pockets, cuff effect on sleeves, etc. Double breasted style with slit in back. Seams, double stitched and taped. Bottom facings, good button stands, well padded, interlined, and lined with extra strong Italian. Pants, full cut knickerbocker style with side pockets, hip pocket, suspender buttons, strap and buckle at knee. **SIZES, 8 to 16 years. Give age of boy.**

$2.75 No. 40R665 EXTRA DURABLE SCHOOL SUIT WITH KNICKERBOCKER PANTS.

Material, strong cheviot cloth. Pattern, medium gray and green mixture with a faint stripe effect. Exactly as illustrated, with stylish long lapels, fancy flaps on all pockets, pretty cuff effect on sleeves, false plaits at side seams, known as a Derby back. Substantially tailored and well trimmed suit at a price which we know cannot be duplicated elsewhere. Extra buttons and a patch piece free. **SIZES, 8 to 16 years. Mention age of boy.**

$2.60 No. 40R667 ONE OF THE NEWEST MODELS OF THE SEASON IN A DOUBLE BREASTED SUIT WITH REGULAR PANTS.

Material, medium weight wool filled cheviot. Pattern, latest olive brown stripe effect. Stylish long roll lapels, fancy shaped flaps on all pockets, neat cuff effect on sleeves, derby back, French seams, canvas fronts, well padded shoulders, bottom facings. Pants, regular style with three buttons at knee, suspender buttons, side pockets, and hip pockets. **SIZES, 8 to 16 years. Give age of boy when ordering.**

$3.25 No. 40R669 AN ALL WOOL KNICKERBOCKER SUIT IN A FANCY MODEL.

Pattern, handsome dark gray stripe effect with colorings in light gray, green, and orange. Material, all wool medium weight cheviot. New style with fancy shaped lapels, neat flaps and buttons on all pockets, stylish cuffs, shaped with a slit in back. Knickerbocker pants with side pockets, hip pocket, belt loops, suspender buttons, and strap and buckle at the knee. Well lined and perfectly tailored garments. **SIZES, 8 to 16 years. Mention age of boy.**

Sig. 25—Ed. 1.

$2.19 TWO-PIECE SAILOR SUITS.

This serviceable and very popular style is made of a good quality navy blue cloth of good weight and smooth finish. The wide sailor collar and yoke are trimmed with narrow braid. Wide plaited skirt is made with attached cambric waist, with dickey front. Knot tie of red mercerized poplin gives the necessary touch of color. Taking it altogether, this is a splendid dress for all seasons of the year and is priced remarkably low. Color, navy blue. Ages, 6 to 14 years. **Be sure to mention age desired.**

No. 38R7590
Price, each..............**$2.19**

$3.89 BEST WORSTED SERGE.

Two-Piece Sailor Suit of extra fine quality navy blue wool serge. Woven from finest worsted yarns. The round sailor collar and neck band are trimmed with numerous rows of silk braid and finished with a red sailor knot tie. The wide plaited skirt is combined with cambric waist that has dickey front, which is neatly trimmed with a silk embroidered emblem. The sleeves are gathered in narrow plaits and finished with braid trimmed cuffs. Silk embroidered emblem on left sleeve. Color, blue. Ages, 6 to 14 years. **Don't forget to state age.**

No. 38R7594
Price, each..............**$3.89**

$1.74 GALATEA CLOTH. WASHABLE.

Recommended by sanitary officers of public schools. This exceedingly handsome and cleverly designed dress is made of splendid galatea cloth, a very fine and closely woven fabric in good weight. Front of dress is made with panel of cloth with the stripes running crosswise, giving the dress the long one-piece front; also trimmed down front with narrow strappings and narrow red piping. The collar, belt and cuffs are neatly trimmed with red piping to match. Color, navy blue with white stripes. Ages, 6 to 14 years. **What age shall we send you?**

No. 38R7647
Price, each..............**$1.74**

$1.75 SHEPHERD CHECK. WASHABLE.

This dress is made in a simple yet charming design. Best quality galatea cloth, very fine, and yet of sufficient weight for winter wear. Front is tastefully trimmed with narrow red piping, with large buttons to match. Trimmed pocket on the right side. Collar, belt and cuffs neatly piped with red. Extra wide kilted skirt with deep hem. Buttons in back from collar to hem, making it easy to launder. School authorities recommend them. Color, the popular black and white shepherd checks. Ages, 6 to 14 years. **State age desired.**

No. 38R7648
Price, each..............**$1.75**

$1.48 FINEST PERCALE. WASHABLE.

Very neat and serviceable dress, made of blue and white striped percale of the finest quality. Wide band on front of waist, with collar and cuffs made of plain navy blue percale, piped around edges with plain white material. Wide plaits running to shoulders. Wide plaited skirt with deep hem. This dress is buttoned from collar to hem, making it an easy matter to press plaits. A dress that will give everlasting service. Color, blue and white stripes. Ages, 6 to 14 years. **State age, please.**

No. 38R7649
Price, each..............**$1.48**

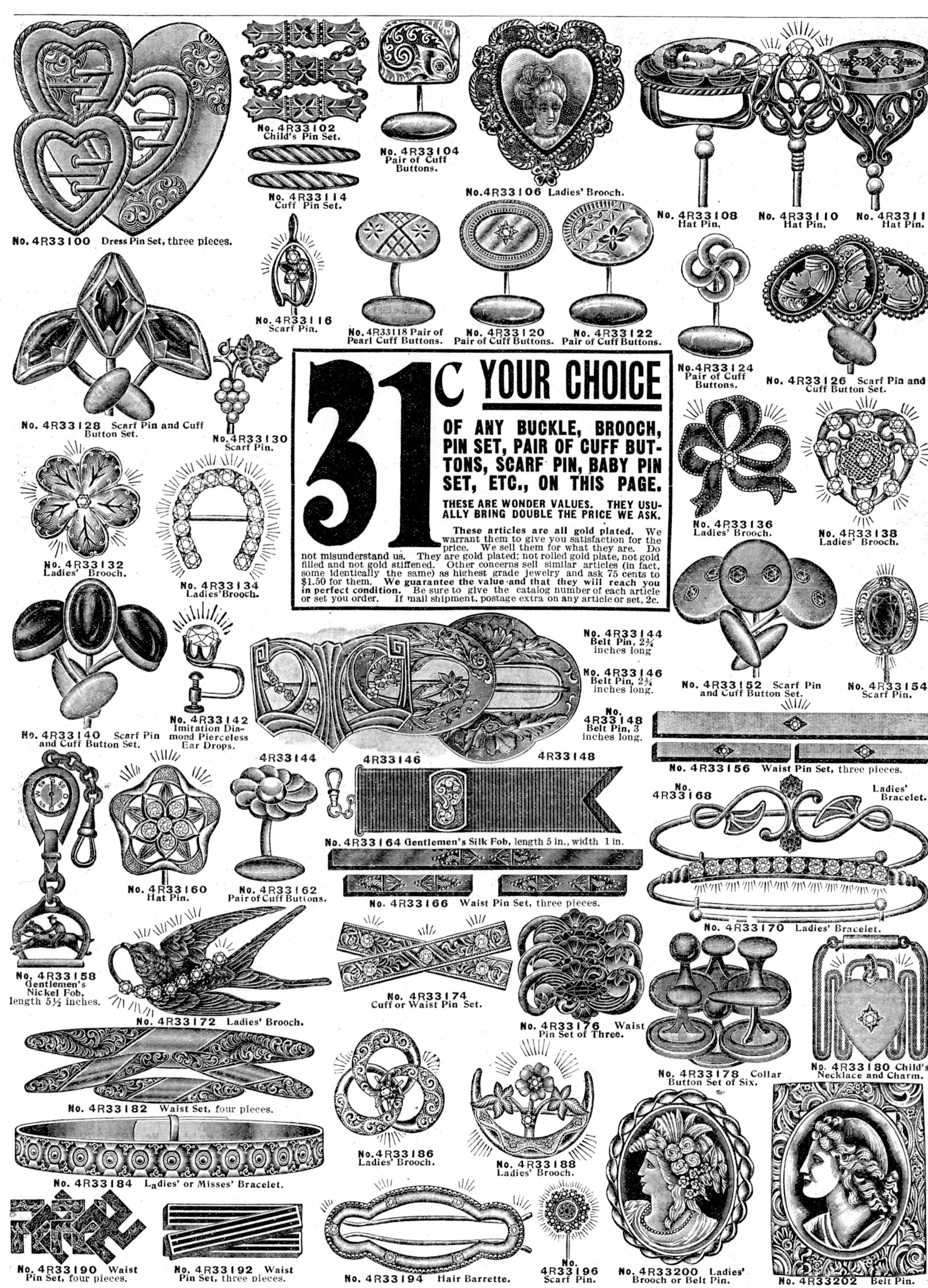

No. 4R33100 Dress Pin Set, three pieces.
No. 4R33102 Child's Pin Set.
No. 4R33104 Pair of Cuff Buttons.
No. 4R33114 Cuff Pin Set.
No. 4R33106 Ladies' Brooch.
No. 4R33108 Hat Pin.
No. 4R33110 Hat Pin.
No. 4R33112 Hat Pin.
No. 4R33116 Scarf Pin.
No. 4R33118 Pair of Pearl Cuff Buttons.
No. 4R33120 Pair of Cuff Buttons.
No. 4R33122 Pair of Cuff Buttons.
No. 4R33124 Pair of Cuff Buttons.
No. 4R33126 Scarf Pin and Cuff Button Set.
No. 4R33128 Scarf Pin and Cuff Button Set.
No. 4R33130 Scarf Pin.
31c YOUR CHOICE
OF ANY BUCKLE, BROOCH, PIN SET, PAIR OF CUFF BUTTONS, SCARF PIN, BABY PIN SET, ETC., ON THIS PAGE.
THESE ARE WONDER VALUES. THEY USUALLY BRING DOUBLE THE PRICE WE ASK.
These articles are all gold plated. We warrant them to give you satisfaction for the price. We sell them for what they are. Do not misunderstand us. They are gold plated; not rolled gold plate, not gold filled and not gold stiffened. Other concerns sell similar articles (in fact, some identically the same) as highest grade jewelry and ask 75 cents to $1.50 for them. We guarantee the value and that they will reach you in perfect condition. Be sure to give the catalog number of each article or set you order. If mail shipment, postage extra on any article or set, 2c.
No. 4R33132 Ladies' Brooch.
No. 4R33134 Ladies' Brooch.
No. 4R33136 Ladies' Brooch.
No. 4R33138 Ladies' Brooch.
No. 4R33140 Scarf Pin and Cuff Button Set.
No. 4R33142 Imitation Diamond Pierceless Ear Drops.
No. 4R33144 Belt Pin, 2¾ inches long
No. 4R33146 Belt Pin, 2¾ inches long.
No. 4R33148 Belt Pin, 3 inches long.
No. 4R33152 Scarf Pin and Cuff Button Set.
No. 4R33154 Scarf Pin.
4R33144
4R33146
4R33148
No. 4R33156 Waist Pin Set, three pieces.
No. 4R33160 Hat Pin.
No. 4R33162 Pair of Cuff Buttons.
No. 4R33164 Gentlemen's Silk Fob, length 5 in., width 1 in.
No. 4R33168 Ladies' Bracelet.
No. 4R33166 Waist Pin Set, three pieces.
No. 4R33170 Ladies' Bracelet.
No. 4R33158 Gentlemen's Nickel Fob, length 5½ inches.
No. 4R33172 Ladies' Brooch.
No. 4R33174 Cuff or Waist Pin Set.
No. 4R33176 Waist Pin Set of Three.
No. 4R33178 Collar Button Set of Six.
No. 4R33180 Child's Necklace and Charm.
No. 4R33182 Waist Set, four pieces.
No. 4R33184 Ladies' or Misses' Bracelet.
No. 4R33186 Ladies' Brooch.
No. 4R33188 Ladies' Brooch.
No. 4R33190 Waist Pin Set, four pieces.
No. 4R33192 Waist Pin Set, three pieces.
No. 4R33194 Hair Barrette.
No. 4R33196 Scarf Pin.
No. 4R33200 Ladies' Brooch or Belt Pin.
No. 4R33202 Belt Pin.

SWEATER COAT SPECIALTIES AND SWEATERS
CARDIGAN AND SMOKING JACKETS
BATH AND LOUNGING ROBES
$1.45 EACH
Colors, Plain Oxford Gray, Oxford trimmed with Navy Blue, Oxford with Brown, Tan with Green or Brown with White.
Black, Brown or Oxford Gray.
$2.45 EACH
IF MAIL SHIPMENT, POSTAGE EXTRA, 1 CENT AN OZ., ACCORDING TO SHIPPING WEIGHT GIVEN
$2.65 EACH
Black, Brown or Oxford Gray.
Oxford Gray or Olive Brown
$4.35 EACH
BE SURE TO STATE SIZE AND COLORS WANTED
LIGHT WEIGHT JERSEY RIBBED SWEATER COAT.
$1.45 EACH No. 33R7855 Colors quoted above. Sizes, 34 to 44 inches State size and color wanted.
Practically All Pure Worsted Light Weight Jersey Knitted Sweater Coat. A serviceable and satisfactory garment for wear indoors or out of doors in mild weather Well made and trimmed Large pearl buttons Retails at $2.50. Shipping wt., 15 oz
FANCY KNITTED CARDIGAN JACKET.
$2.45 EACH No. 33R7908 Colors quoted above. Sizes, 34 to 44 inches State size and color wanted.
Practically Pure Worsted Fancy Knitted Cardigan Jacket, braid bound, and made and finished in best possible manner. Guaranteed to give extraordinary service Shipping wt., 28 oz.
DOUBLE BREASTED CARDIGAN JACKET.
$2.65 EACH No. 33R7911 Colors quoted above. Sizes, 34 to 44 inches. State size and color wanted.
Fancy Zigzag Stitch Double Breasted Cardigan Jacket of fine practically pure worsted yarn, Braid bound Shipping wt., 30 oz.
HUNTER'S SPECIAL SWEATER COAT.
$4.35 EACH No. 33R7859 Colors quoted above. Sizes, 34 to 44 inches. State size and color wanted.
Heaviest Shaker Knitted Pure Wool Sweater Coat, made with open double collar, closed with hooks. Can be worn up for protection or opened back like a coat collar. Pockets lined and bound and stayed at top with strong worsted braid, lower pockets and front closed with large smoked pearl buttons. Shipping wt., 36 oz.
$3.27 EACH
$6.38 AND $3.98 EACH
Dark Blue, Garnet, Brown, Oxford Gray, or Grayish Tan.
No. 33R7898 Colors quoted above. Sizes, 34 to 44 inches. State size and color wanted.
Very Fine Quality Smoking Jacket of double texture wool material Collars, cuffs and pockets faced with plaid back of goods. Fancy silk bound edges and frog fasteners of colors harmonizing with those of jacket Shipping wt., 30 oz
No. 33R7899 Colors as quoted above. Sizes, 34 to 44 inches. State size and color wanted.
Inexpensive Smoking Jacket. Double texture material. Style as above, but not as fine quality Shipping wt., 30 oz.
$2.75 EACH
Dark Green with Brown Trim and Green edge, Smoke Gray with Green Trim and Smoke Edge or Taupe (Olive Green) with Maroon Trim and Taupe Edge.
THE NEW "AUTO" COAT.
No. 33R7853 Colors quoted above. Sizes, 34 to 44 inches. State size and color wanted.
The latest idea in a Sweater Coat, and is certainly very attractive and practical. Nearly pure worsted yarn of fine quality, made with double knitted yoke shoulders, military collar and a new novel idea in contrast trim; the wide strip of facing being in a contrasting color, while the narrow outer edge of the facing is of the same color as body of garment. Large smoked pearl buttons. This coat retails at $4.50 to $5.00. Shipping wt., 26 oz.
Plain Brown or Light Gray.
STYLISH KNITTED VEST.
$1.95 EACH
No. 33R7896 Colors quoted above. Sizes, 34 to 44 inches. State size and color wanted.
One of the most serviceable and sightly vests ever designed for men's wear. Fine closely knitted worsted yarn; armholes, bottom and pockets bound with fine worsted braid. Five smoked pearl buttons. An exceedingly popular garment Shipping wt., 16 oz.
$3.27 EACH
Colors, Blue Figured with Red, Brown with Black, or Gray with Black.
$3.27 EACH No. 33R7635
Sizes, 34 to 48 inches. State size and color wanted.
Blanket Cloth Bath or Lounging Robe for men or women Rich in appearance and very serviceable Shipping wt., 50 oz
Colors, Black and White, Blue and White, or Tan and White.
$3.27 EACH No. 33R7638
Sizes, 34 to 48 inches State size and color wanted.
Terry Cloth Bath Robe for men and women. Similar to Turkish toweling, absorbs moisture, drying the body rapidly Shipping wt., 50 oz.
$1.48 EACH
Navy Blue, Black or Oxford Gray.
MEN'S HEAVY WORSTED FACE SWEATER.
No. 33R7812 Colors quoted above. Sizes, 34 to 44 in. State size and color wanted.
An Extra Heavy, Closely Knitted Pure Worsted Face Sweater, with only a slight mixture of cotton on the inner side, the outer surface being of pure wool yarn. Circular knitted and made with overcast seams, closely ribbed double collar, cuffs and bottom. One of our greatest values as it will wear for several seasons, and always fit snugly and keep its shape Regular retail price for this quality is $2.50 Shipping wt., 24 oz.
$2.39 EACH
Navy Blue, Black or Oxford Gray.
MEN'S HEAVY PURE WORSTED SWEATER.
No. 33R7816 Colors quoted above, Sizes, 34 to 44 inches State size and color wanted.
Closely Knitted Medium Heavy Ribbed Pure Worsted Roll Neck Sweater, made with overcast seams, fancy rickrack knitted shoulders and heavy ribbed double collar and cuffs There is practically no wear out to this garment and the quality and appearance are unsurpassed by any sweater selling at double the price Retails at $3.50. Shipping wt., 25 oz
79c EACH
Navy Blue, Black, Oxford Gray or Maroon.
33c EACH
Combinations of Blue, Black, Oxford Gray, Maroon, Etc.
MEN'S EXTRA HEAVY WOOL SWEATER.
79c EACH No. 33R7804 Colors quoted above. Sizes, 34 to 44 inches. State size and color wanted.
A special value, being made of practically pure wool yarn, closely knitted and extra heavy Closely ribbed double collar, cuffs and bottom, and overcast seams. We are confident that this is a garment that pleases everyone, as its sale has increased by leaps and bounds each succeeding season Shipping wt., 20 oz
Oxford Gray, Navy Blue, Olive Brown.
$3.48 EACH
EXTRA HEAVY SHAKER KNITTED SWEATER.
No. 33R7818 Sizes, 34 to 44. State size and color.
Regular Shaker Knitted Athletic Sweater of pure Australian wool, hand made, heavy ribbed double collar, cuffs and bottom Retails at $5.00 Shipping wt., 34 oz
HEAVY COTTON SWEATER.
33c EACH No. 33R7802 Colors quoted above. Sizes, 34 to 44 inches State size and color wanted.
One of these sweaters will wear three or four seasons. A remarkable value at our price. We bought an immense quantity at half price and offer our customers the full benefit. Ribbed double collar, cuffs and bottom, and overcast seams. Plain or fancy knitted Shipping wt., 24 oz.

$2.98
No. 78K9271½

Particularly becoming style for ladies who can wear a good deep setting shape. Hat is of fine quality smooth finished French felt in royal blue, with wide flange of navy blue and white striped taffeta silk, a folded band of which encircles the crown and is finished at base of trimming with pretty tailored bow. The white fancy feather trimming is of fine quality soft finished quills with curled ends to imitate aigrettes, all wired with soft fluffy marabou feathers. May be ordered in royal blue and white as described; black with white trimming; medium brown with champagne color feathers; black with cardinal red trimming; black with light blue trimming, or all black. **State color.** Shipping weight, 40 ounces.

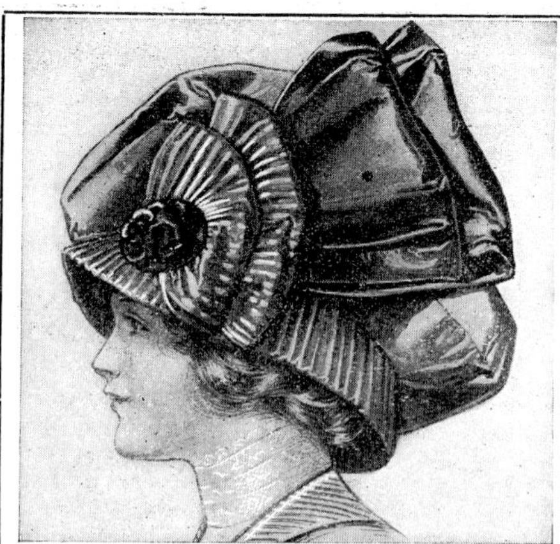

$2.98
No. 78K9276½

This very stylish all velvet turban for misses is called the "Baker's Tam o' Shanter." A good $5.00 value. The close fitting poke shape brim is covered with fluted silk faced paon velvet in dark cerise. The soft tam crown is of the same material. Trimming is of two long wired bows of changeable cardinal and navy blue silk, finished at base with plaited velvet rosettes and jet black cabochon. May be ordered as described in cerise and cardinal; in navy blue, royal blue or dark green, all with changeable silk to harmonize; in black with cerise or light blue silk, or in all solid black. **State color.** Shipping weight, 39 ounces.

$2.98
No. 78K9281½

Stylish, serviceable hat for ladies and misses in the new English walking sailor shape, brim drooping slightly in front and back. The buckram frame is completely covered with black silk faced paon velvet. Trimming is of heavy cream colored lace with upright fancy feather trimming in shaded red and black. Very pretty as described in black with cream color lace and red and black trimming; comes also in cerise top and black under brim; royal blue top and black under brim; in all brown or all navy blue; all hats have cream color lace and shaded feathers to harmonize. **State color.** Shipping weight, 38 ounces.

$2.98
No. 78K9286½

A serviceable low priced hat in most becoming mushroom brim style. Hat is faced with erect pile silk velvet in dark cardinal red. The upper brim and crown is covered with changeable red and blue silk to harmonize. A piping of this silk is laid on the edge of under brim. Trimming is a wide five-loop bow of changeable silk, caught at center with an oval buckle made of the red velvet. Comes in dark red as described; in navy blue or golden brown with changeable silk to harmonize; in black with light blue or primrose red changeable silk; in black with pure white silk, or in solid black. **State color.** Shipping weight, 41 ounces.

$2.98
No. 78K9291½

A splendid value very becoming dress hat with new upright trimming. The shape is of good quality black French felt, bound with silk faced velvet. Trimming is a wide band of imported Oriental lace in white drawn down in points at both sides of brim. The single layer genuine white ostrich feathers in Prince of Wales effect is one of the season's latest novelties. May be ordered in black and white combination as described; black with primrose pink feathers; black with black feathers; navy blue with royal blue feathers; brown with gold color feathers, or dark green with black feathers; all hats have white lace. **State color.** Shipping weight, 56 ounces.

$2.98
No. 78K9296½

Charming bonnet style turban for young ladies. Made on buckram frame with combination of beautiful black silk faced velvet and changeable blue and green taffeta silk. Real $5.00 value. Brim has deep edge of shirred silk with two folds next to velvet. Trimming bows are well wired and finished at base with cabochon and bow knots of silk. Comes in black with changeable blue and green silk as described; in black with changeable cerise and blue silk; black with solid old rose silk; primrose red with changeable silk to match; navy blue with changeable green and blue silk, or in brown with changeable black and old gold silk. **State color.** Shipping weight, 36 ounces.

$2.98
No. 78K9301½

A splendid fitting poke shape turban. The buckram frame is entirely hand covered with black paon silk faced velvet. The trimming is of white imitation marabou feathers with curled ends, each piece wired, making it extremely durable. A knife plaited rosette of pretty silver finished taffeta sets off the base of feathers. Very stylish in black and white combination as described; comes also in all solid black with a touch of gold cloth; in black with rosette of black taffeta silk; in brown with champagne color feathers and gold cloth rosette; all navy blue with gold cloth rosette, or all old rose with gold cloth rosette. **State color.** Shipping weight, 36 ounces.

$2.98
No. 78K9306½

A charming medium size deep setting hat for misses. One of the season's very latest styles. Extra value at a special low price. The buckram frame is faced and partly covered with black silk faced erect pile velvet. The Tam o' Shanter crown in good quality Copenhagen blue mirrored velvet. Trimming of soft fluffy genuine ostrich in white formed into a rosette with two quills sweeping over side of brim. Very pretty as described in black and Copenhagen blue and white ostrich; comes also in black with cerise top and white ostrich, black with cardinal red and black ostrich; all black with white ostrich; navy blue with Copenhagen blue ostrich, or in all solid black. **State color.** Shipping weight, 35 ounces.

$2.98
No. 78K9311½

A smart tailored effect ready to wear hat. Made on a very soft finished bright navy blue shape of fine quality French felt. $5.00 value. The facing and trimming is of changeable green and blue taffeta silk to match, all beautifully shirred and corded. The long quill effect is of folded silk, edged with bright navy blue silk faced velvet to match hat. May be ordered in bright navy blue as described; in brown or cardinal red, both with changeable taffeta silk to harmonize; in black with cerise and royal blue changeable silk; in black with white silk, or in all solid black. **State color.** Shipping weight, 41 ounces.

WOMEN'S CLOTH AND VELVETEEN SUITS

You can safely order a ready made suit from us. Our unique system of sizes which furnishes every size in three different proportions assures you a perfect fit without alterations. If your suit is not all that you desire and perfectly satisfactory, send it back and we will return your money or exchange your suit.

Sizes

Women's Tailored Suits offered on this page are furnished ready to wear only, exactly as illustrated and described. Sizes, 32, 33, 34, 35, 36, 37, 38, 39, 40, 41, 42, 43 and 44 inches bust measure, 22 to 30 inches waist measure, 38 to 50 inches hip measure, and 37 up to and including 43 inches front length of skirt. Each size is furnished in three different proportions, making thirty-nine sizes in all, which guarantees a perfect fit. Skirt will be furnished with hem sewed in length ordered. If open hem is wanted, please mention it in order. We will make larger sizes to special order for 20 per cent extra, or one-fifth more than prices quoted. We require from ten to fourteen days' time in which to make special orders. See inside front cover page for simple measuring instructions. If you wish to see cloth samples of our ready to wear suits, write for Sample Book No. 80K and we will send it to you free and postpaid on request.

AS A PLAIN SUIT SHOWS FINE HAND TAILORING TO BEST ADVANTAGE, we have chosen a strictly tailored style for our finest suit. Material is our finest pure wool chiffon finish broadcloth. Coat made in fashionable 32-inch length with straight French back. Lined with Skinner's guaranteed yarn dyed satin. Slash breast pocket. Ivory buttons. Skirt made in new side trimmed effect, finished with deep lap seam. Closes at left of habit back panel. High waist. Average sweep, 2⅓ yards. **Give measurements.** Shipping weight, 5 pounds.

		EACH
No. 31K1135½	**Black.**	
No. 31K1136½	**Navy blue.**	
No. 31K1137½	**Smoke gray.**	**$22.50**
No. 31K1138½	**Brown.**	

THIS LUSTROUS VELVETEEN is the closest copy of an all silk velvet we have ever sold. Coat made in fashionable 32-inch length with side trimmed back. Closes with handsome silk braid ornaments and braid covered buttons. Trimmed with black silk military braid. Lined throughout with guaranteed satin of yarn dye construction. Skirt cut in six-gore style and finished in fashionable side trimmed effect, raised waist line, panel back. Trimmed to match coat. Average sweep, 2½ yards. **Give measurements.** Shipping weight, 5 pounds.

		EACH
No. 31K1130½	**Black.**	**$20.00**
No. 31K1131½	**Navy blue.**	

THIS MATERIAL IS A SPLENDID HEAVY ALL WOOL CHEVIOT in self stripe effect, very popular this season and an ideal fabric for fall and winter suits. Coat cut in 32-inch length with straight French back, finished with slash pockets, tailor stitching on sleeves and inlaid collar of black velvet. Lined with guaranteed satin. Ivory buttons. Skirt cut in six-gore high waisted style with side trimmed effect front and back. Average sweep, 2¾ yards. **Give measurements.** Shipping weight, 4¾ pounds.

		EACH
No. 31K1140½	**Black.**	**$12.75**
No. 31K1141½	**Navy blue.**	

EXTRA SIZE SUITS—This season we have selected a few stylish models in extra sizes and long coat suits which we offer on page 188 at the same low prices quoted on regular style suits. Every suit guaranteed perfectly satisfactory or your money returned.

THIS IS A SPLENDID TAILORED SUIT for general or dress wear. Material is an all wool worsted in the popular narrow diagonal weave. Coat cut in 32-inch length with round cutaway fronts and straight French back. Trimmed with narrow black silk military braid, salt water pearl buttons and two-tone corded silk in contrasting shade. Braid covered buttons. Lined with guaranteed satin of yarn dye construction. Skirt cut in four-gore style with wide front and raised waist line. Closes at left of habit back panel. Average sweep, 2¾ yards. **Give measurements.** Shipping weight, 5 pounds.

		EACH
No. 31K1145½	**Black.**	
No. 31K1146½	**Navy blue.**	**$17.50**
No. 31K1147½	**Smoke gray.**	

SAMPLES—If you want to see cloth samples of our suits send for our Special Catalog 80K. Free on request.

FUR SET OF GENUINE FOX. Scarf and muff cut in full animal skin effect, each finished with one large natural head, one tail, and skin paws. Set lined with messaline silk. Average shipping weight of set, 47 ounces; scarf, 25 ounces; muff, 30 ounces.

41K6900 Red Fox. Set.... $18.00	41K6901 Scarf only. Red.... $9.00	41K6902 Muff only. Red.... $9.00
41K6905 Gray Fox. Set.... $18.00	41K6906 Scarf only. Gray.... $9.00	41K6907 Muff only. Gray... $9.00
41K6910 Black Fox. Set... $21.00	41K6911 Scarf only. Black. $10.50	41K6912 Muff only. Black. $10.50
41K6915 Isabella Fox. Set.... $18.00	41K6916 Scarf only Isabella.. $9.00	41K6917 Muff only. Isabella... $9.00

FUR SET OF GENUINE SELECTED FOX. Scarf cut in Russian shawl style, trimmed with tails and skin paws. Large down stuffed pillow muff. Set lined with guaranteed satin. Average shipping weight of set, 60 ounces; scarf, 31 ounces; muff, 32 ounces.

41K6920 Black Fox. Set.... $35.00	41K6921 Scarf only. Black. $17.50	41K6922 Muff only. Black. $17.50
41K6925 Natural Red Fox. Set.... $30.00	41K6926 Scarf only. Red... $15.00	41K6927 Muff only. Red.. $15.00
41K6930 Isabella Brown Fox. Set.... $25.00	41K6931 Scarf only. Isabella $12.50	41K6932 Muff only. Isabella $12.50

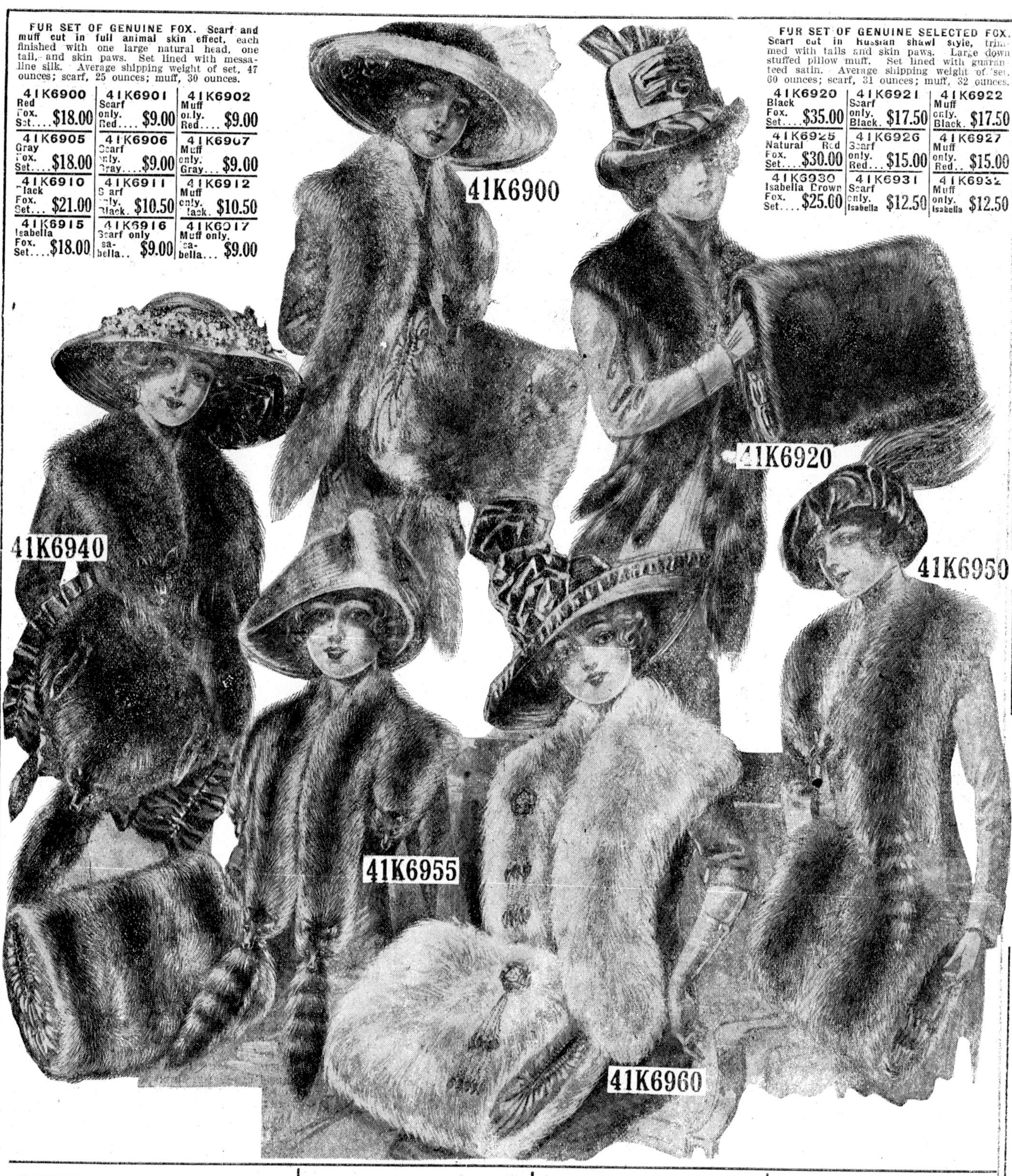

HANDSOME NOVELTY FUR SET. Made of genuine fox in black and natural red. Animal effect scarf. Muff in animal effect combined with changeable messaline silk, which also lines set. Average shipping weight of set, 55 ounces; scarf, 25 ounces; muff, 37 ounces.

41K6940 Black Fox. Set..... $39.50	41K6941 Scarf only. Black... $18.50	41K6942 Muff only. Black... $21.00
41K6945 Natural Red Fox. Set..... $31.50	41K6946 Scarf only. Red... $15.00	41K6947 Muff only. Red.... $16.50

COMPARISON WILL SHOW that the quality of our Furs entitles us to your orders. We offer a better quality than you usually find offered in the average store and our prices mean a large saving.

NATURAL RACCOON SET in new effect. Made from choice selected genuine raccoon, a rich bronze gray fur with darker stripe markings. Scarf cut in double animal skin effect, finished with heads and tails. Muff in half Empire shape stuffed with down. Scarf and muff lined with messaline silk. Average shipping weight of set, 59 ounces; scarf, 30 ounces; muff, 34 ounces.

41K6955 Gray Set.. $29.50	41K6956 Scarf only. Gray $14.00	41K6957 Muff only. Gray $15.50

BEAUTIFULLY TRIMMED WHITE "ICELAND FOX" SET. Made from the fluffy snow white fur of the Thibet lamb (better known as "Iceland Fox"). Large Russian shawl scarf and large well padded semi-barrel muff. Set lined with rich lavender satin, which is combined with silk cord, in hand made rose ornaments which decorate scarf and muff. A very appropriate set for evening or general dressy wear. Average shipping weight of set, 57 ounces; scarf, 21 ounces; muff, 37 ounces.

41K6960 White Set.. $15.90	41K6961 Scarf only. White. $7.90	41K6962 Muff only. White $8.00

GENUINE NATURAL RACCOON SET. Made of natural bronze gray raccoon fur with darker stripe markings. Scarf cut in full animal skin effect, trimmed with head, tail and tabs. Good size pillow muff. Set lined with guaranteed satin. This is a stylish and practical set for general wear. Average shipping weight of set, 44 ounces; scarf, 22 ounces; muff, 30 ounces.

41K6950 Natural gray. Set. $20.75	41K6951 Scarf only. Gray.. $9.75	41K6952 Muff only. Gray $11.00

FUR COATS

GENUINE PONYSKIN COAT. Made from good grade genuine Russian ponyskin with natural moire markings. Coat cut in semi-box style with lapover front, closing with large crochet buttons and loops. Long roll Russian shawl collar. Wide turnback cuffs. Coat lined throughout with rich old rose Skinner's guaranteed satin with facing of black satin at bottom to protect the delicate color of lining. Coat fitted with satin covered arm shields and large shirred inside pocket. Length, 52 inches. Average shipping weight, 9¼ pounds.

No. 41K2810 Black. EACH **$52.50**

GENUINE BEAVER MUFF. Made in large half Empire style, well padded and lined with rich changeable silk. Fur matches collar on No. 41K2815. Average shipping weight, 30 ounces.

No. 41K6175 Muff only. EACH **$23.00**

MARMOT COAT with beaver trimmings. Fur resembles mink in texture, sometimes sold as **"Russian Mink."** Coat cut in semi-box style, closing with large handsome ornament and buttons. Extra large Russian shawl collar and wide turnback cuffs of genuine beaver fur. Coat lined throughout with brown diagonal silk. Has protecting facing of black satin at bottom. Silk covered arm shields, one chamois lined and one fancy inside pocket. Length of coat, 52 inches. Average shipping weight, 8 pounds 5 ounces.

No. 41K2815 Brown. EACH **$59.50**

PLAIN MARMOT COAT. Made in similar style to No. 41K2815, with collar and cuffs of marmot instead of beaver Lined throughout with yellow moire silk. Length of coat, 50 inches. Average shipping wt., 8 lbs.

No. 41K2820 Brown. EACH **$52.00**

41K6175

41K2825

41K2830

41K2810

41K2815

GENUINE PONYSKIN COAT, with dyed raccoon trimmings. Made from choice selected genuine Russian ponyskin of exceptional luster with perfect moire markings. Coat cut in loose semi-box style, closing with large silk braid ornament and braid covered buttons. Genuine raccoon fur dyed black is used to form large Russian shawl collar, which graduates into shaped border extending around lower edge of coat; also forms wide turnback cuffs. Coat lined throughout with beautiful brocaded satin in delicate pastel shades. Fancy chamois lined inside pocket. Length of coat, 50 inches. Average shipping weight, 9 pounds.

No. 41K2825 Black. EACH **$80.00**

GENUINE BLENDED MUSKRAT COAT. Made from beautiful, perfectly matched skins of genuine muskrat. Coat cut in semi-box style with lapover front closing with handsome silk braid ornaments and buttons. Fur is worked in border effect around bottom of coat and outlining deep side vents which are finished with fringed ornaments. Large Russian shawl collar and turnback cuffs. Coat lined with beautiful brocaded satin. Two fancy chamois lined inside pockets. Length of coat, 52 inches. Average shipping weight, 9½ pounds.

No. 41K2830 Brown. EACH **$99.00**

SIZES **ALL LADIES' FUR COATS offered on this page are furnished ready to wear only,** exactly as illustrated and described, in sizes from 32 inches up to and including 42 inches bust measure. We will make larger sizes to special order for 20 per cent extra, or one-fifth more than prices quoted. We require from two to three weeks' time to make coats to special order. **When ordering give bust measure, height and weight.** See inside front cover page for simple measuring instructions.

Women's Dresses Illustrated in Actual Colors

WOMEN'S STUNNING COMBINATION DRESS. This combination of velveteen and suiting material is one of the season's smartest designs and makes a stylish yet practical dress. Material used is mohair or Sicilian with waist and sleeves of self color velveteen of good quality. Dress made in one-piece open front style, with panel habit back skirt. Waist trimmed with turnback cuffs, circular collar and single rever of Sicilian. Finished with self color buttons and silk cord piping. Shipping weight, 21 ounces.

No. 31K1480 Navy blue.
No. 31K1481 Wine.
No. 31K1482 Brown.
No. 31K1483 Black.
EACH **$5.90**

WOMEN'S CHANGEABLE TAFFETA DRESS. We selected the season's most fashionable fabric, changeable pure silk taffeta, and had it made in this striking style copied from a French model, as a special feature for our color page. Dress cut in one-piece open back style, trimmed with the fashionable Macrame lace, which forms turnback cuffs, and new side trimmed effect on back and front of waist. High collar and extension sleeves of fine Oriental allover lace. Shipping weight, 20 ounces.

No. 31K1485 Red and green changeable.
No. 31K1486 Blue and black changeable.
EACH **$13.75**

WOMEN'S DRESS IN NEW EFFECT. The material is a good quality mohair Sicilian in pencil stripe effect. Made in the fashionable new Cossack blouse design. Trimmed with self color velveteen, taffeta covered buttons and loops and white Venise insertion. Skirt has inverted plait in back. Waist finished with fancy shaped velveteen peplum. Open back. Shipping weight, 28 oz.

No. 31K1490 Navy blue.
No. 31K1491 Wine.
No. 31K1492 Gray.
No. 31K1493 Black.
EACH **$5.85**

WOMEN'S DRESS OF WHIPCORD SERGE. A splendid quality wool and cotton mixed wide wale whipcord serge. Trimmed with rich two-tone stripe velveteen in harmonizing shade, taffeta silk and colored pearl buttons. Dress made in one-piece open front style, with extension sleeves and detachable high collar dickey of silk embroidered net. Skirt has habit panel back. Gibson plait at shoulders. Shipping wt., 28 ounces.

No. 31K1495 Brown.
No. 31K1496 Navy blue.
No. 31K1497 Black.
EACH **$5.95**

WOMEN'S PURE WOOL SERGE DRESS. From neck to hem this is at least a $10.00 value. Retail and department stores would sell this dress for $10.00 to $12.00. The material is a fine heavy quality pure wool serge. Trimmed with lustrous black satin. Made in one-piece open front style, with circular habit back skirt. Trimmed with wide braid and buttons. The single rever and heavy silk cord at waist are new features. The finely plaited side frill and sleeve frills of delicate shadow lace edged with black silk braid also add a smart new touch. Shipping weight, 31 oz.

No. 31K1500 Navy blue.
EACH **$6.75**

WOMEN'S BRAID TRIMMED BROADCLOTH DRESS. Even the picture in actual colors doesn't do this dress full justice, as you would never expect to get such fine material at such a low price. Made of pure wool twill back broadcloth. Trimmed with soutache braid, which is applied in new border effect around yoke and down front, which closes with buttons and loops of the braid. Dress made in high waisted open front style, with habit back. Extension sleeves, yoke and collar of self color net. Shipping weight, 36 ounces.

No. 31K1505 Wine.
No. 31K1506 Navy blue.
No. 31K1507 Black.
EACH **$6.85**

SIZES **READ CAREFULLY BEFORE ORDERING. Ladies' Dresses offered on this page are furnished only exactly as illustrated and described, in the following sizes: From 32 up to and including 44 inches bust measure, 23 to 30 inches waist measure and 37 to 43 inches front length of skirt. We will make larger sizes to special order for 20 per cent extra, or one-fifth more than prices quoted. We require from ten to fourteen days' time to make special orders. All dresses will be furnished in skirt length ordered, but with open hem so that length can be adjusted to suit customer. When ordering give your bust measure, waist measure and front length of skirt. For simple measuring instructions see inside front cover.**

Misses' Dresses Illustrated in Their Actual Colors

SCHOOL DRESS OF MIXED SUITING. When you think of it, a calico dress made in this pretty style would be worth $2.75. Then you have only to consider that this material is a good quality wool and cotton mixed suiting which looks like wool, to realize what a big value we are giving you at this price. Dress made in graceful one-piece style, buttoning invisibly in back. Trimmed with mercerized poplin in harmonizing shade, plaid taffeta silk piping and Venise lace. Shipping weight, 26 ounces.

No. 31K1450 Navy blue.
No. 31K1451 Brown.
No. 31K1452 Wine.
Price, each.. **$2.75**

MISSES' VELVETEEN DRESS. If anything could be prettier than this rich wine color velveteen dress it is the same dress in the other two colors. Made in the simple artistic style pictured, closing in front with satin buttons and loops, which form novel trimming. Cut in high waisted effect with panel habit back. Trimmed with pipings, turnback cuffs and tie of messaline silk. Dutch collar of Venise lace. Material is a good quality lustrous velveteen. Shipping weight, 28 oz.

No. 31K1455 Wine.
No. 31K1456 Navy blue.
No. 31K1457 Black.
Price, each.. **$7.95**

MISSES' ALL WOOL SERGE DRESS. This frock has a very smart tailored effect and is especially appropriate for school or general wear. Material is a good quality pure wool serge. Made in one-piece style, with Gibson plait at shoulders and habit panel back skirt. Dutch collar and turnback sleeves scalloped and embroidered with white silk. Dress buttons in front with large black buttons having white pearl centers. Front closing outlined with blue and white silk cord piping. Well made and finished. One of our very best values. Shipping weight, 28 oz.

No. 31K1460 Navy blue.
Price, each.. **$4.95**

MISSES' PARTY DRESS OF ALL WOOL CHALLIS. This dress in the tan with the dainty blue trimmings makes a beautiful girlish looking frock for party or general dress wear. The navy blue with red dots and red trimmings is suitable for more practical wear and is the very embodiment of girlish style. Material is the well known pure wool Botany Challis, with trimmings of fine lustrous messaline silk and silk covered buttons, high collar and extension sleeves of shadow lace. Made in one-piece style, closing in the back. Waist and sleeves lined with lawn. Shipping weight, 22 oz.

No. 31K1465 Tan with blue trimmings.
No. 31K1466 Navy blue with red trimmings.
Price, each.. **$9.95**

MISSES' MESSALINE TRIMMED CHALLIS DRESS. This is a very quaint style, most becoming to slender figures and one of the most popular designs of the season. The material is a good quality part wool challis with trimmings of satin messaline in harmonizing shade. Dress cut in one-piece open front style, with panel habit back skirt. Satin messaline forms circular surplice collar, wide turnback cuffs and plaited frill at waist which gives coat blouse effect. Shipping weight, 20 ounces.

No. 31K1470 Brown.
No. 31K1471 Navy blue.
No. 31K1472 Wine.
Price, each.. **$4.98**

MISSES' CHANGEABLE SILK DRESS. In Paris and New York changeable taffeta silk is the rage for one-piece dresses and the new changeable silks are a delight to the eye. This frock is made of a soft lustrous changeable chiffon taffeta with detachable collar of heavy Macrame lace, another of the season's fancies, and black velvet ribbon which forms quaint tie, trimmings on sleeves and girdle ending in a many looped bow in the back. Dress cut in one-piece habit back style, closing invisibly in back. Shipping wt., 17 ounces.

No. 31K1475 Blue and green changeable.
No. 31K1476 Red and green changeable.
Price, each.. **$8.95**

SIZES **READ CAREFULLY BEFORE ORDERING. Misses' Dresses on this page are furnished in sizes from 32 up to and including 38 inches bust measure, 22 up to and including 27 inches waist measure and 32 up to and including 38 inches front length of skirt. We do not furnish misses' dresses in larger sizes. If larger sizes are required, selection must be made from our line of women's dresses. Small or short women who wear misses' clothing will please remember that a misses' dress, size 38, is no larger in the bust than a women's dress, size 36. All dresses on this page will be sent with skirt finished with open hem unless otherwise requested. See inside front cover for simple measuring instructions.**

Junior Dresses for 13 to 17-Year Old Girls

BRAID AND BUTTON TRIMMED PURE WOOL SERGE DRESS. This is a frock **that is dressy enough for any occasion**, yet made in such a simple style with nothing on it that soils easily, so that it is perfectly practical for everyday school wear. Material is a good quality pure wool storm serge. Made in the popular high waisted style with panel habit back skirt and inset kimono sleeves. Closes invisibly at side front. Trimmed with wide black and white silk novelty braid and silver ball buttons. **Give measurements.** Shipping weight, 30 ounces.

No. 31K1515½ Navy blue. EACH **$6.95**

DIAGONAL SUITING DRESS with solid color trimming. The beauty of a dress of this kind is that it looks like wool, does not soil as readily as ordinary wash fabrics, yet when it is soiled it can be washed as easily as gingham. Material is good heavy quality striped cotton suiting with trimmings of solid navy blue, black and white novelty braid and lacquered buttons. Dress cut in one-piece, open back style, buttoning under fly. Full plaited skirt. **Give measurements.** Shipping weight, 24 ounces.

No. 31K1525 Blue with gray. EACH **$1.95**

BLACK AND WHITE MOHAIR DRESS, with black satin trimmings. If you want the very newest thing in a smart junior dress here it is. In material, style and trimming it is the last word in fashion effects. Made of fine high luster mohair in large black and white shepherd check with trimmings of black satin, detachable white ace collar, emerald green tie and nameled leatherette belt. Dress cut in ne-piece style with panel back skirt and box plaited Russian blouse waist. loses in front. **Give measurements.** Shipping weight, 28 ounces.

No. 31K1540½ Black nd white. EACH **$8.75**

SIZES FOR JUNIOR DRESSES.

Dresses offered on this page furnished only exactly as illustrated and described. Simple measuring instructions will be found on inside front cover page. **Be sure to give girl's age.**

Ages	13	15	17
Average bust measure, inches	32	33	35
Average waist measure, inches	26	26	26
Average length, inches	32	34	36

BRAID TRIMMED PURE WOOL SERGE DRESS. This is a dress that does not go out of style with the seasons. Ask any girl who has one and she will tell you that her sailor dress is her favorite frock. Material used is splendid quality heavy pure wool storm serge. Made in regulation one-piece sailor style, buttoning in front, with extra large sailor collar, button cuffs and detachable dickey, trimmed with red pure silk military braid. Waist finished with red silk tie. Skirt cut with habit panel back. **Give measurements.** Shipping weight, 35 ounces.

No. 31K1535½ Navy blue. EACH **$7.45**

EMBROIDERED NET OVER SILK DROP. For a young girl's party dress nothing could be more charming or girlish than this dainty dress of embroidered Oriental net, over thin silk like "Japonica" drop. Made in one-piece open back style with wide bands of embroidered net over shoulders, giving fichu effect. Waist lined with "Japonica," which looks like silk and wears better. Skirt of embroidered net with band of crochet effect insertion at bottom over "Japonica" drop. Messaline satin girdle to match drop. **Give measurements.** Shipping weight, 18 ounces.

No. 31K1545½ White with white drop.

No. 31K1546½ White with pale blue drop. EACH **$6.45**

SOLID COLOR BROADCLOTH DRESS with striped trimming. Material is a good quality wool and cotton mixed broadcloth with soft smooth finish. Made in neat one-piece style, buttoning invisibly in back. Furnished in navy blue and wine. Navy blue dress trimmed with blue and white stripe mercerized foulard, wine color dress trimmed with wine color and white striped mercerized foulard. Skirt cut in fashionable high waisted style. **Give measurements.** Shipping weight, 32 ounces.

No. 31K1530 Navy blue.
No. 31K1531 Wine. EACH **$2.75**

SHEPHERD CHECK SUITING DRESS with French flannel trimmings. A splendid school dress for a junior. Made of good medium weight shepherd check cotton suiting which looks like wool, yet washes like gingham. Dress cut in one-piece open back style, buttoning under fly. Trimmed with bias stripes of self material, black pipings and new single rever, turnback cuffs and buttons of red French flannel. Waist and sleeves lined with cambric. **Give measurements.** Shipping weight, 24 ounces.

No. 31K1510 Black and white. EACH **$1.59**

PURE WOOL SERGE DRESS with silk braid trimming. A dress that is perfectly practical for general everyday wear and yet has new style touches which make it a dress-up frock. Made of good heavy quality all wool storm serge in navy blue with trimmings of navy blue and dark red silk braid, oxidized buttons with dark red centers and dark blue silk lacing. Cut in one-piece high waisted style, buttoning invisibly in back. **Give measurements.** Shipping weight, 28 ounces.

No. 31K1520½ Navy blue. EACH **$5.98**

SIZES			
Ages, years	13	15	17
Bust measure, inches	32	34	36
Length, inches	45	47	49

Stylish Winter Coats for Juniors

AGES 13, 15 AND 17 YEARS.

Sample of material of any coat sent upon request.

HEAVY WEIGHT WOOL MIXED CLOTH COAT IN A NICE DARK MIXTURE.

The cloth in this garment is very closely woven and of good weight, being about three-quarters wool. Made in one-piece back style, slightly fitted. Front is finished with wide facings of self material, fastening at the side with large fancy buttons. Large full cuffs and patch pockets. Large collar trimmed with small buttons and narrow braid. See size scale above. Shipping weight, 4¾ pounds.

No. 17K5321 Price........ **$3.75**

ALL WOOL CHEVIOT COATS IN NAVY BLUE, GOLDEN BROWN OR GRAY.

This cheviot is all wool, very soft, thick and closely woven. Made in the popular Polo style with full back, having side vents and wide belt. Extra wide double breasted front, fastening at the side. The adjustable collar is a strong feature, as it may be worn as shown in the large illustration or buttoned close to the neck. See size scale. Shipping weight, 5¼ pounds.

No. 17K5334 Navy blue.
No. 17K5335 Go'den brown.
No. 17K5336 Gray.
EACH **$6.95**

ALL WOOL HEAVY WEIGHT CHEVIOT COATS IN BROWN, RED OR NAVY BLUE. TRIMMED WITH IMITATION BABY LAMB.

This cheviot is all pure wool, heavy, soft and pliable. Full back trimmed with half belt. Extra wide lapover front, fastening at the extreme side with large fancy buttons. Deep rolling shawl collar and cuffs of Caucasian cloth, being one of the best imitations of baby lamb manufactured. Pockets trimmed to match the collar and cuffs. See size scale. Shipping weight, 5 pounds.

No. 17K5337 Brown.
No. 17K5338 Red.
No. 17K5339 Navy blue.
EACH **$6.90**

NORFOLK STYLE COATS IN HEAVY ALL WOOL CHEVIOT IN NAVY BLUE OR GRAY.

The cheviot used is a very heavy weight all wool, very closely woven. The Norfolk style is very popular this season. Wide straps down the back. (See back view.) The front fastens with large fancy metal buttons and has straps from the shoulders down. Large patch pockets and wide belt. Collar and cuffs are made of an excellent quality of heavy weight black and white shepherd check wool cloth. See size scale. Shipping weight, 5 pounds.

No. 17K5342 Navy blue.
No. 17K5343 Gray.
EACH **$8.48**

SILK SEAL PLUSH COAT. LINED WITH BLACK MERCERIZED SATEEN.

The silk seal plush used in this garment is a very fine quality, a rich brown black in color and closely resembles real sealskin. Made with one-piece back, slightly fitted and ending in side vents. Extra wide lapover front, fastening at the side with large fancy metal buttons. Large rolling shawl collar. Sleeves finished with full cuffs. The coat is lined throughout with good quality of black mercerized sateen. See size scale. Shipping weight, 6 pounds.

No. 17K5349 Price........................ **$10.00**

WOOL CHINCHILLA CLOTH COATS IN NAVY BLUE OR GRAY. TRIMMED IN CONTRASTING COLORS.

The wool chinchilla cloth used is a heavy weight, having roughish small curl pebbly finish. Full one-piece back, trimmed with wide belt and buttons. Extra wide lapover front, fastened at side with large fancy metal buttons. See size scale. Shipping weight, 5¼ pounds.

No. 17K5344 Navy blue with gray trimming.
No. 17K5345 Gray with navy blue trimming.
EACH **$7.50**

BLACK CARACUL CLOTH OR IMITATION FUR COAT, SOMETIMES CALLED "BROADTAIL."

This caracul cloth is woven in the most furlike pattern of the finest mohair, having deep moire markings in a wavy silky furlike pattern; in fact, it is hard to distinguish it from a real fur. Very durable. One-piece back, slightly fitted, ending in side vents. Extra wide lapover front, fastening at side with large fancy metal buttons. Deep rolling shawl collar and full cuffs. This coat is lined throughout with a very good quality of black mercerized sateen. See size scale. Shipping weight, 5½ pounds.

No. 17K5348 Black. Price.... **$6.98**

PRINCESS SLIPS, CHEMISES, COMBINATION SUITS AND GYMNASIUM SUITS

SIZES.

Slips, combination suits and chemises, 34 to 44 inches bust measure. Gymnasium suits, 32 to 42 inches bust measure. ALWAYS STATE SIZE.

If mail shipment is necessary, send postage extra, 1 cent an ounce.

AVERAGE SHIPPING WEIGHTS:

Princess Slips, about	12 ounces
Combination Suits, about	6 ounces
Chemises, about	10 ounces
Gymnasium Suits	28 ounces
Boudoir Caps	3 ounces

No. 38K2050 Navy blue.
No. 38K2051 Black.
WOMEN'S GYMNASIUM SUIT of fine quality all wool serge. Standard club cut. Made full and on perfect lines, and is beautifully finished. State size.
Price, each.................. **$4.48**

No. 38K6227 WOMEN'S SHORT WHITE CAMBRIC CHEMISE. Yoke trimmed with wide and narrow tucks. Neck and armholes finished with narrow ruffle.
Price, each.................. **39c**

No. 38K6228 WOMEN'S LONG WHITE CAMBRIC CHEMISE. Nearly ankle length. Yoke trimmed with cotton torchon lace insertion, with ribbon draw string. Armholes and bottom ruffle neatly edged with lace. A well made garment.
Price, each.................. **49c**

POPULAR BOUDOIR CAPS.

Three styles, as illustrated, for women and girls. Priced extremely low, very practical and make a neat and inexpensive gift.

No. 38K5986 Made of lace net trimmed with ribbon and rosettes.
Price, each.................. **39c**

No. 38K5987 Better quality of lace net with ribbon trimming.
Price, each.................. **48c**

No. 38K5988 Fine quality lace net trimmed with ribbon and rosebuds. Has double lace ruffle.
Price, each.................. **59c**

No. 38K2052 Black.
No. 38K2053 Navy blue.
GYMNASIUM SUIT of fine quality granite cloth. White braids, shield and tie. Correct lines and ample fullness. State size.
Price, each.......... **$3.68**

No. 38K6230 WHITE LAWN PRINCESS SLIP. Trimmed with Valenciennes lace insertion, embroidered medallions, beading and ribbon draw. Neck, armholes and tucked flounce edged with lace to match.
Price, each.............. **95c**

No. 38K6231 FINE WHITE LAWN PRINCESS SLIP. Yoke trimmed with embroidery beading and ribbon to take in fullness. Embroidery edged neck and armholes. Tucked flounce with beautiful embroidery ruffle.
Price, each........... **$1.18**

No. 38K6235 HANDSOME WHITE LAWN PRINCESS SLIP. Yoke trimmed with fine Valenciennes lace insertion, beading and ribbon draw. Lace edged neck and armholes. Extra deep ruffled flounce trimmed to match. Has protecting underlay.
Price, each........... **$1.39**

No. 38K6207 Corset cover and skirt.
No. 38K6208 Corset cover and drawers.
COMBINATION SUIT. Made of pretty pattern lawn embroidery of good quality; corset cover has embroidery back. Embroidery ribbon beading at waist line. Perfect fitting. Price, each.......... **98c**

No. 38K6237 VERY PRETTY FINE WHITE LAWN PRINCESS SLIP. Back and front yoke of beautiful embroidery, and ribbon beading at bust, and also ribbon draw string at neck to take in fullness. Deep tucked flounce of embroidery to match yoke. Made with protecting underlay. Perfect fitting.
Price, each............ **$1.95**

No. 38K6236 DAINTY WHITE LAWN PRINCESS SLIP. Yoke trimmed with embroidery medallion, and ribbon beading insertions. Neck and armholes edged with fine embroidery. Has embroidery flounce with clusters of tucks. Ruffled underlay.
Price, each........... **$1.69**

Corset Covers and Bust Ruffles

Corset Cover sizes, 34 to 44 inches bust measure.
Average shipping weight, 3 ounces.

No. 38K5905 PLAIN CORSET COVER. Embroidered edge at neck and armholes. Good quality. **Mention bust** measure. Price, each.............. **15c**

No. 38K5901 PRETTY CORSET COVER of soft muslin. Yoke of Valenciennes lace insertion, beading and silk ribbon. Neck and armholes edged with lace. **Mention bust measure.** Price, each.......................... **19c**

No. 38K5912 CORSET COVER. Front is made of lawn embroidery, plain back, trimmed at neck with embroidery edge. Ribbon draw string. Armholes edged with torchon lace. **State bust measure.** Price, each.......................... **24c**

No. 38K5972 CORSET COVER. Made of nainsook, trimmed with wide band of lace beading, with silk ribbon. Neck and armholes lace edged. A remarkable value. **State bust measure.** Price, each.......................... **29c**

No. 38K5924 VERY PRETTY EMBROIDERY CORSET COVER, with draw string at neck. Armholes and back are edged with lace. **State bust measure.** Price, each.......................... **39c**

No. 38K5956 FLUFFY RUFFLE CAMBRIC CORSET COVER and Bust Ruffles combined. Lace edged ruffles and draw string at neck. **State bust measure.** Price, each.......................... **44c**

No. 38K5952 ELABORATE CORSET COVER. Embroidery back and front with ribbon draw string at neck. Armholes edged with Valenciennes lace. **State bust measure.** Price, each.......................... **48c**

No. 38K5968 ALLOVER EMBROIDERY CORSET COVER in an exquisite pattern. Ribbon draw string at neck. Exceptional value. **State bust measure.** Price, each.......................... **58c**

BUST RUFFLES.

No. 38K5985 BUST RUFFLES. Made of four ruffles of attractive embroidery. Finished with ribbon beading and lace. Each.... **48c**

No. 38K5984 WHITE LAWN BUST RUFFLES. Improved style. Trimmed with lace beading, ribbon inserting and bow. Ea. **39c**

No. 38K5982 LAWN BUST RUFFLES. Trimmed with Valenciennes lace insertion and lace edge. Each.............. **29c**

If mail shipment, send postage extra, 1 cent an ounce.

White Underskirts

Lengths, 38, 40 and 42 inches.
Average shipping weight, 20 ounces.

No. 38K5762 WHITE CAMBRIC UNDERSKIRT of good quality. Trimmed at bottom with a deep and pretty pattern lawn embroidery flouncing. Made with underlay. Good value. **State length.** Price, each......... **59c**

No. 38K5736 BEAUTIFUL WHITE UNDERSKIRT of good quality cambric. Deep flounce trimmed with tucks and very deep ruffle of pretty and durable embroidery. Underlay with dust ruffle. **State length.** Price, each......... **88c**

No. 38K5744 WHITE CAMBRIC UNDERSKIRT of good quality. Full flounce trimmed with tucks, embroidery insertion and full ruffle to match. Ruffled underlay. **State length.** Price, each......... **98c**

No. 38K5782 WHITE CAMBRIC UNDERSKIRT of good quality. Deep flounce trimmed with clusters of hemstitched tucks and neat embroidery ruffle. Ruffled underlay. **Give length.** Price, each...... **$1.48**

No. 38K5765 VERY PRETTY WHITE CAMBRIC UNDERSKIRT of good quality. Exceptionally deep flounce trimmed with tucks, Valenciennes lace insertion; wide band embroidery beading with wash ribbon inserting and Valenciennes lace edge. Deep ruffled underlay. **State length.** Price, each...... **$1.95**

No. 38K5767 SOFT FINISH CAMBRIC UNDERSKIRT of fine quality. Trimmed with wide band embroidery beading with silk ribbon inserting and bow, also full ruffle of embroidery in a very pretty pattern. Ruffled underlay. **State length.** Price, each...... **$2.48**

No. 38K5754 WHITE CAMBRIC UNDERSKIRT of good quality. Very full flounce trimmed with hemstitched tucks, embroidery insertion and embroidery ruffle to match. Full width. Ruffled underlay. **State length.** Price, each.......... **$1.29**

No. 38K5784 WHITE CAMBRIC UNDERSKIRT of good quality. Made as illustrated. Trimmed with embroidery beading, wash ribbon inserting and deep flounce of beautiful embroidery. Ruffled underlay. **State length.** Price, each.......................... **$1.68**

Ucanttear BRAND SUITS FOR LITTLE FELLOWS

No. 40K314

$3.35 PRETTY BROWN AND GRAY MIXTURE SUIT of good weight all wool cassimere. Coat has yoke effect, plaits trimmed with tape, slash pockets, derby back, bottom facings and English twill lining. Knickerbocker pants with side pockets, one hip pocket and strap and buckle at knee. **SIZES—5 to 9 years. State boy's age.**

No. 40K316

$1.75 LITTLE FELLOWS' MILITARY COLLAR RUSSIAN SUIT of good weight soft finish wool and cotton mixed Union cassimere. Coat is trimmed with black tape and silk embroidered emblem. Silk handkerchief effect in breast pocket, and belt of same material. Bloomer pants with elastic bottoms, full lining and taped seams. **SIZES—2½ to 6 years.**

No. 40K318

$1.90 BLUE RUSSIAN BLOUSE SUIT of good weight soft finish wool and cotton mixed cassimere. Sailor collar trimmed with soutache. Detachable shield, silk handkerchief effect in breast pocket, silk tie, and belt of same material. Bloomer pants with elastic bottoms; double stitched and taped seams. **SIZES—2½ to 6 years. State boy's age.**

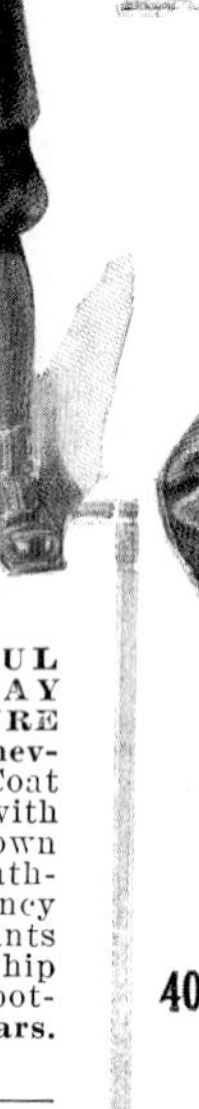

40K310

40K314

40K316

40K318

No. 40K310

$2.95 BEAUTIFUL FANCY GRAY AND BROWN MIXTURE SUIT of good weight cheviot (not all wool). Coat buttons to the neck with collar trimmed with brown tape. Slash pockets, leather lined belt and fancy cuff effect. Bloomer pants with side pockets, one hip pocket and elastic bottoms. **SIZES—4 to 8 years. State boy's age.**

No. 40K326

$4.50 FANCY RUSSIAN STYLE SUIT with sailor collar. Strictly all wool worsted material in pretty brown mixture. Detachable silk embroidered shield in cream color, leather belt, black silk tie and plaited cuffs made to button. Full lined bloomer pants. **SIZES—2½ to 6 years. Mention boy's age.**

No. 40K312

$3.50 DARK NAVY BLUE ALL WOOL WORSTED SERGE SUIT. Double breasted effect with yoke, fancy plaits and derby back. English twill lining. Full lined knickerbocker pants with side pockets, hip pocket and strap and buckle at knee. **SIZES—5 to 9 years. Mention boy's age.**

No. 40K328

$4.00 STRICTLY PURE WOOL WORSTED NAVY BLUE SERGE SUIT. Fancy sailor collar trimmed with silk soutache and silk braid, detachable silk embroidered white shield, breast pocket with silk handkerchief effect, and leather belt. Full lined bloomer pants with elastic bottoms. **SIZES—2½ to 6 years. State boy's age.**

No. 40K320

$2.50 ETON RUSSIAN BLOUSE SUIT in bluish gray all wool material. Coat buttons on the side and has silk embroidered emblem, silk handkerchief effect in breast pocket, black tie, and belt of same material. Bloomer pants have side pockets, one hip pocket and elastic bottoms. **SIZES—2½ to 6 years. State boy's age.**

No. 40K322

$2.75 LITTLE FELLOWS' SUIT in popular Eton Russian style. Made of excellent quality cotton worsted. Coat collar trimmed with brown tape, leather lined belt, cuff effect and ivory buttons. Bloomer pants with double stitched and taped seams, side pockets, one hip pocket and elastic bottoms. **SIZES—4 to 8 years. State boy's age.**

No. 40K324

$3.75 VERY DRESSY SUIT of medium weight all wool cassimere, in gray mixture with light blue trimmings. Coat has gray silk tie, silk embroidered emblem on left sleeve, leather belt and fancy trimmed cuffs made to button. Bloomer pants with elastic bottoms. Finely tailored. **SIZES—2½ to 6 years. Mention boy's age.**

ILLUSTRATIONS SHOW GARMENTS IN THEIR ACTUAL STYLES AND COLORS. Note descriptions for sizes, and when ordering state boy's age and whether he is large, small or average size. Average shipping weight of suits on this page, each, 2¼ pounds.

Ucanttear
BRAND SUITS
Let your boy become a member of the U-CANT-TEAR club of boosters for U-CANT-TEAR brand clothes. We furnish a handsome club button, as illustrated, with each suit. You'll be a booster, too, when you see the clothes. They are the best boys' suits on the market. Made and sold exclusively by us.
Illustrations show suits in their actual styles and colors. Sizes are mentioned in each description. State boy's age and whether he is large, small or of average size. Average shipping weight of suits on this page, each, 3 pounds.
UCANTTEAR CLUB
No. 40K232
$2.25 NEAT MEDIUM GRAY KNICKERBOCKER KNEE PANTS SUIT. Material is a strong wool and cotton mixed cassimere. Coat has silk handkerchief effect in breast pocket, sleeves finished with vent and buttons, derby back and twill lining. Knickerbocker pants with belt loops, side pockets, one hip pocket, and strap and buckle at knee. U-CANT-TEAR club button, also extra buttons and patch piece included. SIZES—8 to 16 years. State boy's age.
No. 40K236
$3.95 BOYS' DOUBLE BREASTED SUIT with two pairs of knickerbocker pants. Latest brown pencil stripe effect in wool and cotton mixed fabric. Coat has English twill lining, bar tacks on all pockets and silk handkerchief effect in breast pocket. Knickerbocker pants have belt loops, side pockets, hip pocket made to button, watch pocket, extension waistband and taped seams. Extra buttons, patch piece and a handsome U-CANT-TEAR club button included free. SIZES—8 to 16 years. State boy's age.
No. 40K240
$3.00 BOYS' DARK BLUE UNION CASSIMERE KNICKERBOCKER SUIT. (Not all wool). Double breasted coat with silk handkerchief effect in breast pocket, bottom facings, bar tacks on pockets and English twill lining. Full cut knickerbocker pants with strap and buckle at knee. U-CANT-TEAR club button furnished with each suit. SIZES—8 to 16 years. State boy's age.
40K230
40K232
40K240
No. 40K230
$1.50 BOYS' STRAIGHT STYLE KNEE PANTS SUIT. Made of strong cotton worsted in dark stripe pattern. Three-button coat with Italian lining. Regular straight style knee pants with side pockets, one hip pocket, taped seat and three buttons at knee. Strongly made. U-CANT-TEAR club button included free. SIZES—8 to 16 years. State boy's age.
No. 40K244
$4.85 BOYS' NAVY BLUE SERGE SUIT with two pairs of knickerbocker pants. Made of medium weight splendid wearing cotton serge. Coat has bottom facings, bar tacks on all pockets and silk handkerchief effect in breast pocket. Slit in back. Full peg top knickerbocker pants with belt loops, strap and buckle at knee, and full lining. Watch pocket is made to button. U-CANT-TEAR club button, also extra buttons and patch piece furnished free. SIZES—8 to 16 years. State boy's age.
40K236
40K234
No. 40K234
$2.50 BOYS' DARK BROWN KNICKERBOCKER KNEE PANTS SUIT. Made of an exceptionally strong wool and cotton mixed fabric. Silk handkerchief effect in breast pocket, derby back and English twill lining. Knickerbocker pants with belt loops, side pockets, hip pocket, and strap and buckle at knee. Patch piece and buttons included free. SIZES—8 to 16 years. State boy's age.
40K242
No. 40K242
$3.60 BOYS' BROWN AND GRAY MIXTURE KNICKERBOCKER SUIT. Medium weight soft finish all wool material. Coat has double welt breast pocket with silk handkerchief effect, bottom facings, bar tacks on pockets and English twill lining. Full cut knickerbocker pants with belt loops, strap and buckle at knee and hip pocket made to button. U-CANT-TEAR club button, also extra buttons and patch piece furnished with each suit. SIZES—8 to 16 years. State boy's age.
No. 40K238
$3.35 BOYS' OLIVE BROWN KNICKERBOCKER SUIT of soft finish medium weight Union cassimere. (Not all wool.) Coat has silk handkerchief effect in breast pocket, bar tacks on pockets, bottom facings and English twill lining. Pants have folded side seams, strap and buckle at knee, side pockets, hip pocket and watch pocket made to button. With each suit we furnish U-CANT-TEAR club button, also extra buttons and patch free. SIZES—8 to 16 years. State boy's age.
40K238
40K244

WOMEN'S MESSALINE DRESS. **One of the season's new tucked shoulder styles.** Made of good quality silk messaline in black, blue or brown. Piped and trimmed in contrasting colors of messaline and messaline covered buttons. Yoke and collar made of tucked net, trimmed with a good size plaited net jabot with hairlines of red. Tie made of a pretty combination of silk messaline. Sleeves trimmed with frills of net. Skirt has plait down front. Cut in one-piece style, buttoning invisibly in back. Average sweep, 74 inches. **Give measurements.** Shipping weight, 2 lbs.

No. 31N4770½ Black.
No. 31N4771½ Blue.
No. 31N4772½ Brown. EACH **$10.50**

WOMEN'S BEAUTIFULLY EMBROIDERED NET DRESS. **Lined with net and has net drop** which is trimmed around bottom with scalloped lace. Neat frill of Valenciennes lace on yoke, neck and sleeves. Wide crushed girdle of good quality white silk messaline. Top of skirt has small tucks and rows of pin tucks at bottom. Comes in one-piece style, closing invisibly in back. A dress that can be worn on any distinguished occasion and also makes a good wedding gown. Average sweep, 2 yards. **Give measurements.** Shipping weight, 2 pounds.

No. 31N4775½ White. EACH **$7.48**

WOMEN'S ELABORATELY EMBROIDERED WOOL VOILE DRESS. **An exceedingly tasteful dress,** being a modified copy of one of the season's latest styles. The material is of a good quality wool voile. Comes in either black or blue. Waist lined with silk and has good quality silk messaline drop. Collar, yoke and cuffs of a neat pattern silk embroidered net. Front and back of waist and sleeves very elaborately embroidered with a good quality silk braid. Has a three-fold silk messaline girdle with a messaline covered buckle. Skirt is very modestly draped on one side with neat embroidered medallion. Has wide panel back. One-piece style, closing invisibly in front. Average sweep, 68 inches. **Give measurements.** Shipping weight, 2½ lbs.

No. 31N4780½ Black.
No. 31N4781½ Blue. EACH **$13.75**

WOMEN'S EMBROIDERED SILK TAFFETA DRESS. **Made of a good quality silk taffeta,** heavily embroidered with silk on both waist and skirt. Yoke and collar of silk embroidered net. Waist has double plait over shoulders and the new plaited sleeves with trimmings of self covered buttons to match buttons down front of dress. Row of plaits below knee on skirt gives it a comfortable fullness without sacrificing its straight hanging lines. Panel back. One-piece style, buttoning invisibly in back. Average sweep, 80 inches. **Give measurements.** Shipping weight, 2 pounds.

No. 31N4785½ Black.
No. 31N4786½ Blue.
No. 31N4787½ Gray. EACH **$7.90**

WOMEN'S BEAUTIFUL MESSALINE DRESS. **This dress combines style and quality seldom found in a model under twice its price.** Yoke of tucked net, prettily trimmed with embroidered lace and outlined with tan silk messaline. Cuffs of embroidered lace and tan silk messaline to match. Messaline covered buttons in front of waist and skirt. Skirt is modestly draped at each side and has panel back. One-piece style, buttoning invisibly in back. Average sweep, 2 yards. **Give measurements.** Shipping weight, 1¾ pounds.

No. 31N4790½ Navy blue.
No. 31N4791½ Black. EACH **$7.65**

WOMEN'S WOOL VOILE DRESS. **A refined dress made of fine quality pure wool crisp voile** with pipings of messaline silk. Hand made ornaments and crushed girdle of silk messaline. The laydown messaline collar is prettily embroidered with silk braid. Yoke and standing collar are made of a silk embroidered net in color to match, excepting the gray dress, which has white yoke and collar. Messaline trimmings on all three colors are in black. Waist and sleeves lined with silk. Skirt has knee plaits each side of front panel and at sides. Panel back. Cut in one-piece style, buttoning invisibly in back. Average sweep, 86 inches. **Give measurements.** Shpg. wt., 2½ lbs.

No. 31N4795½ Black.
No. 31N4796½ Blue.
No. 31N4797½ Gray. EACH **$9.95**

SIZES Women's Dresses offered on this page will be furnished only as illustrated and described, in sizes 32 up to and including 44 inches bust measure, 22 up to and including 30 inches waist measure and skirt lengths up to and including 43 inches front length. The misses' dresses will be furnished in sizes 14 to 20 years, or 32 up to and including 38 inches bust measure and from 32 up to and including 38 inches front length of skirt. All dresses on this page sent in lengths ordered with wide basted hem. Be sure to give measurements.

WOMEN'S SILK CREPE METEOR DRESS. A beautiful dress of excellent quality silk crepe meteor. Made in one-piece style, fastening invisibly in front. Front of blouse waist of white accordion plaited crepe de chine attached to underwaist of silk mull. Crushed girdle, cuffs and edging on front of waist of old gold colored silk messaline. Ornament on girdle of gilt soutache and black braid, with suspended spangles to match. Round collar scalloped and embroidered in ecru color on cream silk. Jet buttons on front of waist and skirt. Skirt made in new French echarpe drape effect at each side, with gathered back. This identical dress is on sale today in Chicago and New York at $40.00 retail. Average sweep, 68 inches. **Give measurements.** Shipping weight, 1¾ pounds.

No. 31N4740½ Black. No. 31N4741½ Navy blue. EACH **$22.50**

WOMEN'S PARTY OR DANCING DRESS. An exact copy of an imported model sold at more than four times our price. With the revival of dancing, dresses of this character have become very popular, but have never been offered before in good quality at this price. Made of a heavy silk charmeuse in one-piece style, fastening in back. Waist of fine net with over drapery of wide shadow lace, trimmed with beaded braid and an elaborate medallion of pearl and gold color beads. Bouquet of artificial flowers on wide crushed girdle. Skirt one-piece gathered back with draped front and rows of small buttons all the way down each side. Average sweep, 64 inches. **Give measurements.** Shipping weight, 1¾ lbs.

No. 31N4745½ Pale blue. No. 31N4746½ Nell rose. EACH **$16.50**

WOMEN'S BEAUTIFUL MESSALINE EVENING GOWN. Made of our best silk messaline in one-piece style, fastening in front of waist and at side of skirt. Front of waist, extension sleeves, lapels and half round collar in back of a fine fillet lace. Dress trimmed throughout with hand made ornaments of self material and piping in harmonizing shades. Waist full lined with silk mull. Skirt has latest style gathered back and is modestly draped in front, as per illustration, with plait below draping at side. A high quality dress, conforming to the demands of fashion and still modest enough for any occasion. Average sweep, 64 inches. **Give measurements.** Shipping weight, 1¾ lbs.

No. 31N4750½ Cream-white. 31N4751½ Pale blue. EACH **$17.50**

MISSES' PARTY OR DANCING DRESS. Made of a high grade silk messaline with draped overwaist and draped tunic of silk chiffon. Richly trimmed with rhinestone buttons and rhinestone studded buckles set in rosettes of chiffon to match. Wide crushed girdle and streamers or sash in back made of messaline. Cut in one-piece style, fastening invisibly in back. Average sweep, 78 inches. **Give measurements.** Shipping weight, 1¾ lbs.

No. 31N4755½ Pink. No. 31N4756½ Pale blue. 31N4757½ White. EACH **$13.75**

WOMEN'S BROCADED MESSALINE DRESS. A charming one-piece open front style. Made of high grade silk messaline in a printed brocade. Wide laydown collar of Plauen lace in baby Irish effect. Yoke and extension sleeves of dotted net and edged with silk to match dress. Panel front in waist of silk chiffon with fancy gold and green braid across gathers at top and large self covered buttons on each side. Three-piece skirt with inverted box plait panel front. Draped and button trimmed at center seam in back. Average sweep, 66 inches. **Give measurements.** Shipping weight, 1½ lbs.

No. 31N4760½ Cream-white. No. 31N4761½ Copenhagen blue. EACH **$16.75**

WOMEN'S DRESS of silk embroidered net over messaline. Made of a good quality silk messaline with fichu effect on waist and tunic overskirt of silk embroidered net. Trimmed with beaded braid on front and back of waist. Five-fold girdle of messaline. Waist and sleeves interlined. Average sweep, 78 inches. **Give measurements. Shipping** weight, 2 lbs.

No. 31N4765½ White. EACH **$14.75**

WE WANT YOUR HAT ORDER

And Will Surely Get It if Style and Quality at a Big Saving Appeals to You.

$4.25 No. 18N9083½ Dainty poke bonnet shape, one of our most popular hats. Entirely covered with fine brown velvet. Wide genuine ostrich band in natural brownish gray shade. Cluster of bright colored winter berries with frosted foliage is trimmed on one side. Bow of wide gold color soft taffeta ribbon at opposite side. Becoming to misses and young women. In brown with natural color ostrich band, as described; royal blue with navy blue ostrich; navy blue with taupe gray, or shaded Nell rose to black ostrich; taupe gray with royal blue ostrich; black with royal blue, or shaded Nell rose to black ostrich; all with flower and ribbon trimming to harmonize.

Good Fitting Modified Tricorne Hat.

$3.65 No. 18N9109½ Becoming, modified tricorne all velvet hat. Sets well down over the hair. Frame covered with fine navy blue silk velvet. Wide ostrich band in shaded Nell rose to black trimmed around crown and over brim in back. Cluster of small silk covered buds in bright Bulgarian shades give a finishing touch. Comes in navy blue with Nell rose to black shaded ostrich; black with shaded Nell rose to black ostrich, or royal blue to black ostrich; rich golden brown with shaded Alice blue ostrich, or in solid black; all hats with silk covered, bright colored buds to harmonize.

A Perfect Fitting High Grade Hat.

$4.25 No. 18N9098½ Handsome wide vulture aigrettes in splendid imitation of the very costly and popular numidi trimming are effectively placed on this most becoming Tam o' Shanter crown dress hat. Shape is covered with dark taupe gray silk plush, which is faced with dark gray taffeta silk. The aigrettes are shaded from taupe gray to black, harmonizing perfectly. While we illustrate this charming hat on a youthful face, it is also most becoming to mature women. The style is perfect and the materials are of high quality. May be ordered in taupe gray shades, as described; in rich dark brown with touch of orange in aigrettes; pretty navy blue or dark royal purple, both with shaded aigrettes to match hat, or in all solid black.

Hat With Plumes, Well Worth $7.00.

$4.45 No. 18N9088½ Combination quality and style at a real bargain price. A most becoming medium size shape which sets well on head. Hat is of shirred black taffeta silk with wide silk velvet flange. Two black plumes are of good quality, each 14 inches long. Elaborate rosette trimming of the black silk drawn through circular jet black ornament. A splendid serviceable hat in all black, as described. Comes also in black with white plumes; navy blue with Alice blue plumes; navy blue with black plumes; dark old rose with black plumes, or medium brown with brown plumes.

A Truly Becoming Rich Looking Dress Hat.

$3.65 No. 18N9114½ Four good medium size black ostrich tips form principal trimming of this dress hat. Head size is just right to set firmly and comfortably. Upper brim and crown of good black silk faced velvet with wide flange of velvet on under brim. Facing of good black taffeta silk. Wide band of spangled jet on lavender silk foundation is laid around crown. Pretty in black with soft lavender, as described; comes also in black with old rose or Alice blue silk behind the jet; in all black, or black with shaded black and white tips.

Genuine Velour Hat With Rich Silk Velvet.

$3.98 No. 18N9093½ A fine quality genuine velour felt shape with most artistic trimming of rich silk faced velvet and silk covered winter berries in bright Bulgarian shades make this one of our most stylish and very becoming dress hats. The shape is in black, as illustrated, with Nell rose color velvet, perfectly wired to hold its shape. A splendid hat in black as described, with Nell rose color velvet; comes also with royal blue, cardinal red, old rose, emerald green or gold color velvet; all silk covered berries in Bulgarian shades to harmonize.

Specially Priced Silk Velvet Poke Bonnet.

$3.38 No. 18N9104½ Here is the smartest poke bonnet shape for dress wear, motoring or driving that we have ever offered to our customers. A $5.00 value. Becoming short brim with modified Tam o' Shanter crown, all of good black silk faced velvet. Long ties are of finest quality, soft finished light blue chiffon, formed into rosette at each side and centered with hand made silk ribbon jacque roses surrounded with silk velvet foliage. The ties are 21 inches wide and long enough to be used as a veil if desired. A hat which can be worn in the coldest weather. Very pretty in black, as described, with light blue ties. Comes also in black with pink or old rose ties; in navy blue with light blue ties, or in golden brown with light blue ties; all silk ribbon roses to contrast with chiffon.

Average Shipping Weight for Hats on This Page. 3 Pounds.

Fine Ribbon Roses Make a Handsome Trimming.

$4.65 No. 18N9119½ An unusually smart looking all velvet hat made of our best quality silk faced black velvet. Becoming to either women or misses. A beautiful trimming wreath of fine quality satin taffeta ribbon roses in popular Nell rose pink shade with velvet foliage is a feature of hat. Four-loop wired bow of all silk wide flowered ribbon is trimmed most artistically over side of crown. Very pretty in black with Nell rose pink roses, as described. Comes also in black with Alice blue or old rose color roses; navy blue with American beauty red or Alice blue roses; all with wide flowered ribbon to harmonize.

BRACELET WATCHES

THE LATEST FAD AND THE LATEST CRAZE. AN ORNAMENT EVERY LADY WANTS.

We show different makes and different grades so as to meet the pocketbooks of all. These bracelets, except the leather, are gold filled and made resilient with springs that are self adjusting so as to fit any wrist. The watches are stem wind and stem set, exact size as illustration shows in every instance, guaranteed to give entire satisfaction and warranted against defective material and workmanship. Shipping weight, 5 ounces.

$6.25 $12.00 $9.00 $12.25

No. 4N6700 Leather Bracelet Watch, 10-year guaranteed gold filled case fitted with fine imported Swiss lever movement. Price **$6.25**
No. 4N6701 Same style and case, fitted with 7-jeweled Elgin or Waltham movement. Price **$9.45**

No. 4N6703 Gold Filled Bracelet Watch, guaranteed for twenty years, fitted with Elgin or Waltham movement.
Price **$12.00**

No. 4N6705 Gold Filled Bracelet Watch. Guaranteed for ten years. Fitted with fine 7-jeweled Swiss lever movement.
Price **$9.00**
No. 4N6707 Same style, fitted with genuine 7-jeweled Elgin or Waltham movement.
Price **$11.25**

No. 4N6709 Wide Style Bracelet Watch, guaranteed for twenty years, fitted with Elgin or Waltham movement. Price......**$12.25**
No. 4N6711 Same style, fitted with fine 7-jeweled imported Swiss lever movement.
Price **$9.95**

$9.60 $24.50 $35.00 $24.25

No. 4N6713 Gold Filled Bracelet Watch, guaranteed for twenty-five years, fitted with 7-jeweled imported Swiss lever movement.
Price **$9.60**
No. 4N6715 Same style, fitted with 7-jeweled Elgin or Waltham movement.
Price **$13.00**

No. 4N6717 Extra Small Size Watch with Narrow Style Bracelet. The acme of perfection in watch bracelets. Gold filled, guaranteed for twenty-five years, fitted with an Elgin movement. Price..........**$24.50**
No. 4N6719 Same style, in solid gold, 14-karat, fitted with Elgin movement.
Price **$37.50**

No. 4N6721 14-Karat Solid Gold Bracelet Watch, fitted with extra small Elgin movement and narrow bracelet.
Price **$35.00**

No. 4N6723 14-Karat Solid Gold Bracelet Watch, fitted with Elgin or Waltham movement.
Price **$24.25**

$4.85

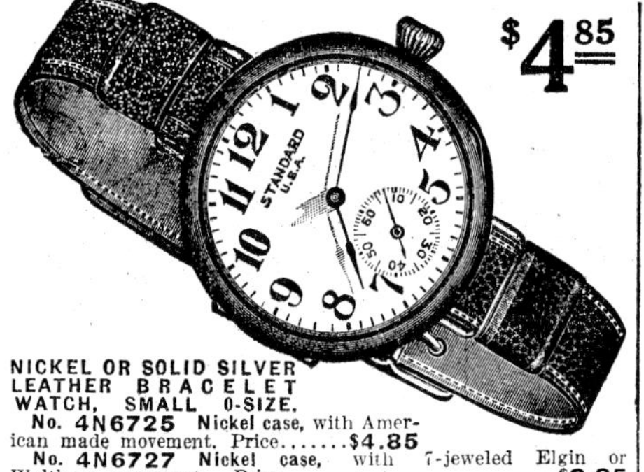

NICKEL OR SOLID SILVER LEATHER BRACELET WATCH, SMALL 0-SIZE.
No. 4N6725 Nickel case, with American made movement. Price.......**$4.85**
No. 4N6727 Nickel case, with 7-jeweled Elgin or Waltham movement. Price..............**$8.85**
No. 4N6729 Solid silver case, with American made movement. Price..............**$6.00**
No. 4N6731 Solid silver case, with 7-jeweled Elgin or Waltham movement. Price..............**$9.90**

$6.95 FOR THIS HANDSOME BRACELET WATCH.

The watch is exact size as illustration shows, imported from Switzerland. Stem wind and pendant set. The bracelet is adjustable, **gold filled,** fits any size wrist.
No. 4N6733 Gold Filled Bracelet Watch.
Price **$6.95**

$8.90

No. 4N6735 Gold Filled Royal Bracelet Watch, guaranteed for twenty years, with 7-jeweled American made movement, skylight dial.
Price **$8.90**
No. 4N6737 Same style Bracelet Watch, same quality, with 7-jeweled Elgin or Waltham movement. Price...**$12.85**

$7.50 to $13.50 for These Ladies' High Grade Gold Filled 6-Size Watches. Guaranteed for Twenty Years' Continual Wear.

You will observe the designs are beautifully engraved, all come hunting style, and all have the new antique crown and bow. We do not mention the manufacturers' names on account of the reduced prices. However, the manufacturers' names are plainly stamped on the inside lid with their guarantee. You assume no risk whatsoever. Order one of these watches, and if after you receive it you are not pleased with the make, engraving; in fact, if for any reason at all you don't want it, you are at liberty to return the watch to us and have your money returned, together with transportation charges. We guarantee absolute satisfaction. $7.50 may seem a very little money for a very good watch, still, we are able to send you for this sum a watch that we know will please you.

$7.50 AND UP $7.50 AND UP

No. 4N6740 Guaranteed for twenty years.
No. 4N6742 Guaranteed for twenty years.
No. 4N6744 Guaranteed for twenty years.
No. 4N6746 Guaranteed for twenty years.

We fit these 6-size cases with the following 6-size movements. Prices quoted are for the complete watch, movement and case.

7-Jeweled American Made Movement, cut balance and Breguet hairspring. Price..**$7.50**
7-Jeweled Elgin or Waltham Movement. Price..............**9.40**
15-Jeweled Elgin or Waltham Movement. Price..............**$11.50**
16-Jeweled Lady Waltham Movement, adjusted grade. Price..............**13.50**

WOMEN'S FASHIONABLE SPRING AND FALL COAT in the correct three-quarter length style. The material used in this garment is a heavy rich quality of brilliant black satin. The coat is fashioned after one of the new models on loose fitting lines. The fronts have wide facings of self material, and fasten with attractive satin cord ornament and braid covered button. The wide sleeves are the new kimono style made in one piece together with the back of coat, and are finished with wide round cornered turnback cuffs. The square back collar is made of heavy cord moire silk in contrasting shade, and tastefully embroidered in Persian pattern and shades. The long graceful revers have over-revers of heavy ecru macrame lace, which may be readily removed if desired. Length, about 45 inches. Sizes, 34 to 46 inches bust measure. **State size.** Average shipping weight, 1⅝ pounds.
No. 17R7721 Price................ **$6.98**

WOMEN'S AND MISSES' ATTRACTIVE COAT in the regulation three-quarter length. The material used is a good quality closely woven black silk mixed moire. The garment is cut along straight and loose lines. The fronts have wide facings of self material, and fasten with heavy moire cord ornament and covered button. The long stylish square back shawl collar is of heavy quality black satin, and has overcollar of rich heavy ecru macrame lace, which may be removed when desired. Matches the satin cuffs which finish the wide kimono or raglan slip on sleeves that are made in one piece together with the back of coat. There is a wide black satin girdle knotted at center, back finished with black silk fringes at ends. See back view. Length, about 45 inches. Sizes, 34 to 46 inches bust measure. **State size.** Average shipping weight, 2 pounds.
No. 17R7723 Price................ **$7.48**

WOMEN'S OR MISSES' UP TO DATE THREE-QUARTER LENGTH COAT. The material used in this garment is a good rich quality silk mixed black moire which is very fashionable this season. The coat is cut loose fitting, and is lined throughout with good quality self striped satin showing floral design in light Dresden shades. The handsome square back collar is made of a heavy brocaded silk vesting in contrasting shades, over a black groundwork. The front is trimmed with novelty style rich black satin revers, finished with black silk tassel. The coat fastens with smoke pearl buttons. The fancy turnback cuffs are also made of black satin and silk vesting, and add a finish to the wide kimono sleeves which are made with the new drop shoulders. Length, about 40 inches. Sizes, 34 to 46 inches bust measure. **State size.** Average shipping weight, 2 pounds.
No. 17R7728 Price.............. **$12.50**

SIZES

Women's Regular Size Tailored Suits offered on this page are furnished only as illustrated and described, in the following sizes: From 32 to 44 inches bust measure, and from 36 to 44 inches front length of skirt. Open basted hem. Please mention if you wish hem stitched down in length ordered. Samples of materials sent free and postpaid on request. When taking waist measure for high girdle skirts, take measure at regular waist line. Do not make allowance for high girdle. For women's extra size suits see page 247. When ordering state bust measure, waist measure and front length of skirt. See page 825 for simple measuring instructions.

WOMEN'S SUIT made of all wool granite crepe. Lined throughout with satin, guaranteed for two seasons' wear. Mannish collar, lapels and sleeves with cuffs. Single breasted front, closing with novelty self covered buttons. Tailored breast pocket. See small illustration for fancy tailored back, trimmed with small self covered buttons to match front. Arm shields and coat weights. Stylish skirt with raised waist, closing in center back with patented Koh-i-noor fasteners. Long overskirt tunic hanging free from waist line all around. Furnished in women's sizes only, from 32 to 44 inches bust measure. Samples of materials sent free and postpaid on request. **When ordering state bust measure, waist measure and front length of skirt.** Average shipping weight, 4½ pounds.

No. 31T8220½ Navy blue.
No. 31T8221½ Brown.
No. 31T8222½ Black.

PRICE $10.98

WOMEN'S TAILORED SUIT made of our standard all wool double twisted warp serge. Lined throughout with satin, guaranteed for two seasons' wear. Single breasted front, closing with velvet and braid combination buttons. Mannish sleeves with cuffs. Velvet collar with mannish lapels trimmed with small buttons. V shaped openings on both sides, finished off with hand embroidered arrow heads. Arm shields and coat weights. See small illustration for plain French back. Straight hanging skirt. Raised waist, closes with patented Koh-i-noor fasteners. One sided effect with full length stitched down tailored tucks, trimmed with small velvet buttons. Furnished in women's sizes only, from 32 to 44 inches bust measure. Samples of materials sent free and postpaid on request. **When ordering state bust measure, waist measure and front length of skirt.** Average shipping weight, 4 pounds.

No. 31T8225½ Navy blue.
No. 31T8226½ Black.
No. 31T8227½ Dark green.

PRICE $9.98

WOMEN'S TAILORED SUIT with fashionable ruffle flounce of self material. Made of fine quality all wool wide wale storm serge. Lined throughout with guaranteed satin. Marie Antoinette collar of caracul cloth. Sleeves with bell shaped cuffs to match ruffles on coat and skirt. Single breasted front, closing with imported novelty celluloid buttons. See small illustration for back. Stylish skirt. Overskirt tunic effect with wide ruffles of self material in front and back to correspond with coat. Raised waist fastening at left front with patented Koh-i-noor fasteners. Furnished in women's sizes only, from 32 to 44 inches bust measure. Samples of materials sent free and postpaid on request. **When ordering state bust measure, waist measure and front length of skirt.** Average shipping weight, 4½ pounds.

No. 31T8230½ Navy blue.
No. 31T8231½ Black.

PRICE $12.48

SIZES Women's Regular Size Skirts offered on this page are furnished only from 22 up to and including 32 inches waist measure and from 36 to 44 inches front length of skirt. For larger sizes make your selection from women's extra sizes offered on page 246. When taking your waist measure take at the regular waist line. Make no allowance for high girdle. Samples of materials sent free and postpaid on request. Don't forget to give your waist measure and front length of skirt when ordering. See page 825 for simple measuring instructions.

WOMEN'S SKIRT. Made of good quality mercerized moire, at a remarkably low price. Loose hanging tunic overskirt in front and back. Trimmed with small self covered ball shape buttons. Raised waist. (See small illustration for back.) Furnished in women's regular sizes only, from 22 to 32 inches waist measure and 36 to 44 inches front length of skirt. **When ordering be sure to state waist measure and front length of skirt.** Average shipping weight, 1¾ pounds.
No. 31T7845 Black. EACH **$2.48**

Give Measurements.

31T7835

WOMEN'S SKIRT. Made of good quality wool mixed broadcloth in fall and winter weight. Overskirt effect in front and back. Raised waist. Trimmed with combination buttons. Furnished in women's regular sizes only, from 22 to 32 inches waist measure and from 36 to 44 inches front length of skirt. **When ordering state waist measure and front length of skirt.** Average shpg. wt., 1¾ lbs.
No. 31T7835 Black.
No. 31T7836 Navy blue.
No. 31T7837 Brown.
No. 31T7838 Medium gray. EACH **$1.95**

31T7835 31T7840

Samples of Material Sent Free and Postpaid on Request.

31T7840

WOMEN'S SKIRT. Made of all wool double twisted warp serge. In one-sided effect with cluster of plaits to give fullness for comfortable walking. Raised waist. Self covered buttons. Fancy habit back. (See small illustration.) Furnished in women's regular sizes only, from 22 to 32 inches waist measure and 36 to 44 inches front length of skirt. For larger sizes see extra size skirts offered on page 246. **When ordering state waist measure and front length of skirt.** Average shipping weight, 1¾ pounds.
No. 31T7840 Black.
No. 31T7841 Navy blue.
No. 31T7842 Medium gray. EACH **$3.25**

31T7845

31T7850

WOMEN'S SKIRT. Made of wool mixed novelty suiting in popular Roman stripe pattern. Long stylish loose hanging tunic overskirt in front and back. Trimmed with self covered buttons. Raised waist. Furnished in women's regular sizes only. **When ordering state waist measure and front length of skirt.** Average shipping weight, 1¾ pounds.
No. 31T7850 Blue stripe.
No. 31T7851 Brown stripe. EACH **$2.98**

31T7855

WOMEN'S SKIRT. Made of wool mixed novelty plaid suiting in pleasing colors. Tunic overskirt effect in front, with cluster of plaits at side to give fullness for comfortable walking. Plain habit back. (See small illustration.) Raised waist. Furnished in women's regular sizes only. **When ordering state waist measure and front length of skirt.** Average shipping weight, 1¾ lbs.
No. 31T7855 Green and blue plaid.
No. 31T7856 Brown plaid. EACH **$2.65**

31T7845 31T7850 31T7855

SUMMER COATS

See Inside Front Cover Page for Simple Measuring Instructions.

WOMEN'S OR MISSES' FASHIONABLE SUMMER COAT, made of closely woven tan color French linen, which is a cotton fabric resembling real linen. The fronts are finished with wide facings and have large patch pockets. The back is loose and easy fitting. The very attractive fancy collar is trimmed with strappings of leather brown linons and small pearl buttons, and matches the trimming shown on pocket lapels and the deep novelty cuffs which finish the new style sleeves. The shoulder seams, which are double stitched, show wide welt effect and trimming of leather brown buttons. Sizes, 32 to 46 inches bust measure. **State size.** Average shipping weight, 2 pounds.
No. 17R7557 54-inch length.
No. 17R7558 50-inch length. Price...**$3.78**

WOMEN'S OR MISSES' VERY STYLISH SUMMER COAT of tan color French linen, which is a cotton fabric closely woven and resembles real linen. Fronts are finished with wide facings and pointed lapel pockets. The back is cut straight and loose. The wide collar with a deep square back is elaborately embroidered with white in scroll design over strappings of lavender color linon, matching the wide turnback cuffs, soutache braid and small buttons on lapels. The buttons which fasten the new style front are tan color with lavender center. Sizes, 32 to 46 inches bust measure. **State size.** Average shipping weight, 2 pounds.
No. 17R7560 54-inch length.
No. 17R7561 50-inch length. Price...**$3.48**

WOMEN'S OR MISSES' VERY STYLISH SUMMER COAT of tan color French linen, which is a cotton fabric closely woven and having the appearance of real linen. The fronts are finished with wide facings. The back is loose and easy fitting. The new style drop shoulders and kimono sleeves make this a strictly up to date garment. The wide fancy collar of new blue French linen is trimmed with ornaments of black velvet and pearl rings, and elaborately embroidered in shades of light blue and white in a floral and scroll design over tan strappings, to match the deep turnback cuffs where there is also a trimming of soutache braid. The piping and buttons shown on the sleeves and wide belt (which terminates at the side seams) are of new blue to match collar and cuffs. Length, about 48 inches. Sizes, 32 to 46 inches bust measure. **State size.** Average shipping weight, 2 pounds.
No. 17R7563 48-inch length. Price................ **$3.79**

WOMEN'S OR MISSES' EXTRA FINE QUALITY TAN COLOR PURE LINEN SUMMER COAT, strictly up to date with new style raglan sleeves. The fronts are finished with wide facings and large pockets having fancy pointed lapels, and fasten with four large linen covered buttons. The back is cut full and loose, being slightly gathered at the waist line, with wide belt buttoning on to side seams with large linen covered buttons. The sleeves have deep turnback cuffs and the wide collar and lapels may be buttoned up closely about the neck, forming a high collar to be used for driving purposes when desired. Sizes, 32 to 46 inches bust measure. **State size.** Average shipping weight, 2 pounds.
No. 17R7566 54-inch length.
No. 17R7567 50-inch length. Price..**$3.75**

NURSING WAISTS

Style, comfort and convenience have been attained in the designing and making of these waists. There are side vents in all these waists, very neatly and cleverly hidden, and fastening invisibly under the side plaits. These vents enable the mother to nurse baby with absolute comfort to herself and baby, and without any embarrassment, whether at home or in public. When the vents are closed there is no sign of the waist being a nursing waist. Sizes, 34 to 46 inches bust measure. **State size. See inside front cover page for simple measuring instructions.**

NURSING WAIST of tub silk, a fine silk and cotton material that washes and launders perfectly and keeps its color. The front shows two wide side plaits, under which the waist may be opened while nursing baby, and four yoke depth plaits to add fullness. Also two revers with piping in harmonizing color to match the finish on fancy cuffs and the trimming down front, where there are also two cord and button ornaments. The small V shaped front and high collar are of white Brussels net. The back is plain and fastens invisibly down center. **State size.** Shipping weight, 12 ounces.

No. 27R2280 White with blue.
No. 27R2282 White with lavender.
No. 27R2283 White with black.
Price **$1.79**

NURSING WAIST of good quality white cotton voile, with beautifully embroidered vest effect, edged with imitation baby Irish lace insertion to match heading of voile frill on sleeves which have two clusters of lengthwise tucks. The front also has four wide side plaits and two rows of cluster tucks. The high collar and small yoke are of pretty pattern shadow lace. The back has four rows of cluster pin tucks and opens down center, fastening invisibly. **State size.** Shipping weight, 7 ounces.

No. 27R2277 Price............................ **98c**

NURSING WAIST of fine sheer white lawn. The back has clusters of fine pin tucks and fastens with pearl buttons of good quality. The front and yoke are made of panels of very dainty allover Swiss embroidery and Valenciennes lace insertions. Imported embroidered medallion forms centerpiece of yoke. Wide cluster of tucks at shoulder, and the vents are cleverly concealed and fasten invisibly under the wide side plaits. The sleeves have two rows of clusters of four pin tucks lengthwise, with lace insertion between. The neck is trimmed with Valenciennes lace and finished with frill ruching of net with lace edge. **State size.** Shipping weight, 7 oz.

No. 27R2278 Price......................... **$1.38**

NURSING WAIST of white cotton voile with panels of heavy embroidery in conventional design and rows of Valenciennes insertion, as well as two wide side plaits and three rows of cluster tucks. The high collar has rows of Valenciennes insertion and the new drop shoulders have imitation baby Irish lace insertion to match that about the upper arms and wrists, where there is a plaiting of voile. The back is plain and opens down center, fastening invisibly. **State size.** Shipping weight, 7 ounces.

No. 27R2279 Price......................... **$1.18**

NURSING WAIST of fine quality lingerie cotton voile. The front has two wide side plaits, with vents fastening invisibly under them. The embroidery work is very artistic and well done, being of mercerized cotton floss in raised design. The sleeves show the new drop shoulders. Lace beading on the sleeves, shoulders and front trims the waist prettily. Full plaited ruching on collar and cuffs. Fastens invisibly down front under the ruching. **State size.** Shipping weight, 12 ounces.

No. 27R2281 Price................. **$1.88**

NURSING WAIST of good quality white cotton voile, beautifully embroidered in two panels; under the outer edge of each one the waist fastens invisibly, and opens for nursing purposes. This opening is made with continuous facing to prevent tearing. The front also shows V shaped yoke and row of imitation baby Irish lace insertion, together with four rows of cluster tucks and two of side plaits. The upper yoke, collar and cuffs are of tucked Brussels net to match one another. Sleeves have three long rows of cluster tucks. The back opens down center and fastens with pearl buttons. On each side are two rows of cluster tucks and one side plait. **State size.** Shipping weight, 7 ounces.

No. 27R2284 Price......................... **$1.48**

Crepe de Chine, Lace and Messaline Waists.

See Page 825 for Simple Measuring Instructions.

CREPE DE CHINE SILK WAIST. The material is **a good quality soft highly lustrous silk crepe.** The waist is made after the latest blouse models with elastic band at waist line. The front fastens invisibly down center between ruching of fine embroidered cream Brussels net, which continues about the back of neck where there is a double row, as illustrated. The low cut neck is finished with hemstitched revers and heavy silk cord and tassels. The three-quarter length kimono sleeves have open beading about the shoulders and are finished with ruching to match the front. Sizes, 32 to 46 inches bust measure. **State size.** Shipping weight, 13 ounces.

No. **27T2641** Peach.
No. **27T2642** Light blue.
No. **27T2643** White.
No. **27T2644** Navy blue.
No. **27T2645** Black.
Price.................................. **$2.98**

CREPE DE CHINE SILK WAIST of good quality soft bright finished silk crepe. The garment is made in the latest blouse style with elastic band at waist line. The front has vest effect of beautifully embroidered sheer, crisp white organdy muslin matching the hemstitched embroidered collar. The full length kimono sleeves are finished with wide hemstitched organdy muslin cuffs and cord piping. The gathering above the busts provides fullness to allow the garment to fall in soft graceful lines. Sizes, 32 to 46 inches bust measure. **State size.** Shipping weight, 13 ounces.

No. **27T2625** White.
No. **27T2626** Light blue.
No. **27T2627** Peach.
No. **27T2628** Champagne.
Price.................................. **$2.98**

SILK MESSALINE WAIST. The material used in this waist is an excellent quality of silk messaline with high lustrous finish and splendid wearing texture—a messaline that we positively recommend. The style is strictly up to date, showing fancy vest effect with cord and tassels, on one side of which the waist fastens invisibly. The sleeves are finished with frill of black net and have the new drop shoulders which form a deep front yoke. There is a low cut hemstitched collar as well as an embroidered net high collar. This net collar and small front yoke may be removed if desired, changing the style of the waist to a low neck effect. The garment is easy fitting and may be worn in soft blousy effect. Sizes, 32 to 46 inches bust measure. **State size.** Shipping weight, 14 ounces.

No. **27T2634** Black.
No. **27T2635** Navy blue.
No. **27T2636** Brown.
Price.................................. **$2.48**

BROCADED TUSSAH SILK WAIST. The material is **a good quality of silk and cotton mixed fabric** showing a rich pattern of silk brocade throughout. The waist is made on the correct easy fitting lines. The front has wide side plaits forming vest effect down the center of which the waist fastens with ball buttons. The full length kimono sleeves are finished with wide cuffs. The low cut collar is made square at back and is finished with cord and tassels at front. Sizes, 32 to 46 inches bust measure. **State size.** Shipping weight, 13 ounces.

No. **27T2637** Ivory.
No. **27T2638** Light blue.
No. **27T2639** Navy blue.
No. **27T2640** Black.
Price.................................. **$1.48**

SHADOW LACE WAIST. The material is **a real soft fine quality of cream color shadow lace.** The garment is cut to fall in soft graceful fullness with elastic band at waist line. There is a beautiful vest effect of flesh color chiffon folds and rich artistic Oriental lace shown between two rows of Brussels net ruching, under one of which the waist fastens invisibly. The low cut neck has high ruching of lace about the back. The full length kimono sleeves are finished with ruching of Brussels net and folds of flesh color chiffon. The waist is lined throughout with good quality Brussels net. Sizes, 32 to 46 inches bust measure. **State size.** Shipping weight, 13 ounces.

No. **27T2632** Cream.
Price.................................. **$2.98**

ALLOVER EMBROIDERED WHITE COTTON BRUSSELS NET WAIST of good quality, heavily and tastefully embroidered. The neck is finished with soft frill of net continuing down sides of the front opening, which is fastened with pearl buttons. The front shows yoke effect and a pale blue shadow girdle, as well as silk bow of the same shade. The sleeves are three-quarter length with drop shoulders and frilling of Brussels net. The body of the garment is lined with Brussels net. Sizes, 32 to 46 inches bust measure. **State size.** Shipping weight, 5 oz.

No. **27T2633** White.
Price.................................. **$1.48**

WHITE SHADOW LACE WAIST of good fine quality shadow lace. The waist is made on loose fitting lines. The front fastens invisibly between rows of wide soft shadow lace ruching, which continues about the neck, where there is a frill of Brussels net and fold of flesh color chiffon. The full length sleeves have drop shoulders and are finished with frills of Brussels net. The body of the garment is lined with flesh color Brussels net. Sizes, 32 to 46 inches bust measure. **State size.** Shipping weight, 13 ounces.

No. **27T2631** White.
Price.................................. **$1.98**

WOMEN'S WOOL MIXED CHALLIS DRESS. Made of excellent quality soft half wool challis. Vestee effect with cross plaited yoke and high collar of net, edged at top with hemstitched braid. Raglan shoulders with full length sleeves, finished off with frills of plaited net. Wide revers which extend around neck under laydown collar. Turnback cuffs and wide girdle of silk moire. Round collar of brocaded messaline in contrasting color, backed with silk moire. Waist trimmed with row of jet buttons in front and has box plait from neck to girdle in back. Skirt is entirely new and very pleasing. Made with loose hanging overskirt ending in long points at each side, trimmed with silk tassels and silk moire covered buttons. Bottom of skirt has the new "kick" plaits on each side. Dress fastens in front. Women's sizes only. **Give measurements.** Average shipping wt., 2 lbs.

No. 31T7760½ Navy blue
No. 31T7761½ Wine.
No. 31T7762½ Brown.
EACH **$5.98**

SIZES **Dresses on this page will be furnished only as illustrated and described and in the following sizes: From 32 up to and including 44 inches bust measure; waist measure up to and including 33 inches, and front skirt length of 39 or 42 inches, with wide basted hem. If you desire larger sizes, see dresses for stout women on page 219. BE SURE TO GIVE BUST MEASURE, WAIST MEASURE AND FRONT LENGTH OF SKIRT. See page 825 for simple measuring instructions. Samples of materials sent on request.**

WOMEN'S EMBROIDERED FRENCH SERGE DRESS. Fine quality all wool French serge made in one-piece style. Waist front handsomely embroidered in self color with just enough contrasting color to bring out the embroidery plainly. Yoke and high collar of fine allover lace, collar piped at top with silk messaline. Tucked girdle and large bow of silk messaline. Long false coat effect skirt, trimmed in front with self covered buttons and has wide box plait panel back with plaits, in addition to the new small plaits at each side of front at bottom. Dress closes invisibly in back. Women's sizes only. **Give measurements.** Av. shpg. wt., 2 lbs.

No. 31T7765½ Navy blue.
No. 31T7766½ Black.
No. 31T7767½ Wine.
EACH **$6.98**

WOMEN'S WOOL CREPE DRESS. Fine quality all wool unfinished crepe, the material so much in demand this season. Long shoulders with three-quarter length sleeves. Plaited frills of shadow lace on waist front, around neck and on sleeves. Tabs on waist front and sleeves trimmed with bows of silk messaline and fancy buttons give added attractiveness. Skirt made with loose hanging overskirt or tunic, set off by wide box plaits in front and back. Lap seam running full length. Dress closes invisibly in front. One of the prettiest dresses in our line. Women's sizes only. **Give measurements.** Average shipping weight, 1¾ pounds.

No. 31T7770½ Navy blue.
No. 31T7771½ Brown.
No. 31T7772½ Purple.
EACH **$5.90**

WOMEN'S WOOL BROADCLOTH DRESS. A dress of just the right weight for fall, winter or spring use. All wool broadcloth in drop shoulder effect, with three-quarter length sleeves. Yoke, round laydown collar and attractive cuffs of velveteen. Plaited frills of shadow lace in scalloped effect on each side of yoke, around neck and on cuffs. Latest style skirt having loose overskirt at back which is plaited in at each side of front and trimmed with rows of fancy buttons. Lap seam down center of skirt and on each side from overskirt to bottom. Dress closes invisibly in front. **Give measurements.** Average shipping weight, 2¼ pounds.

No. 31T7775½ Wine.
No. 31T7776½ Navy blue.
No. 31T7777½ Black.
EACH **$5.85**

WOMEN'S WOOL GRANITE CREPE DRESS. A one-piece dress made of all wool worsted granite crepe, with drop shoulders in Raglan effect and three-quarter length sleeves. Attractive laydown collar of silk messaline extending to a point in back and ending in points over the waist front. Plaited frill on waist front and turnback cuffs of silk messaline. Waist trimmed in front with row of self covered buttons. Skirt made with medium long false tunic and wide ruffle of self material, trimmed with covered buttons. Dress closes invisibly in front. A beautiful garment in a popular and serviceable material. Women's sizes only. **Give measurements.** Average shpg. wt., 2 lbs.

No. 31T7780½ Mahogany.
No. 31T7781½ Navy blue.
No. 31T7782½ Dark green.
EACH **$6.75**

WOMEN'S SILK EMBROIDERED NET OVER MESSALINE DRESS. Made of fine quality silk messaline with fichu effect on waist and long overskirt of silk embroidered net. Yoke of embroidered net with handsome beaded ornament on left side extending over shoulder. High collar trimmed with row of beaded braid and three-quarter length sleeves having three tucks, row of beaded braid and edging of silk net in embroidered design. Waist and sleeves lined with lawn. Tucked girdle with large silk messaline bow and long sash on left side. Dress fastens in back. An ideal wedding dress. Women's sizes only. **Give measurements.** Average shipping weight; 1¾ pounds.

No. 31T7790½ White. EACH **$13.75**

WOMEN'S SILK CREPE DE CHINE DRESS. An exceptionally attractive dress made of high grade silk crepe de chine. Drop shoulders in raglan effect with three-quarter length sleeves. Vestee, standing collar and new style cuffs of shadow lace, cuffs trimmed with narrow bands of self material. Skirt made with false tunic and extra wide gathered ruffle of self material, extending to a point low down on front of skirt. Slit in front at bottom which can be closed if so desired. Dress closes invisibly in front. Women's sizes only. **Give measurements.** Average shipping weight, 1¼ pounds.

No. 31T7795½ Navy blue.
No. 31T7796½ Terra cotta.
No. 31T7797½ Black. EACH **$11.25**

WOMEN'S SILK CREPE POPLIN DRESS. Material is entirely new, having the moire water mark on silk crepe poplin material, which gives a high luster and a very rich appearance. Yoke of good quality velvet and wide revers of Plauen Oriental lace. Box plaited collar of silk moire in contrasting color. Raglan shoulders with three-quarter length sleeves, set off by attractive cuffs of self material and wide frills of Oriental lace. Tucked velvet girdle. Double loose hanging coatee skirt trimmed with velvet covered buttons. Short cutaway slit at bottom. Dress closes invisibly in front. Women's sizes only. **Give measurements.** Average shipping wt., 1¾ pounds.

No. 31T7800½ Navy blue.
No. 31T7801½ Russian green.
No. 31T7802½ Black. EACH **$14.50**

WOMEN'S SILK TAFFETA DRESS. Made of excellent quality silk taffeta in a style especially suitable for middle aged or elderly women, but at the same time not too plain for younger women. Shadow lace vestee set off by embroidered net in jabot effect trimmed with cameo buttons. Long shoulders with full length sleeves, trimmed with wide frills of embroidered net in scalloped design. Crushed girdle of self material. Cutaway false coat effect skirt, trimmed with self covered buttons in front and has inverted box plaits at each side on bottom. Women's sizes only. **Give measurements.** Average shipping weight, 1½ pounds.

No. 31T7785½ Black.
No. 31T7786½ Navy blue.
No. 31T7787½ Brown. EACH **$8.95**

SIZES **WOMEN'S dresses on this page will be furnished in the following sizes only: From 32 up to and including 44 inches bust measure; waist measure up to and including 33 inches, and front skirt length of 39 or 42 inches, with wide basted hem. In ordering be sure to give bust measure, waist measure and front length of skirt. See page 825 for simple measuring instructions. Samples of materials sent on request.**

MISSES' PARTY OR DANCING DRESS. Fine quality silk embroidered chiffon over China silk. Elbow length kimono sleeves. Plaited frills on sleeves and inset on back of waist and at bottom of skirt in front of fine quality shadow lace. Trimming of shadow lace in fan effect above girdle on waist front. Wide shirred girdle and large bow of good quality silk messaline. Loose hanging overskirt with gathered ruffle. Entire dress richly embroidered in silk in contrasting colors. Fastens invisibly in back. One of the daintiest dresses we have ever offered. Misses' sizes only. **Give measurements.** Average shipping weight, 1¼ pounds.

No. 31T7805½ Pink.
No. 31T7806½ Light blue.
No. 31T7807½ White.
No. 31T7808½ Nile green. EACH **$8.85**

SIZES **MISSES' dresses will be furnished in sizes 14, 16, 18 and 20 years, or 32, 34, 36 and 38 inches bust measure with average skirt lengths of 34, 35, 37 and 38 inches, with wide basted hem. Be sure to give bust measure, waist measure and front length of skirt. Simple measuring instructions on page 825.**

Homestead Brand House Dresses

WOMEN'S SHEPHERD CHECK HOUSE DRESS. Made of good quality washable flannelette or percale. Buttons visibly down front with pearl buttons. Gibson shoulders and buttoned cuffs. **Give bust measure.** Average shipping weight, 2 pounds.

No. 31T7005 Shepherd check flannelette.
No. 31T7006 Shepherd check percale.
No. 31T7007 Blue striped percale.
EACH **92c**

WOMEN'S CHAMBRAY HOUSE DRESS. Made of good washable chambray. Plain trimmed with stripe, and stripe trimmed with plain. Buttons visibly down front with row of pearl buttons. Piped with heavy mercerized cord. **Give bust measure.** Average shipping wt., 1½ pounds.

No. 31T7025 Plain blue.
No. 31T7026 Blue stripe.
No. 31T7027 Tan stripe.
EACH **98c**

WOMEN'S COTTON SERGE DRESS. Made of good quality washable striped cotton serge. Trimmed with highly mercerized sateen. Buttons visibly in front. Gibson shoulders. Buttoned cuffs. Skirt piped all the way down front. Suitable for street or house wear. **Give bust measure.** Average shipping weight, 1¾ pounds.

No. 31T7000 Blue.
No. 31T7001 Black.
EACH **$1.79**

WOMEN'S CHAMBRAY HOUSE DRESS with cap. Made of a good quality chambray in light colors. Cap and dress trimmed with substantial white embroidery. Buttons visibly down front with pearl buttons. Full and roomy adjustable cap. **Give bust measure.** Average shipping weight, 1¾ pounds.

No. 31T7035 Blue check.
No. 31T7036 Black check.
No. 31T7037 Lavender check.
Dress with Cap **$1.15**

WOMEN'S PERCALE HOUSE DRESS with cap. An exceptional value in a house dress. Made of good strong washable percale, with full roomy adjustable cap to match. Buttons visibly down front with pearl buttons. Neatly piped with striped percale. **Give bust measure.** Average shipping weight, 1½ pounds.

No. 31T7015 Fancy blue.
No. 31T7016 Fancy gray.
Dress with Cap **89c**

WOMEN'S CHAMBRAY HOUSE DRESS. Made of good quality washable chambray in plain colors. Trimmed with plaid collar and cuffs to match. Neatly piped in heavy mercerized cord. Has latest drop shoulder effect. Fastens invisibly down front, and has plait all the way down front of skirt. Back of waist also trimmed. **Give bust measure.** Average shipping weight, 1¾ pounds.

No. 31T7010 Blue.
No. 31T7011 Gray.
No. 31T7012 Lavender.
EACH **$1.19**

WOMEN'S FLANNELETTE HOUSE DRESS. Made of good quality washable flannelette, cut in the one-piece open front style, with the latest drop shoulders. Neat velvet tie. Skirt has two-tier effect now so popular. A dress suitable either for street or house wear. **Give bust measure.** Average shipping weight, 1¾ pounds.

No. 31T7020 Fancy blue.
No. 31T7021 Fancy gray.
EACH **$1.48**

SIZE SCALE.

Women's House Dresses on this page will be furnished in sizes 32, 34, 36, 38, 40, 42 and 44 inches bust measure. Be sure to mention size when ordering.

WOMEN'S FLANNELETTE HOUSE DRESS. Made of a good quality fancy striped washable flannelette, prettily piped throughout with washable rick-rack braid in red. Buttons visibly down front with neat colored pearl buttons which form part of the trimming. Gibson shoulders. Plait runs all the way down front of skirt. **Give bust measure.** Average shipping weight, 2 pounds.

No. 31T7030 Fancy blue.
No. 31T7031 Fancy gray.
EACH **$1.15**

WOMEN'S CHAMBRAY HOUSE DRESS. Made of a good quality striped chambray. Trimmed with plain color to match stripes and neat edging of white embroidery. Back of waist also trimmed. Is slightly high waisted. Fastens visibly down front and has plait running all the way down front of skirt. Can be worn for house or street wear. **Give bust measure.** Average shipping weight, 2 pounds.

No. 31T7040 Blue stripe.
No. 31T7041 Black stripe.
No. 31T7042 Lavender stripe.
EACH **$1.39**

MATERNITY DRESSES

No. 29T965½ Blue with white stripe. INEXPENSIVE MATERNITY DRESS made of hairline striped cotton serge. Lapels and cuffs neatly trimmed with a highly mercerized cotton fabric. Plaited girdle and sash to match. Square lace collar. Tucked white net chemisette. Adjustable elastic waistband. Button trimmed gored skirt. Sizes, 32 to 46 inches bust measure. **State size.** Average shipping weight, 1⅞ pounds. Price, each.................. **$3.98**

No. 29T972½ Wistaria. MATERNITY DRESS of all wool Canton crepe with latest style raglan sleeves. Sleeves at elbow draped and button trimmed, finished with frilled lawn and lace trimmed cuffs. Fancy pearl button trimmed vest to match. Boned lawn collar trimmed with neat lace insertion. Button trimmed tabs on waist finished with ball ends. Wide crushed sash of self material. Dress retains its natural contour and does not pull up in front or sag, as the waist line is fitted at back and front with a series of fasteners which can be adjusted from time to time. Sizes, 32 to 44 inches bust measure. **State size.** Average shipping weight, 1⅞ pounds. Price, each..... **$9.98**

No. 29T970½ Wine.
No. 29T971½ Navy blue.
ATTRACTIVE MATERNITY DRESS made of all wool poplin, a material that will give excellent service and satisfaction. Deep collar and cuffs trimmed with fancy printed silk. Fancy button trimmed lace vest, finished at neck with lace Gladstone collar. Front of waist trimmed with deep plait on each side. Deep shoulders with set-in sleeves. Plaited messaline girdle with tailored bow. Elastic waistband. Fancy draped skirt with corded ornamentation. Sizes, 32 to 46 inches bust measure. **State size.** Average shipping weight, 1⅞ pounds. Price, each........... **$8.98**

No. 29T968½ Navy blue.
No. 29T969½ Brown.
PRACTICAL MATERNITY DRESS of all wool challis. Waist artistically trimmed with deep messaline collar, finished with tabs of self material fastened in surplice effect at sides. Vest trimmed with fancy crystal buttons. White lace chemisette lined with net. Elastic waistband finished with plaited messaline girdle. Button trimmed skirt finished with double box plait at back. Sizes, 32 to 46 inches bust measure. **State size.** Average shipping weight, 1⅝ pounds. Price, each..... **$6.98**

Our range of maternity dresses comprises practical garments suitable for morning wear, conservative styles for street wear and more elaborate styles for afternoon wear. Each garment is selected with the utmost care to provide the greatest comfort to the wearer. The styles are in keeping with the latest fashions in women's apparel; can be worn throughout the period of pregnancy and easily remodeled to normal size after confinement. If you are contemplating the purchase of a maternity dress, order one of these attractive garments with the assurance of satisfaction or your money returned if for any reason the garment does not please you.

No. 29T966½ Navy blue. PRETTY MATERNITY DRESS of half wool challis. Made with yoke front and drop shoulders. Cuffs and rever collar neatly trimmed with wide messaline silk band. Fancy button trimmed lace yoke and Gladstone collar. Vest trimmed with messaline covered buttons. Elastic waist line finished with plaited messaline girdle and bow. Gored skirt trimmed with wide plait to give tunic effect; button trimmed. Sizes, 32 to 46 inches bust measure. **State size.** Average shipping weight, 1⅝ pounds. Price, each........... **$4.98**

No. 29T974½ Copenhagen blue.
No. 29T975½ Taupe.
STYLISH MODEL MATERNITY DRESS of a beautiful quality silk poplin. Fancy raglan sleeves with button trimmed cuffs and lace frill. Dainty lace vest trimmed with pearl buttons. High lace collar. Bottom of skirt trimmed with small silk covered buttons. Waist line fitted both back and front with a series of fasteners which can be adjusted from time to time, preventing dress from pulling up in front, or drawing across the abdomen. Waist lined. Wide poplin sash. A dressy garment and one that is sure to please. Sizes, 32 to 44 inches bust measure. State size. Average shipping weight, 1⅝ pounds. Price, each..................... **$15.95**

Pretty Hats for Children

Average Shipping Weight. Each, 1½ Pounds.

FOR CHILDREN 5 TO 7 YEARS OF AGE.

$1.10 No. 18T6504 Hat of good quality heavy ribbed corduroy, with durable facing. Trimming of closely gathered, good quality satin taffeta ribbon and wreath of silk ribbon rosebuds. **Colors, white with pink or light blue trimming; navy blue with light blue trimming; brown with pink, or all cardinal red.**

FOR CHILDREN 4 TO 6 YEARS OF AGE.

$1.19 No. 18T6508 The Rah-Rah hat of beautiful velvet, with trimming band and bow; also of velvet with piping of satin messaline. Imported brush like fancy feather completes the trimming. **Colors, navy blue, brown, cardinal red, or black with light blue band. State color.**

FOR CHILDREN 3 TO 5 YEARS OF AGE.

89c No. 18T6512 Close-fitting hat of good quality smooth felt, with narrow rolling brim. Band and accordion plaited upright trimming of all silk plaid ribbon in bright colors to match color of hat. **Colors, navy blue, Alice blue, brown or cardinal red. State color.**

FOR CHILDREN 3 TO 5 YEARS OF AGE.

58c No. 18T6516 Becoming hat of good quality velvetta. Band of narrow satin taffeta ribbon across front, with small bows at each side of crown. Very special value. **Colors, all navy blue, all cardinal red, brown with light blue ribbon, or navy blue with light blue ribbon. State color.**

FOR CHILDREN 3 TO 5 YEARS OF AGE.

98c No. 18T6520 Tam o' Shanter crown of good quality velvetta. Brim covered with fluted satin taffeta ribbon. Bow and band of same. Silk ribbon rose at side. **Colors, navy blue crown with light blue brim trimming; all navy blue; brown with light blue brim trimming, or black crown with pink or light blue brim trimming.**

FOR CHILDREN 4 TO 6 YEARS OF AGE.

$1.10 No. 18T6524 Tam o' Shanter crown with fluted brim of good quality velvetta. Ruche of milliners' mull gathered under edge. Satin taffeta ribbon band set with bow and two small rosebuds. **Colors, navy blue with light blue trimming; all navy blue; brown with pink trimming; or black with pink or light blue trimming.**

FOR CHILDREN 3 OR 4 YEARS OF AGE.

98c No. 18T6528 Wreath of eight new style all silk roses with foliage surrounds the crown of this good quality velvetta bonnet. Pretty rosette of satin taffeta ribbon at left side. Very special value. **Colors, navy blue, brown or black; all with mixed pink and light blue flower wreath. State color.**

FOR GIRLS 5 TO 7 YEARS OF AGE.

$1.48 No. 18T6532 Beautifully made hat of good quality black velvet, trimming of fine satin taffeta ribbon, with close accordion plaits. Ribbon rosette centered with large velvet button. **Colors, black with pink or light blue ribbon; all navy blue, or navy blue with light blue ribbon. State color.**

FOR GIRLS 8 TO 10 YEARS OF AGE.

98c No. 18T6536 Good quality smooth felt hat, which sets well down on head. Exceptionally full trimming band and large rosette bow of good quality satin ribbon, over 3 inches wide. **Colors, navy blue, brown, cardinal red, or navy blue with Alice blue ribbon. State color.**

FOR GIRLS 6 TO 9 YEARS OF AGE.

$1.58 No. 18T6540 Most becoming hat of long nap rich looking plush, wide trimming band laid in fine accordion plaits and large rosettes of satin taffeta ribbon. **Colors, navy blue with Alice blue ribbon; all navy blue; brown with light blue ribbon; cardinal red, or black with pink or light blue ribbon. State color.**

FOR GIRLS 5 TO 7 YEARS OF AGE.

$1.48 No. 18T6544 Most becoming hat of good quality felt, Daintily trimmed with satin faced ribbon, fluted around edge of brim. Ribbon chin strap to match trimming. One of our best hats. **Colors, navy blue, cardinal red, navy blue with Alice blue trimming, or black with pink or light blue trimming.**

FOR GIRLS 7 TO 10 YEARS OF AGE.

95c No. 18T6548 Hat of good quality smooth felt. Trimming of good quality satin taffeta ribbon, draped and knotted around crown with pretty bow and streamers at side. **Colors, navy blue, brown or cardinal, or navy blue with light blue trimming. State color.**

FOR GIRLS 7 TO 10 YEARS OF AGE.

$1.10 No. 18T6552 Deep setting poke bonnet style of good quality felt. All around band trimming and large rosettes are of good quality satin taffeta ribbon, about 1⅛ inches wide. **Colors, light brown with dark brown ribbon; all navy blue; all cardinal, or navy blue with Alice blue trimming. State color.**

FOR GIRLS 9 TO 12 YEARS OF AGE.

$1.58 No. 18T6556 Good quality velvet, hand laid over buckram frame. A beautiful trimming of satin messaline ribbon, with large knotted rosette at side of crown near top. **Colors, navy blue with white or light blue ribbon; all cardinal red; all light blue, or old rose with pink ribbon. State color.**

FOR GIRLS 9 TO 12 YEARS OF AGE.

98c No. 18T6560 Crown and upper brim of good quality velvetta, facing of satin messaline. Trimming band and streamers of satin taffeta ribbon. Large lace rosettes. **Colors, navy blue with Alice blue ribbon; all navy blue; cardinal red; black with pink or light blue ribbon. State color.**

FOR GIRLS 6 TO 8 YEARS OF AGE.

95c No. 18T6564 Serviceable school hat of good quality smooth felt. A very attractive shape. Trimming band of 1½-inch velvetta ribbon, finished at left side in neatly tailored bow. **Colors, Alice blue hat with navy blue ribbon; all navy blue; medium brown, or cardinal red. State color.**

VERY BEAUTIFUL SPRING AND FALL COAT to fit children 6 to 12 years of age. Made of a good quality all wool worsted finished serge. Coat is cut straight and loose fitting and is lined throughout with navy blue mercerized sateen. Front fastens with large fancy buttons. Silk plaid sash comes in attractive combination of colors to harmonize with color of coat, blending perfectly with the rich embroidery shown on the deep circular collar and turnback cuffs. **State age.** See scale of sizes. Average shipping weight, 1½ lbs.
No. 17R7858 Navy blue.
No. 17R7859 Brown.
Price........................ **$4.95**

STYLISH SPRING AND FALL COAT to fit girls from 6 to 14 years of age. Material is a real good quality all wool twilled granite cloth. The fronts fasten with fancy covered buttons. The circular collar is inlaid with black satin to match the cuffs. **State age.** See scale of sizes. Average shipping weight, 1½ pounds.
No. 17R7870 Copenhagen blue.
No. 17R7871 Old Rose. Price........ **$4.98**

SPRING AND FALL COAT to fit children from 2 to 14 years of age. Material is a good quality navy blue all wool serge. Coat is lined throughout with sateen. Fronts show four fancy metal buttons. Deep square back sailor collar embroidered in white with cardinal star design on back and front. **State age.** Average shipping weight, 1½ pounds.
No. 17R7860 Ages, 8 to 14 years.
Price................ **$3.98**
No. 17R7862 Ages, 2 to 6 years.
Price................ **$2.79**

BLACK SATIN COAT to fit girls 8 to 14 years of age. Good heavy quality of black satin, and the garment is cut full in every particular. Lined throughout with black mercerized sateen. Large collar is finished with overcollar made of white pique trimmed with lace and insertion. Cuffs are also finished to match the collar. Fancy metal buttons fasten and trim the front. **Sta'e age.** Average shipping wt., 1¾ lbs.
No. 17R7867 Black
Price.................. **$5.00**

SPRING AND FALL COAT to fit girls from 6 to 14 years of age. Material is a fine all wool serge. Also comes in fine worsted black and white Shepherd check, with cotton warp. The fronts fasten with large covered buttons. Wide sash bow is finished at ends with handsome silk cord ornaments and tassels. Sleeves are the new kimono style forming wide front and back yokes. **State age.** Average shipping weight, 1½ pounds.
No. 17R7874 Navy blue.
No. 17R7875 Shepherd check. Price.... **$5.48**

SPRING AND FALL COAT to fit girls 6 to 14 years of age. Material is a good quality closely woven all wool worsted finished serge. The fronts fasten with large fancy colored buttons to match those shown on the turnback cuffs. The collar is the neat tailor coat style. The garment throughout is cut on straight loose fitting lines. **State age.** See scale of sizes. Average shipping weight, 1¾ pounds.
No. 17R7868 Navy blue. Price....... **$3.48**

WASH COAT to fit children 6 to 14 years of age. Material is a tan color closely woven cotton fabric resembling Irish linen. Fronts fasten with good white pearl buttons. The turnback cuffs, patch pockets and also large shawl collar are inlaid with Copenhagen blue, in same material as coat, and trimmed with soutache braid. **State age.** See scale of sizes. Average shipping weight, 1½ lbs.
No. 17R7866 Tan.
Price.................. **$1.28**

SPRING AND FALL COAT to fit girls 6 to 14 years of age. Material is an all wool Bedford cord. Garment throughout is lined with mercerized sateen. Fronts are fastened with large colored buttons. Square backed collar is inlaid with a rich quality corded silk brocade in contrasting colors to match the turnback cuffs. Kimono sleeves are made in two pieces without seams. The back shows wide Balkan belt effect. **State age.** Average shipping weight, 1½ lbs.
No. 17R7861 Navy blue.
No. 17R7863 Biscuit tan.
Price.................. **$5.95**

Our Own Ucanttear Make. Finest Washable Suits

This line is equal to the best made wash suits in the country. All garments are made of perfect washable material, cut especially full and roomy. | Note sizes in which each number can be furnished. **Order by age.** Average shipping weight, each suit, 1 pound.

$1.05 No. 40R2272 **Handsome Sailor Blouse Suit** in blue and white striped madras cloth. Embroidered white rep collar. Tie, breast pocket. Bloomer pants. **SIZES—5 to 10 years. State age.**

$1.15 No. 40R2274 **Hydegrade Galatea Sailor Suit** in brown and white stripes. Brown sailor collar. Tie, breast pocket. Cuffs made to button. Bloomer pants. **SIZES—5 to 10 years. State age.**

$1.25 No. 40R2276 **Sailor Suit** in white lawn. Fly front, sailor collar, detachable silk embroidered shield. Plaited cuffs. Breast pocket. Bloomer pants. **SIZES—5 to 10 years. State age.**

$1.60 No. 40R2280 **Handsome Tan and White Checked Sailor Suit.** Made of Renfrew madras. Fancy collar, detachable silk embroidered shield. Pearl buttons. Bloomer pants. **SIZES—5 to 10 years. State age.**

$1.68 No. 40R2282 **Double Breasted Sailor Suit.** Splendid brown and white washable Renfrew madras. Fancy brown collar, silk embroidered white shield. Cuffs button. Bloomer pants. **SIZES—5 to 10 years. State age.**

$1.75 No. 40R2284 **Pure Linen Sailor Suit.** Natural linen color with red trimmings. White rep silk embroidered shield. Cuffs made to button. Bloomer pants. **SIZES—5 to 10 years. State age.**

$1.15 No. 40R2286 **Little Fellows' Very Pretty Military Suit.** Plain white rep with light blue silk trimmings, as illustrated. Breast pocket, belt. Bloomer pants. **SIZES—2½ to 6 years. State age.**

$1.05 No. 40R2288 **Fancy Russian Suit** made of tan and white striped madras. Fancy shaped, neatly trimmed white sailor collar. Shield, belt, breast pocket. Bloomer pants. **SIZES—2½ to 6 years. State age.**

$1.35 No. 40R2278 **Balkan Blouse** in the latest style. Made of white cotton middy cloth with dark navy blue trimmings. Half shield made detachable, large tie. Cuffs, bottom and pocket trimmed in dark blue and white. Full cut, straight pants with blue trimming at bottoms. **SIZES—3 to 8 years. State age.**

$1.45 No. 40R2292 **Wonderful value in the popular light blue rep, double breasted Russian Sailor Suit.** Large rolling collar scalloped in white with white embroidery on each side. Silk embroidered detachable white shield. Breast pocket, belt. Cuffs made to button. Full cut bloomer pants with elastic at bottoms. **SIZES—2½ to 6 years. State age.**

$1.35 No. 40R2290 **The latest effect in Little Fellows' Beach Suit,** made of crinkled seersucker. White and brown stripes, with fancy brown and white trimmings. Short sleeves. Roomy straight pants with fancy trimmed bottoms. **SIZES—2½ to 6 years. State age.**

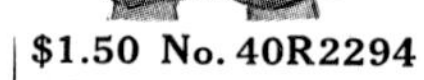

$1.50 No. 40R2294 **Great effect in Little Fellows' Russian Suit,** plain white cotton Devonshire cloth with light blue trimmings. Belt, collar and pocket trimmed with white tape. Cuffs made to button. Bloomer pants. **SIZES—2½ to 6 years. State age.**

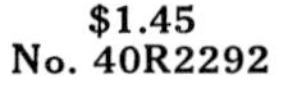

$1.75 No. 40R2296 **Russian Suit** in gray pinchecked pure linen crash. Collar trimmed in blue, detachable shield. Tie. Bloomer pants. **SIZES—2½ to 6 years. State age.**

$1.60 No. 40R2298 **Handsome Little Military Suit** in light blue rep embroidered with white trimmings. Embroidered plait down front. Bloomer pants. **SIZES—2½ to 6 years. State age.**

Every suit on this page is an unusual value. Positively none better made.

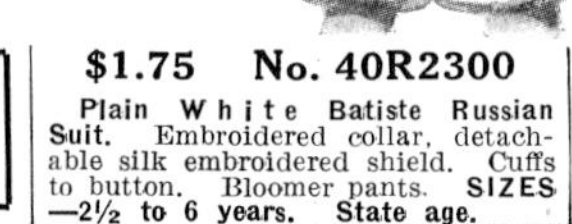

$1.75 No. 40R2300 **Plain White Batiste Russian Suit.** Embroidered collar, detachable silk embroidered shield. Cuffs to button. Bloomer pants. **SIZES—2½ to 6 years. State age.**

$1.65 No. 40R2302 **Russian Suit** in tan color rep, white trimmings, silk embroidered detachable shield. Cuffs to button. Bloomer pants. **SIZES—2½ to 6 years. State age.**

Girls' Cloth and Wash Dresses

The scale below will help you to decide on the correct size. If your child is large or small for her age, order accordingly. Sizes of children of the same age vary a great deal. Measurements may vary slightly, owing to the different styles. We cannot give you the service you expect unless you order according to these specifications. **Be sure to state age.**

Ages	2	3	4	5	6
Average length, inches	20	22	23	24	26
Average bust, inches	22	23	24	25	26

No. 29T7728 Navy blue check.
BALKAN DRESS of very fine quality Galatea, trimmed with embroidered edging, soutache braid and buttons; tunic skirt. Ages, 2 to 6 years. **State age.** Av. shpg wt., 9 oz. Price, each.. **$1.19**

No. 29T7719 White.
WHITE LAWN DRESS, smartly trimmed with embroidery in the latest effect. Wide satin ribbon sash and bow. Ages, 2 to 6 years. **State age.** Av. shpg. wt., 7 ounces. Price, each... **$1.48**

No. 29T7721 Blue and white.
GIRLS' HEAVY WEIGHT WASH DRESS of striped Galatea, trimmed with plain blue percale, embroidered braid and piping. Ages, 2 to 6 years. **State age.** Av. shpg. weight, 8 ounces. Price, each...... **59c**

No. 29T7806 Re[d] plaid.
No. 29T7807 Blu[e] plaid.
GIRLS' WAR[M] DRESS, made of woven cotton plaid material. Neatly trimme[d] with cotton serge, pipings and pearl buttons. Waist lined. Ages, [2] to 6 years. **State age.** Average shpg. wt., 6 o[z]. Price, each.......... **48[c]**

No. 29T7723 Blue and white.
SERVICEABLE DRESS of washable pin striped Galatea. Waist neatly embroidered on front; plain blue collar, cuffs and strappings. Dress fastens down side front with loops and pearl buttons. Latest semi-plaited skirt with tunic. Ages, 2 to 6 years. **State age.** Average shpg. weight, 9 ounces. Price, each....... **88c**

No. 29T7716 Blue check.
No. 29T7717 Tan check.
LITTLE TOTS' BELTED RUSSIAN DRESS of good quality gingham. Trimmed with solid color chambray in contrasting color. Sizes to fit ages 1 to 4 years. **State age.** Average shipping weight, 6 ounces. Price, each........ **49c**

No. 29T7709 White.
PRETTY LAWN DRESS. Waist attractively trimmed with wide pattern embroidery and tucked lawn panel. Embroidery trimmed skirt joined to waist with ribbon drawn lawn beading. Good value. Ages, 2 to 6 years. **State age.** Average shipping weight, 5 ounces. Price, each....... **98c**

No. 29T7793 Blue plaid.
No. 29T7794 Pink plaid.
WARM DRESS of good quality light plaid flannelette. Neatly trimmed with plain percale, striped pipings and pearl buttons. Ages, 2 to 6 years. **State age.** Average shipping weight, 8 ounces. Price, each...... **44c**

No. 29T7722 Blue.
GIRLS' BALKAN DRESS. Full blouse of plain blue percale, with blue and white checked gingham skirt, belt, collar and cuffs. Ages, 2 to 6 years. **State age.** Average shipping weight, 7 oz. Price, each....... **69c**

No. 29T7729 Blue.
No. 29T7730 Tan.
SERVICEABLE HEAVY WEIGHT GALATEA DRESS. Waist attractively trimmed with checked inserts and artistic red embroidered design. Collar and cuffs of fancy checked novelty cloth. Ages, 2 to 6 years. **State age.** Av. shpg. wt., 9 oz. Price, each **$1.12**

No. 29T7720
SPECIAL BARGAIN—Three choice gingham dresses in different patterns of blue plaid, black and white Shepherd check and blue stripe. Waist trimmed with solid color yoke and red embroidered panel. Sold only in sets of three dresses. Excellent value. Ages, 2 to 6 years. **State age.** Average shipping weight, for three, 1¾ lbs. Price, 3 dresses for. **$1.00**

No. 29T7718 Blue Polka Dot.
GIRLS' WASH DRESS of good weight Playtime Suiting. Attractively trimmed with blue and white striped Galatea, red pipings and fancy buttons. Ages, 2 6 years. **State age.** Average shipping wt., 8 oz. Price, each....... **48c**

No. 29T7724 Tan plaid.
No. 29T7725 Blue plaid.
GIRLS' REVERSIBLE GINGHAM DRESS, neatly trimmed with light bias binding and pearl buttons. Double breasted reversible coat front; when one side is slightly soiled it can be reversed and clean side buttoned on top. Tape and adjustable patent clasp on inside of dress prevents the under side from sagging. Ages, 2 to 6 years. **State age.** Average shipping weight, 9 ounces. Price, each............ **98c**

No. 29T7726 Blue.
No. 29T7727 Pink.
GOOD WEIGHT WASHABLE COTTON REP DRESS, daintily **embroidered and trimmed with scalloped embroidered band, pipings and pearl buttons.** Ages 2 to 6 years. **State age.** Average shipping weight, 9 oz. Price, each ... **$1.18**

No. 29T7896 Black and whit[e] check.
GIRLS' WARM DRESS made of a woven cotton material. Attractivel[y] trimmed with re[d] flannel bands and strappings; gilt buttons. Ages, 2 to 6 years. **State age.** Average shipping weight, 8 ounces. Price, each......... **79c**

BOYS' OVERALLS AND JACKETS

SIZES—3 to 15 Years.

No. 41R734

Sizes, 3 to 8 years....**42c**
Sizes, 9 to 15 years....**47c**

BOYS' HEAVY WEIGHT BLUE DENIM OVERALLS. Made just like dad's. This is a large full cut garment. One hip pocket, two front pockets. Wide suspenders, large double gilt buckles; double sewed seams, reinforced pocket corners. **State age and note prices for sizes as listed above.** Average shipping wt., 1¼ pounds.

No. 41R731

Sizes, 3 to 8 years, **42c**
Sizes, 9 to 15 years, **47c**

BOYS' HEAVY WEIGHT BLUE DENIM JACKET. Made just like dad's, to match our No. 41R734 Overalls. Double sewed seams, sleeve cuffs made to button. **State age and note prices for sizes as listed above.** Average shipping wt., 1 pound.

No. 41R735

Sizes, 3 to 8 years....**45c**
Sizes, 9 to 15 years....**49c**

BOYS' TWO-IN-ONE DOUBLE KNEE AND SEAT OVERALLS. Made of good quality double and twist blue denim; two front pockets and one hip pocket, riveted corners, detachable suspenders with elastic ends. **State age and note prices for sizes as listed above.** Average shipping weight, 12 ounces.

YOUTHS' OVERALLS

SIZES—26 to 32 Inches Waist Measure, to Fit Boys From 12 to 18 Years.

No. 41R725 69c

YOUTHS' TWO-IN-ONE DOUBLE KNEE OVERALLS. Material is a heavy weight gold back blue denim. One hip pocket in addition to those shown; suspenders with elastic ends, riveted pocket corners and double sewed seams. Sizes, 26 to 32 inches waist measure, lengths accordingly. **State waist measure.** Average shipping weight, 1⅜ pounds.

No. 41R726 49c

YOUTHS' WABASH STRIPED MEDIUM WEIGHT DENIM OVERALLS. Made with one hip pocket in addition to those shown, attached suspenders, double stitched seams and patent buttons. Sizes, 26 to 32 inches waist measure, lengths accordingly. **State waist measure.** Average shipping weight, 1 pound.

Men's Auto and Driving Dusters

SIZES—34 to 48 Inches Breast Measure.

No. 41R33 $2.25

MEN'S SINGLE BREASTED TAN LINEN DUSTER. Made of natural color pure linen with sleeve tabs, slash pockets and double sewed seams. Average length, 51 inches. **State breast measure taken over vest.** Average shipping weight, 1½ pounds.

No. 41R39 $4.95

MEN'S SMOKE GRAY MOHAIR DUSTER. This is a cool, comfortable, neat appearing duster; double breasted front, wide facing, detachable belt in back, two deep slash pockets and one breast pocket. Average length, 52 inches. **State breast measure taken over vest.** Average shipping weight, 2⅛ pounds.

No. 41R37 $2.55

MEN'S DOUBLE BREASTED DIAGONAL STRIPED DARK TAN COTTON DUSTER. A neat serviceable garment; wide facings, standing collar, sleeve tabs, deep slash pockets and slit in back. Average length, 52 inches. **State breast measure taken over vest.** Average shipping weight, 2⅛ pounds.

Boys' Rubber and Oiled Slicker Raincoats

SIZES—26 to 34 Inches Breast Measure, to Fit Boys From 8 to 16 Years.

No. 41R831 $2.35

BOYS' DULL FINISHED BLACK RUBBER COAT. Made the same as our men's rubber coats. Has white sheeting lining and pure gum rubber surface; two outside pockets with flaps, slit in back, and front closes with hook and slot buckles. **State age and breast measure.** Average shipping weight, 4 pounds.

No. 41R980 $1.75

BOYS' OR GIRLS' BLACK OILED SLICKER RAINCOAT. Made of a soft, flexible oiled material, absolutely waterproof. Made double throughout sleeves and body to the waist line; velveteen collar and fly front. **State age and breast measure.** Average shipping wt., 3 pounds.

No. 41R985 $1.95

BOY SCOUTS' ARMY DRAB COLOR OILED SLICKER RAINCOAT. Also worn by girls. Material is a very soft, flexible slicker cloth. Has fly front, velveteen collar. Made double to the waist and throughout the sleeves. **State age and breast measure.** Average shipping weight, 3 pounds.

GIRLS', JUNIOR AND MISSES' SIZE SWEATERS

FOR AGES 13 to 20 Years, BUST MEASURE, 34 and 36 In. Suitable for Small Women, Too.

Price, $2.48 Each

No. 38T3682 Red.
No. 38T3683 White.
No. 38T3684 King's blue.

SCHOOLGIRLS' OR SMALL WOMEN'S SWEATER COAT of finest quality 100 per cent pure wool zephyr yarn. Half belt in back. Soft and warm and an exceptional value. Sizes, 34 and 36 inches bust measure. **State size.** Shipping weight, 1½ pounds.

Price, $2.48 Each

No. 38T3685 Red, navy blue and white plaid.
No. 38T3686 Gray, navy blue and white plaid.

MISSES' OR SMALL WOMEN'S MACKINAW COAT. Knitted from soft wool yarn, brushed up blanket finish, with a closely woven cotton mesh underneath to maintain its shape. Sizes, 34 and 36 inches bust measure. Fully guaranteed. **State size.** Shipping weight, 1½ pounds.

Price, $2.98 Each

No. 38T3687 Maroon.
No. 38T3688 Kelly green.
No. 38T3689 Seal brown.

MISSES' OR SMALL WOMEN'S FINE QUALITY SOFT PURE WOOL ZEPHYR WORSTED NORFOLK COAT. Trimmed with the stylish Robespierre collar; wide belt; pockets and turnback cuffs. Sizes, 34 and 36 inches bust measure. **State size.** Shipping wt., 1⅝ lbs.

Price, $1.89 Each

No. 38T3671 Maroon.
No. 38T3672 Navy blue.

MISSES' OR SMALL WOMEN'S CO-ED SWEATER COAT in the plain Cardigan stitch. A mixture of equal parts pure wool worsted and cotton yarns. Sizes, 34 and 36 inches bust measure. **State size.** Shipping weight, 1 lb. 7 oz.

Price, $1.59 Each

No. 38T3664 Maroon.
No. 38T3665 Navy blue.
No. 38T3666 Gray.
No. 38T3667 Seal brown.

MISSES' OR SMALL WOMEN'S LIGHT WEIGHT JERSEY SWEATER. Made of 100 per cent pure wool worsted yarn. Military close fitting collar fastened with snaps. This coat is standard jersey weight and very warm. Sizes, 34 and 36 inches bust measure. **State size.** Shipping weight, 1 pound.

Price, $2.98 Each

No. 38T3690 Maroon.
No. 38T3691 Navy blue.
No. 38T3692 Gray.

MISSES' OR SMALL WOMEN'S EXTRA HEAVY SHAKER KNIT ALL WOOL WORSTED SWEATER COAT in the popular mannish effect. Double "Ruff-Neck" collar. Heavy weight and is an exceptional value. Sizes, 34 and 36 inches bust measure. **State size.** Shpg. wt., 2¼ lbs.

BOY SCOUTS' OUTFIT

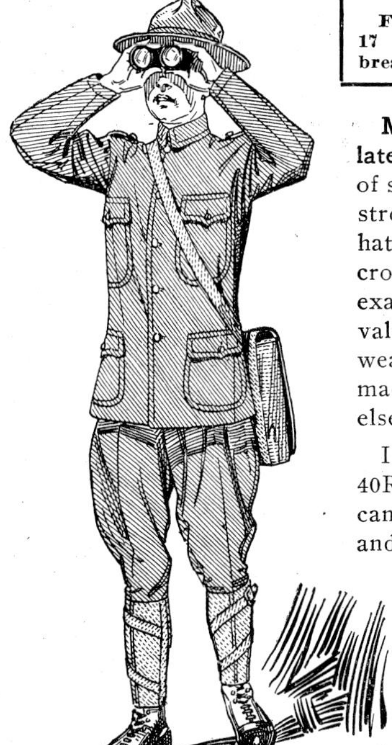

No. 40R2570

Furnished in sizes to fit average size boys from 12 to 17 years. Order by age. Not larger than 33 inches breast measure.

Made of a splendid quality of khaki cloth in the latest olive tan color. Complete uniform consists of scout coat, scout breeches laced below the knee, strong puttees made of army duck, a campaign hat of khaki cloth, with ventilation eyelets in crown, and the latest style haversack. All made exactly like illustrations. An outfit of practical value, not only as a uniform, but for general wear, at a much more reasonable price than well made goods like these can possibly be obtained elsewhere.

If you want the complete uniform, order No. 40R2570, price, $3.65. Any part of the uniform can be obtained by ordering under the numbers and at prices listed below.

No. 40R2570 Complete Scout Outfit.. **$3.65**
Shipping weight, 3½ lbs.

No. 40R2560 Scout Coat............ **$1.25**
Shipping weight, 1¾ lbs.

No. 40R2562 Scout Breeches........... **98c**
Shipping weight, 1⅜ lbs.

No. 40R2564 Scout Campaign Hat... **40c**
Sizes, 6½, 6⅝, 6¾, 6⅞, 7 and 7⅛.
Shipping weight, 12 oz.

No. 40R2566 Scout Haversack........ **54c**
Shipping weight, 9 oz.

No. 40R2568 Scout Puttees.......... **48c**
Shipping weight, 9 oz.

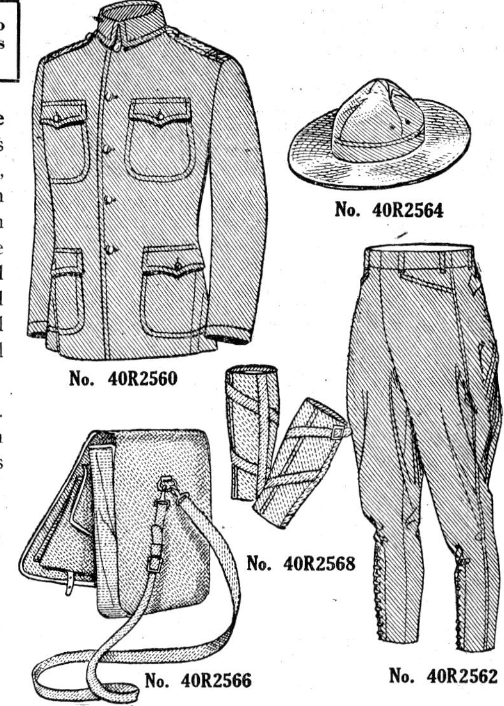

No. 40R2564

No. 40R2560

No. 40R2568

No. 40R2566

No. 40R2562

$10.00 Remarkable Special Clothing Offer $10.00
FOR YOUNG MEN

Furnished in sizes from 33 to 37 inches breast measure. See about taking measurements, as explained on page 825.

$10.00

Full Satin Lined Pure Wool Navy Blue Serge Suit.

Full 13-ounce material. Three-button single breasted sack coat with three outside pockets, one inside pocket, vent and three small buttons on sleeves. Slit in back. Latest style high cut six-button vest with narrow notched collar, four outside pockets and one inside pocket. Conservative peg top pants with belt loops, side buckle straps, side pockets, two hip pockets with tab and button on one, watch pocket, and 2-inch cuff bottoms. Coat and vest back lined with the well known Belden satin. Handsome trimmings to match. Average shipping weight, 5½ pounds.

No. 40T1080

Young men's suit, **sizes, 33 to 37 inches breast measure. Give measurements.**

$10.00

The Latest English Swagger Style Coats Which Are All the Rage for Young Men.

Something entirely new in the overcoat line. A coat warm enough to ward off chills, but light so as not to be oppressive. **Made of all wool cheviot cloth in fancy light gray and black, or handsome brown and olive mixtures.** Waterproofed by the well known Priestley process, which keeps out dampness and gives a good protection in ordinary rains. Silk yoke, silk sleeve lining. Slash pockets. Cuff effect on sleeves. Raglan shoulders. Box back. Slings on inside of coat for arm rests. **SIZES —To fit average size young men from 17 to 21 years of age, or measuring 33 to 37 inches breast measure. State size.** Average shipping weight, 4½ pounds. Note catalog number for each color.

No. 40T1442 Gray.
No. 40T1444 Brown.

Khaki Suits

Khaki Suits Are Noted for Their Serviceability and Wear Resisting Qualities

These khaki suits are guaranteed not to fade or turn color when exposed to weather conditions. Cut, fashioned and made by tailors, not simply thrown together; they are strongly sewed and neatly finished. The motorcycle suits are equipped to suit the needs of motorcyclists, the Protector collar shielding from wind and dust; the inverted pockets are large and can carry needed articles securely, as they button through. The breeches are reinforced in the seat, insuring double service and wear. For the man who is going hunting, camping or for the man who works out of doors, there is nothing better than khaki clothing as, in addition to its serviceability, it does not soil easily nor show dust.

$5.25

STRONGLY MADE BRONZE FUSTIAN CLOTH MOTORCYCLE SUIT.

Fustian cloth is an extremely durable fabric that is noted for its wear resisting qualities. This well made motorcycle suit will withstand the wear and tear that is usually given a suit of this kind. The illustration above shows the fabric and the style. The jacket is made with the yoke effect and box plaits in back, through which a belt is drawn, fastening with a buckle. Four bellows pockets, with flaps that button, insure the contents when riding at a high speed. Protector collar. Breeches lace around the calves. Average shipping weight, 5 pounds.

No. 45V6288

Price for jacket and breeches.....**$5.25**
Give measurements.

$4.75

STRONGLY SEWED BEAVER BROWN KHAKI MOTORCYCLE SUIT.

A medium shade of brown similar to the shade used by the U. S. Government. It is a very practical color, as it will not soil or show dust easily. The illustration above brings out the style details. The jacket is made with yoke effect and box plaits in back, through which a belt is drawn, fastening in front with a buckle. Four pockets that have inverted plaits and flaps that button. Protector collar shields from wind and dust. Breeches are full and roomy through the hips and fit close around the calves, fastening with laces. Average shipping weight, 5 lbs.

No. 45V6290

Price for jacket and breeches.....**$4.75**
Give measurements.

SIZES The two-piece khaki suits offered on this page are furnished in sizes from 34 to 44 inches breast measure and 30 to 42 inches waist measure, and 30 to 36 inches inseam measure. When ordering give BREAST, WAIST and INSEAM measures. When ordering a motorcycle suit give BREAST and WAIST measures. In all cases give HEIGHT AND WEIGHT. See page 732 for simple measuring instructions.

$3.85

YOKE EFFECT BEAVER BROWN KHAKI NORFOLK SUIT.

A strong wear resisting khaki fabric in a beaver brown shade that is similar to the shade used by the U. S. Government. In the illustration directly above we illustrate this suit. Coat has the yoke effect front and back from which extend two box plaits, through which a belt is drawn. The belt is adjustable and can be worn as a half belt in back, or all around waist as shown above. Coat is unlined and has patch pockets to button. Pants have tunnel belt loops and cuff bottoms. Average shipping weight, 5 pounds.

No. 45V6287

Price for coat and pants............**$3.85**
State measurements.

$3.50

YOKE EFFECT WALNUT SHADE KHAKI NORFOLK SUIT.

Walnut is a light shade of brown verging into an olive. Khaki cloth is very durable and will stand the wear and tear. It does not soil easily. Made in the Norfolk style, as illustrated above, with yoke front and back, from which extend two box plaits through which a belt is drawn, fastening in front. This belt is made in three parts and can be worn in the back as a half belt, or all around the waist as shown in the illustration. Pants have cuff bottoms and tunnel belt loops. Average shipping weight, 5 pounds.

No. 45V6284

Price for coat and pants..........**$3.50**
Give measurements.

$2.20

DURABLE TAN KHAKI SUIT. SINGLE BREASTED SACK STYLE.

A light tan shade verging into an olive. Khaki cloth is especially serviceable, as it wears well and does not soil easily. The illustration above pictures this suit. Round cut sack style with patch pockets. Pants have cuff buttons. Neatly made. Average shipping weight, 4 pounds.

No. 45V6280

Price for coat and pants...........**$2.20**
State measurements.

$3.85

BEAVER BROWN KHAKI SUIT. SINGLE BREASTED SACK STYLE.

A round cut sack style khaki suit with four patch pockets to button. Pants have belt loops and cuff bottoms. Neatly sewed and finished. All seams strongly sewed to withstand wear. The cloth is a medium brown shade similar to the color adopted by the U. S. Government. Average shipping weight, 4 pounds.

No. 45V6286

Price for coat and pants...........**$3.85**
Give measurements.

$2.75

DARK DRAB KHAKI SUIT WITH THE MILITARY STYLE COLLAR.

A round cut sack suit with five buttons, has a small standup collar similar to those used on military suits. Three patch pockets that are made to button through. Pants are comfortably fitting and have belt loops and cuff bottoms. Cloth is a dark drab shade verging into gray. Strongly sewed and well finished. Will not soil easily. Average shipping weight, 4 lbs.

45V6282

Price for coat and pants..........**$2.75**
State measurements.

$7.65

$10.75

FOR DESCRIPTION AND PRICES SEE PAGE 222

Milady's Slipper Problems Solved

The extensive line of Women's hand turned shoes shown on this and other pages are made in our own factories. They carry the usual high standard of SEARSMADE QUALITY.

No. 15V199 The Pair, $2.50

All Patent Colt Tango Sandal—Flexible Hand Turned Sole—Comfortable Toe—Low Heel.

Sizes 2½ to 8. Widths, D to EE. Shipping wt., 1½ lbs.

No. 15V3212 The Pair, $2.50

All Dull Kid Welt — White Rubber Sole and Heel — Stylish, Comfortable and Noiseless — Searsmade.

Sizes, 2½ to 8. Widths, D to EE. Shipping wt., 1⅞ lbs.

Our showing of Women's low shoes combine the snap and elegance of the newest models now being shown in the big city style centers. Each detail is correct.

Convincer.

No. 15V3215 The Pair, $2.50

Patent Colt Baby Doll Pump—Welt—New White Ivory Leather Sole—White Rubber Heel—Searsmade.

Sizes, 2½ to 8. Widths, D to EE. Shipping weight, 1⅞ lbs.

No. 15V34 The Pair, $2.50

All Patent Coltskin Pump—Welt—Detachable Strap—Raised Toe—Low Heel—Searsmade.

Sizes, 2½ to 8. Widths, C to EE. Shipping weight, 1 lb. 11 oz.

No. 15V94 The Pair, $2.50

Handsome Black Suede Sandal—Welt—Made Over a Stylish Last With Cuban Heel—Searsmade.

Sizes, 2½ to 8. Widths, D to EE. Shipping wt., 1 lb. 9 oz.

No. 15V3214 The Pair, $3.00

Patent Colt—Newest Barred Front Effect—Semi-Pointed Toe—Cuban Heel—Welt—Style Direct From Paris—Searsmade.

Sizes, 2½ to 8. Widths, D to EE. Shipping weight, 1⅝ lbs.

No. 15V7 The Pair, $3.00

Patent Colt Tango Sandal—New Last—Latest Cuban Louis Heel—Hand Turned Sole.

Sizes, 2½ to 8. Widths, D to EE. Shipping wt., 1 lb. 5 oz.

No. 15V3006 The Pair, $3.00

All Patent Colt Turn—Newest Open Throat One-Piece Slashed Strap Effect—Celluloid Louis Heel—Searsmade.

Sizes, 2½ to 8. Widths, D to EE. Shipping wt., 1½ lbs.

Convincer.

No. 15V3007 The Pair, $2.50

Handsome Dull Kid Strap Sandal — Hand Turned — Attractive Black Bead Trim — City Last—Cuban Heel—Searsmade.

Sizes, 2½ to 8. Widths, D to EE. Shipping wt., 1 lb. 9 oz.

No. 15V200 The Pair, $3.00

Famous Castle Tango Pump of Patent Colt—Black Cloth Quarter—Rubber Inlaid Turned Sole—Wood Louis Heel.

Sizes, 2½ to 8. Widths, D to EE. Shipping wt., 1¼ lbs.

No. 15V3203 The Pair, $2.75

All Dull Kid Colonial—Welt—Short Vamp—White Rubber Sole and Heel — Stylish, Comfortable and Noiseless—Searsmade.

Sizes, 2½ to 8. Widths, D to EE. Shipping wt., 1⅞ lbs.

No. 15V38 The Pair, $3.00

Patent Colt Colonial — Welt — Cut Steel Buckle — Attachable Strap—City Last—Cuban Heel—Searsmade.

Sizes, 2½ to 8. Widths, D to EE. Shipping weight, 1 lb. 11 oz.

No. 15V8 The Pair, $2.50

Patent Colt Tie—Dull Collar—Welt—Snappy Hi-Toe and Cuban Heel—Searsmade.

Sizes, 2½ to 8. Widths, C to EE. Shipping wt., 1 lb. 11 oz.

No. 15V22 The Pair, $3.00

All Patent Colt—Welt—Made Over a Smart Hi-Toe Crest Last With Cuban Heel—Searsmade.

Sizes, 2½ to 8. Widths, D to EE. Shipping weight, 1 lb. 11 oz.

$3.98
78V9533

We Can Please You

No. 78V9528 **$2.48**

Stylish good fitting narrow brim sailor, all hand made of pyroxylin braid on light weight buckram frame. The upright bows and trimming across the front are of good quality silk taffeta ribbon, 3 inches wide. Six medium quality roses with green foliage and small buds are prettily arranged. **COLORS:** White with pink trimming, as illustrated; white with Alice blue trimming; black with pink, or in navy blue with Alice blue trimming. **State color.**

No. 78V9533 **$3.98**

Splendid dress hat on most becoming shape. Hand made of crimped pyroxylin braid. There are three good quality extra large ostrich tips, a pretty cluster of pink roses, a quantity of natural looking lilacs and foliage, all arranged in charming effect with good quality 3-inch silk taffeta ribbon. A single rose with lilacs sets off the facing. **COLORS:** White with pink roses, as illustrated; white with light blue roses; black with American beauty red or pink roses, or champagne with cream color tips and light blue roses. **State color.**

No. 78V9538 **$2.48**

A becoming hand made hat with deep folds of fine figured silk net around the crown, over the pyroxylin braid. In a pretty rosette of this net is a large imported American beauty rose with natural looking green foliage. **COLORS:** Black with American beauty red rose, as illustrated; black with pink or light blue rose; brown with pink or tea color rose, or navy blue with tea color or American beauty red rose. **State color.**

No. 78V9543 **$2.98**

A pleasing sailor hat. Splendidly made of pyroxylin braid with corded edge facing of good quality messaline silk. Bow and band around crown of good quality satin taffeta ribbon, 3 inches wide. Neat arrangement of good roses with foliage and tiny buds. **COLORS:** White with old rose trimming and facing, as illustrated; white with pink trimming and facing; all black with pink trimming; champagne with light blue trimming and facing, or navy blue with Alice blue trimming and facing. **State color.**

No. 78V9548 **$2.75**

A stunning black and white trimming is a feature of this straight brim sailor. The hat is all hand made of closely woven, imported braid. The sides of crown are completely covered with a wide folded band of good quality taffeta silk. A large full blown rose with green foliage is correctly placed. **COLORS:** Black with black and white silk and white rose, as illustrated, or with pink, light blue or American beauty red rose. **State color.**

No. 78V9553 **$2.48**

A splendid turban with perfect imitation heron aigrettes, set off with tiny ostrich tips, and a wreath of nine silk centered velvet pansies. Top of crown is of pyroxylin braid, while sides of brim are covered with silk shadow lace laid over taffeta silk. **COLORS:** Black with natural purple pansies, as illustrated; black with light blue pansies; brown or navy blue, both with natural purple pansies; all hats with black aigrettes. **State color.**

No. 78V9558 **$4.45**

A beautiful dress hat with genuine full ostrich plumes of good quality held in place by a double bow design of good quality satin taffeta ribbon, 3½ inches wide. A deeply folded band of this ribbon extends around crown completely covering the sides. Top and wide binding are of closely woven, corded braid with facing of pyroxylin braid. A tailored bow of ribbon is placed on under brim. **COLORS:** Black with old rose plumes and trimming, as illustrated; in all solid black, or in white with white plumes, and white, pink, or light blue ribbon trimming. **State color.**

No. 78V9563 **$2.98**

A pleasing hat of moderate size made of pyroxylin braid in pretty raised design. Sides of crown entirely covered with jet spangled all-over net, laid over taffeta silk. A medium quality ostrich plume, is set off with three large silk velvet pansies. **COLORS:** Black with natural purple pansies, as illustrated, or in brown or navy blue, both with natural purple pansies. **State color.**

No. 78V9568 **$2.65**

This becoming hat of good, smooth, chip braid is prettily trimmed by five full blown roses with imported forget-me-nots and cleverly arranged bands of good quality satin taffeta ribbon, 3 inches wide; one band of which is brought over edge to underbrim. **COLORS:** Burnt color with pink roses and light blue ribbon, as illustrated; white with light blue or old rose trimming; black with pink or American beauty red trimming. **State color.**

Average shipping weight, 3 pounds.

Average shipping weight, 3 pounds.

Appropriate Suit for warm weather and outing wear. Can be had in women's or misses' sizes, from 32 to 44 inches bust measure, 22 to 32 inches waist measure, and from 34 to 44 inches front length of skirt. Made of the well known all wool Palm Beach cloth in natural color. Coat is unlined, made in Norfolk style with patch pockets. Sleeves with cuffs. See small illustration for back. **When ordering state bust measure, waist measure and front length of skirt.** Average shipping weight, 3½ pounds.

No. 31V9720½ Women's and Misses' sizes. Natural Palm Beach color. EACH **$6.95**

Same style as above, made of wool mixed covert cloth. **When ordering state bust measure, waist measure and front length of skirt.** Average shpg. wt., 3½ lbs.

No. 31V9721½ Tan covert. EACH **$7.95**

Women's Suit in strictly new style. Made of fine quality all wool poplin. Spring length. Lined throughout with guaranteed peau de cygne silk. Robespierre collar covered with fancy ribbed silk. Gathered yoke, single breasted front, closing with self covered buttons. Set-in sleeves with split bell shape cuffs trimmed with silk to match collar. See small illustration for fancy back with slot seams and small buttons. Yoke top skirt with wide plaited flounce and raised waist closing at left front. Plain back. Women's regular sizes only. **When ordering state bust measure, waist measure and front length of skirt.** Samples of material sent free on request. Average shipping weight, 4 pounds.

No. 31V9730½ Navy blue.
No. 31V9731½ Dark Copenhagen blue.
No. 31V9732½ Dark green. EACH **$15.95**

Women's Suit made of wool mixed broadcloth in spring and summer weight. Coat in spring length and lined throughout with mercerized sateen. Single breasted front, closing with composition buttons. Plain mannish collar and lapels trimmed with stitched down braid and buttons. Set-in sleeves and French back trimmed with braid and buttons to match lapels. See small illustration. Skirt in divided false tunic style. Raised waist closing at left front. Women's regular sizes only. For larger sizes see stout women's suits on page 226. **When ordering state bust measure, waist measure and front length of skirt.** Samples of material sent free and postpaid on request. Average shipping weight, 4 pounds.

No. 31V9715½ Navy blue.
No. 31V9716½ Brown.
No. 31V9717½ Black. EACH **$6.45**

Women's Suit at a special low price. Made of our standard all wool double twisted warp serge. Single breasted front, closing with composition buttons. Snug fitting long rolled lapels and mannish collar. Set-in sleeves with cuffs and buttons. Lined with fine quality guaranteed satin. See small illustration for back with belt and slot seam in center. Fashionable skirt with long loose hanging divided tunic. Raised waist closing at left front. Women's regular sizes only. For larger sizes see stout women's suits on page 226. **When ordering state bust measure, waist measure and front length of skirt.** Average shipping wt., 4 lbs.

No. 31V9725½ Navy blue.
No. 31V9726½ Brown.
No. 31V9727½ Black. EACH **$9.60**

SIZES Women's Regular Size Tailored Suits offered on this page are furnished only as illustrated and described, in the following sizes: From 32 to 44 inches bust measure, 22 to 32 inches waist measure and from 36 to 44 inches front length of skirt. Open basted hem. Please mention if you wish hem stitched down in length ordered. Samples of material sent free and postpaid on request. When taking waist measure for high girdle skirts, take measure at regular belt line. Do not make allowance for high girdle. For women's extra sizes see page 226. **State bust and waist measure and front length of skirt.** See page 732 for measuring instructions.

Women's or Misses' Spring and Fall Coat. Made in the cutaway front style in the new 45-inch length of a wool mixed fancy gray striped mixture. The back is slightly fitted and finished with wide plaits at each side trimmed with self covered buttons with black satin centers. The fancy cut collar has trimming of black satin and small buttons. Fancy patch pockets. Sizes, 32 to 42 inches bust measure. **Give size.** Sample of material sent free on request. Average shipping weight, 2 pounds 5 oz.

No. 17V9400 Gray mixture.
Price................. **$3.98**

Women's or Misses' Wool Mixed Fancy Mixture Spring and Fall Coat. Made in the becoming 45-inch length, plain tailored style, of a very pretty mixture material woven in a small check pattern. The collar is of unfinished broadcloth in color to harmonize. The back of the coat hangs straight and loose. Large lapel pockets. The cutaway fronts are finished with wide facings and fasten with fancy buttons. Sizes, 32 to 44 inches bust measure. **Be sure to state size.** Sample of material sent free on request. Average shipping weight, $2\frac{1}{4}$ pounds.

No. 17V9402 Tan mixture.
No. 17V9403 Gray mixture.
Price.................. **$4.95**

Women's or Misses' Black Moire Spring and Fall Coat. The material is a good quality mercerized poplin with deep moire markings. This is a very dressy model, made in the becoming 36-inch length. The back is cut full and loose, held in at waist line with tabs of self material at each side and finished with large jet buttons. The coat fastens with loops and jet buttons. The collar is trimmed with small band of black velvet and small buttons. Lined throughout with black mercerized sateen. Sizes, 32 to 44 inches bust measure. **State size when ordering.** Sample of material sent free on request. Average shipping weight, $2\frac{1}{8}$ pounds.

No. 17V9408
Black. Price.......... **$5.48**

Women's or Misses' Stylish Fancy Checked Spring and Fall Coat. Made in the loose box style in 34-inch length. The material is a very handsome wool mixed novelty cloth of fancy basket weave design in small broken checks and pretty color effects. The fronts have fancy patch pockets and fasten with self covered buttons. The stylish back is cut full with wide belt, button trimmed. The collar has inlay of black silk moire. Sizes, 32 to 42 inches bust measure. **State size.** Sample of material sent free on request. Average shipping weight, 2 pounds 11 ounces.

No. 17V9405 Black and white check.
No. 17V9406 Tan and gray check.
Price................. **$5.25**

Women's Fur Sets and Coats

No. 41D2518 Natural Light Brown **$39.50**
No. 41D2519 Blended Dark Brown **$43.50**

WOMEN'S NATURAL LIGHT BROWN OR BLENDED DARK BROWN WATERMINK FUR COAT. Made of selected Northern winter muskrat fur. Beautiful light brown natural shade, or blended dark brown. Made with a neat pointed collar, semi-raglan sleeves, deep cuffs, large sweep, and lined with Skinner's guaranteed satin. Length of coat in back, 38 inches. Sizes, 32 to 42 inches bust measure. Larger sizes made to order at an extra charge of 20 per cent. **State bust measure.** See page 708 for simple measuring instructions. Average shipping weight, 6 pounds.

No. 41D2740 Natural Brown and Gray Set **$22.50**
No. 41D2741 Natural Brown and Gray Scarf **$10.50**
No. 41D2742 Natural Brown and Gray Muff **$12.00**

WOMEN'S NEW STYLE NOVELTY RACCOON FUR SET. Fur is a selected brown body, gray tipped natural raccoon. Single animal style fur boa with fur on both sides, fastens with snap head or hook and chain. Large melon shape muff with fancy tucked silk cuff ends and silk lining. Average shipping weight of set, 3 pounds; scarf, 1½ pounds; muff, 2¼ pounds.

No. 41D2735 Natural Brown and Gray Set **$18.95**
No. 41D2736 Natural Brown and Gray Scarf .... **$ 7.20**
No. 41D2737 Natural Brown and Gray Muff **$11.75**

WOMEN'S ANIMAL STYLE NATURAL RACCOON FUR SET. Fur is a beautiful selected Northern raccoon. Dark brown under fur and gray tipped hairs. Large single animal style scarf with silk ruching around the neck. Extra large pillow muff with fancy set-in bed, tucked and shirred silk ends. Both scarf and muff lined with silk. Average shipping weight, of set, 3⅜ pounds; scarf, 1¼ pounds; muff, 2⅝ pounds.

No. 41D2516 Black. $19.50

WOMEN'S THREE-QUARTER LENGTH RUSSIAN PONYSKIN FUR COAT. Made of imported, well marked black ponyskins. Has a neat square collar, wide flaring skirt, Skinner's satin lining and single breasted front. Length of coat in back, 36 inches. Sizes, 32 to 42 inches bust measure. At the time this catalog goes to press it appears that European conditions will cause a shortage of these Russian Pony Skins and therefore we are unable to guarantee delivery on any sizes larger than the above. **State bust measure.** See page 708 for simple measuring instructions. Average shipping weight, 5⅝ pounds.

Women's or Misses' Raincoats

Samples of Material Sent on Request.

17V9840 $5.48

Women's or Misses' Silk Mixed Raincoat. The material is a fine bright gloria silk mixed fabric, light in weight with a coating of elastic rubber on the inside, making it thoroughly waterproof. Stylish for sunshine as well as rain. The coat is cut loose and easy fitting with belt across back. Fronts have facings of same material. Finished with slash pockets and a neat turnover French band collar. Sizes, 34 to 46 inches bust measure; lengths, 52 and 56 inches. **State size and length.** Average shipping wt., 2 lbs. 3 oz.

No. 17V9840 Tan.
No. 17V9841 Navy blue.
No. 17V9842 Silver gray. Price............ **$5.48**

Waterproofed Hat of same material. **State color.** Average shipping weight, 12 ounces.
No. 17V9869 Price.... **48c**

17V9850 $7.98

Women's or Misses' Raincoat, made of good quality closely woven wool mixed serge, in very attractive dark color broken checks. The coat is thoroughly waterproofed by a good coating of rubber on the inside and is fashioned after one of the latest models, cut loose and full, with wide facings of self material. The collar is the convertible style and may also be worn buttoned up closely about the throat. (See small illustration). There is a long full cape about the shoulders, made so as to properly protect the arms, forming a loose sleeve and cuff effect at front. A stylish coat for either clear or stormy weather. Sizes, 34 to 46 inches bust measure. Lengths, 52 and 56 inches. **State size and length.** Average shipping weight, 3½ pounds.

No. 17V9850 Navy blue and green.
No. 17V9851 Navy blue and brown.
Price.. **$7.98**

17V9844 $6.48

Women's or Misses' Rainproof Coat. The material is a very fine silk finished cotton rep, dressy and serviceable. The coat is cut along loose easy fitting lines, having attractive belt and buttons across back. The kimono sleeves have deep cut armholes and are finished with wide cuffs and buttons. The fronts have wide facings of self material and fancy patch pockets with lapels. There is also a neat inlaid velvet collar. The garment is thoroughly waterproofed throughout with good coating of rubber on the inside. Sizes, 34 to 46 inches bust measure. Lengths, 52 and 56 inches. **State size and length.** Av. shpg. wt., 3 lbs.

No. 17V9844 Navy blue.
No. 17V9845 Tan.
No. 17V9846 Gray.
Price.. **$6.48**

17V9847 $8.48

Women's or Misses' Raincoat. One of the best waterproof coats made. The material is a fine closely woven all wool cashmere on the outside and a gloria silk on the inside, with good coating of rubber between the two fabrics, making the coat thoroughly waterproof. The garment is made on loose straight lines and has wide facings of cashmere. Convertible collar that may be worn buttoned up about the throat. (See small illustration.) Straps on sleeves. All seams are sewed, cemented and strapped. Sizes, 34 to 46 inches bust measure. Length, 52 and 56 inches. **State size and length.** Average shipping weight, 3½ pounds.

No. 17V9847 Tan.
No. 17V9848 Navy blue.
No. 17V9849 Oxford gray.
Price.................. **$8.48**

No. 17D2220 Price, $10.98
Heavy Weight Pebble Cheviot, Unlined.

No. 17D2225 Price, $11.98
Silk Seal Plush, Guaranteed Sol Satin Lining.

SAMPLES OF MATERIALS SENT FREE ON REQUEST.

WHEN YOU VOTE, the cross mark in the little square on the ballot is the important thing. When you order by mail, the SIZE is important. We must know size wanted to fill your order. See page 708 for simple measuring instructions.

Silk Crepe de Chine Waist, $2.39

The material is a fine quality richly finished pure silk crepe de chine. The fronts are slightly gathered on yoke to provide fullness, and fasten down center between rows of beautiful heavy ivory white Venise lace insertion. On all colors quoted, the front opening and the collar are bound with wide band of ivory white crepe de chine, matching the wide cuffs that finish the three-quarter length sleeves. Sizes, 32 to 46 inches bust measure. **State size.** Average shipping weight, 14 ounces.

No. 27D3234 Ivory white.
No. 27D3235 Flesh pink.
No. 27D3236 Light blue.
Price.................................. **$2.39**

Women's or Misses' Winter Coat of Plush. This attractive coat which comes in 45-inch length is made in the popular belted style with wide flaring skirt of silk seal plush, one of the best plushes used in women's or misses' coats. It has a thick heavy pile and is a rich brown black in color and resembles the real seal fur. The fullness in front and back forms wide box plait effect and is held in place by wide belt which is fastened with loops and plush buttons. The sleeves are finished with cuffs, button trimmed. Coat can also be worn buttoned closely around the neck. Lined throughout with guaranteed Sol satin, an imported Venetian of good weight, a rich lustrous black with a wonderful bright satin finish and guaranteed to give perfect satisfaction. Sizes, 32 to 46 inches bust measure. **Give size.** Average shipping weight, 6 pounds.

No. 17D2225 Black.
Price.................................. **$11.98**

Muff to match. Satin lined. Average shipping weight, 2½ pounds.
No. 17D2409 Black.
Price.................................. **$1.98**

Women's or Misses' Winter Coat of Pebble Cheviot Cloth. This coat is fashioned after one of the latest models. It is made with slightly fitted back, with a wide flaring skirt which drapes in wide graceful folds. The material used is a thick all wool heavy cheviot cloth, of good winter weight and finished with a real fine pebbly surface. The wide lapover front is finished with two rows of plush buttons in military effect and may be worn open with revers as per small view. Collar and deep pointed cuffs are of black silk seal plush to match the wide band of plush which trims the bottom of coat. The coat is made in 50-inch length and comes in bust measures from 32 to 46 inches. **State size.** Average shipping weight, 6¾ pounds.

No. 17D2220 Navy blue.
No. 17D2221 Brown.
No. 17D2222 Black.
Price.................................. **$10.98**

No. 27D3222 Voile Waist. $1.98

Embroidered Voile Waist. Material is a real fine quality sheer white cotton voile. The waist is fashioned after the latest loose fitting style, being plaited on to the lace trimmed front yoke to allow fullness. The fronts fasten down center with small buttons and are beautifully trimmed with rows of heavy fillet lace insertion and embroidered in rich artistic floral design to match the back. (See small back view.) The collar is also made of the same embroidery and edged with fillet lace, matching perfectly the full length embroidered sleeves that are finished with wide turnback lace trimmed cuffs. Sizes, 32 to 46 inches bust measure. **State size.** Shipping weight, 13 ounces.

No. 27D3222 White.
Price.................................. **$1.98**

Women's or Misses' Pebble Cheviot Winter Cloth Coat in 45-inch length. A most becoming model made in the latest style with slightly fitted back, with flaring skirt which drapes in graceful folds. The material is a closely woven all wool cheviot, very thick and close, with a real fine pebbly surface. The fronts, which fasten with large plush buttons, have side slit pockets, button trimmed. Collar is of silk seal plush. The sleeves have deep cuffs of plush to match collar. Wide band of silk plush around the bottom gives this coat a stylish finish and adds greatly to its appearance. Sizes, 32 to 46 inches bust measure. **Give size.** Average shipping weight, 6¼ pounds.

No. 17D2170 Black.
No. 17D2171 Navy blue.
No. 17D2172 Brown.
Price.................................. **$9.75**

Women's or Misses' Fur Trimmed Velour Corduroy Coat. This stylish garment comes in 42-inch length and is made in the popular belted style of a heavy corded corduroy, which is exceedingly lustrous and has all the appearance of a silk velvet. It is very heavy and warm and a splendid wearing material. Coat is cut along straight loose fitting lines and fastens with self covered buttons and braid loops. Lined throughout with black guaranteed Sol satin, an imported Venetian with a wonderfully lustrous satin finish and of extraordinary durability. The large collar is Siberian marten, otherwise known as black opossum fur. Sizes, 32 to 46 inches bust measure. **State size.** Average shipping weight, 5¾ pounds.

No. 17D2175 Navy blue.
No. 17D2176 Copenhagen blue.
No. 17D2177 Brown.
No. 17D2178 Black.
Price.................................. **$9.98**

No. 17D2170 Price, $9.75
Heavy Weight Pebble Cheviot, Unlined.

No. 17D2175 Price, $9.98
Velour Corduroy, Fur Collar, Sol Satin Lining.

SAMPLES OF MATERIALS SENT FREE ON REQUEST.

"IT'S SURPRISING" **Said the manager of our Cloak and Suit Department, "how many customers forget to state size." We must know size wanted to fill your order. See page 708 for simple measuring instructions.**

The Shoemaker's Latest Triumph

The Military Lace—Fashion's Newest Sensation

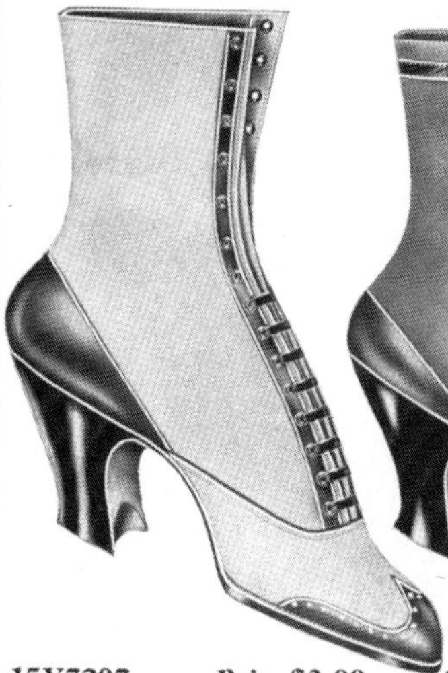

15V7207 Pair, $3.00
Putty Color Cloth Military Lace—Gunmetal Calf Wing Tip, Foxing and Lace Stay—Goodyear Welt Sewed—Leather Louis Heel—Searsmade.
Sizes, 2½ to 8. Widths, D to EE. Shipping wt., 1¾ lbs.

15V7206 Pair, $3.50
Imperial Brown Nu-Buck Military Lace—Gunmetal Calf Diamond Tip, Foxing and Lace Stay—Goodyear Welt Sewed—Leather Louis Heel—Searsmade.
Sizes, 2½ to 8. Widths, D to EE. Shipping wt., 1⅞ lbs.

15V7208 Pair, $3.50
White Nu-Buck Military Lace—Tan Calf Diamond Tip, Foxing and Lace Stay—Goodyear Welt Sewed—Leather Louis Heel—Searsmade.
Sizes, 2½ to 8. Widths, D to EE. Shipping wt., 1⅞ lbs.

Convincer.

15V7202 Fawn Top. Pair, $2.95
15V7203 Gray Top. Pair, 2.95
15V7204 Nigger Brown Top. Pair, 2.95
15V7205 Black Top. Pair, 2.95
Patent Colt Military Lace—Cloth Top—Welt—Short Stage Vamp—French Heel—Searsmade.
Sizes, 2½ to 8. Widths, D to EE. Shipping wt., 1⅛ lbs.

15V3218 Pair, $2.95
Patent Coltskin Military Lace Oxford—Fashionable Diamond Tip—Nigger Brown Cloth Top—Goodyear Welt Sewed—Leather Louis Heel—Searsmade.
Sizes, 2½ to 8. Widths, D to EE. Shipping wt., 1⅝ lbs.

15V41 Pair, $3.00
Patent Coltskin—Dull Kid Top—Goodyear Welt—Hi-Toe—Cuban Heel—Searsmade.
Sizes, 2½ to 8. Widths, C to EE.

15V36 Pair, $3.00
Gunmetal Calfskin.
Sizes, 1 to 8. Widths, C to EE. Shipping wt., 1⅞ lbs.

15V7044 Pair, $3.45
Fine Bronze Kid—Brown Cloth Quarter—Goodyear Welt—Recede Toe—Leather Louis Heel—Searsmade.
Sizes, 2½ to 8. Widths, D to EE. Shipping wt., 1¾ lbs.

15V7500 Pair, $2.50
Tan Russia Calfskin—New English Last—White Rubber Sole and Low Heel—Searsmade.
Sizes, 2½ to 8. Widths, D to EE. Shipping wt., 2¼ lbs.

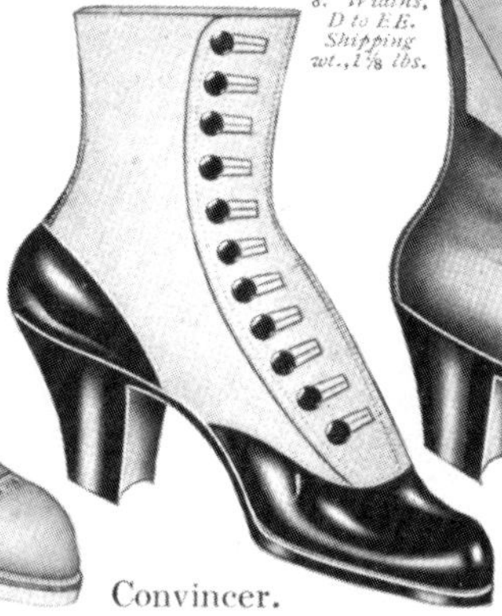

Convincer.

15V7210 Fawn Top. Pair, $2.75
15V7211 Gray Top. Pair, 2.75
15V7212 Black Figured Brocade Top. Pair, 2.75
Patent Coltskin—Stylish Cloth Spat Top Effect—Welt—Short Stage Vamp—New Cuban Heel—Searsmade.
Sizes, 2⅛ to 8. Widths, D to EE. Shipping wt., 1⅞ lbs.

Convincer.

15V4011 Pair, $2.65
All Dull Kid Button Boot—Goodyear Welt—Short Stage Vamp—Cuban Heel—Searsmade.
Sizes, 2½ to 8. Widths, D to EE. Shipping wt., 1⅝ lbs.

Individual Styles for Men Who Care

No. 15D4072
The Pair, $3.75
Patent Coltskin—Fawn Cloth Top—Military Lace—English Last—Sensible Heel—Goodyear Welt—Light Sole—Searsmade.
Sizes, 5 to 11. Widths, C to EE. Shipping wt., 2¾ lbs.

No. 15D4071
The Pair, $3.75
Gunmetal Calfskin—Gray Cloth Top—Military Lace—English Last—Low Heel—Goodyear Welt—Single Sole—Searsmade.
Sizes, 5 to 11. Widths, C to EE. Shipping wt., 2¾ lbs.

No. 15D4073
The Pair, $3.75
Dark Tan Calf—Fawn Cloth Top—Military Lace—English Last—Low Heel—Goodyear Welt—Single Sole—Searsmade.
Sizes, 5 to 11. Widths, C to EE. Shipping wt., 2¾ lbs.

No. 15D4075
The Pair, $3.75
Patent Coltskin—Fawn Cloth Top—English Last—Low Heel—Goodyear Welt—Single Sole—Searsmade.
Sizes, 5 to 11. Widths, C to EE. Shipping wt., 2¾ lbs.

No. 31D2680½ Navy blue.
No. 31D2681½ Bottle green.
No. 31D2682½ Uniform blue.

EACH $12.48

Misses' Suit at $12.48 in popular military style. Made of good wearing quality all wool poplin. Belted coat in fall and winter length. Single breasted front, buttons up to neck with novelty metal buttons. Standing military collar trimmed with velvet and buttons. Slit pocket at each side. Set-in sleeves with cuffs. Lined throughout with satin, guaranteed for two seasons' wear. See small illustration for belted back. Skirt with raised waist closes at left front. Stylish box plait at each side. Average sweep, 72 inches. Furnished in misses' sizes only, from 32 to 38 inches bust measure. For larger sizes see women's regular size suits. **When ordering state bust measure, waist measure and front length of skirt.** Average shipping weight, 4 pounds.

No. 31D2690½ Navy blue.
No. 31D2691½ Bottle green.
No. 31D2692½ Dark brown.

EACH $13.65

Misses' Suit, trimmed with popular silk military braid, at $13.65. Made of fine quality all wool worsted poplin. Single breasted coat in fall and winter length. Pocket at each side. Sleeves and collar edged with silk military braid. Lined throughout with satin, guaranteed for two seasons' wear. See small illustration for gathered belted back, trimmed with braid and braid buttons to match front of coat. Box plaited skirt with raised waist closing at left front. Average sweep, 80 inches. Furnished in misses' sizes only, from 32 to 38 inches bust measure, 22 to 28 inches waist measure and from 34 to 38 inches front length of skirt. For larger sizes see women's regular size suits. **When ordering state bust measure, waist measure and front length of sk.rt.** Average shipping weight, 4 pounds.

ALL WOOL SERGE, lined with satin.

No. 31D2685½ Navy blue.
No. 31D2686½ Dark brown.
No. 31D2687½ Black.

EACH $8.65

ALL WOOL MEN'S WEAR SERGE, lined with yarn dye construction satin.

No. 31D2688 Navy blue.
No. 31D2689 Bottle green.

EACH $12.75

Misses' or Small Women's Suit. Furnished in our standard all wool double twisted warp serge or in heavy quality all wool men's wear serge at prices quoted above. Strictly tailored conservative style in popular fall and winter length. Single breasted front, closing with ivory buttons. Mannish collar and lapels. Set-in sleeves with button trimmed cuffs. Tailored slit pocket at each side. See small illustration for belted button trimmed back. Skirt with raised waist closes at left front. Full length tailored fold in center of front. Furnished in misses' sizes only. For larger sizes see women's regular size suits. **When ordering state bust measure, waist measure and front length of skirt.** Average shipping weight, 3½ pounds.

SIZES Misses' or Small Women's Suits offered on this page can be furnished only as illustrated and described, in the following sizes: From 32 up to and including 38 inches bust measure; and 22 up to and including 28 inches waist measure, proportionate hip measure, and from 34 up to and including 38 inches front length of skirt. Open basted hem. If you wish hem stitched down in length ordered, please mention on order. When taking measure for high girdle skirt, take measure at regular belt line. Do not make allowance for high girdle. **When ordering state bust measure, waist measure and front length of skirt.** See page 708 for simple measuring instructions.

SPECIAL NOTE—Write for our Special Sample Book No. 80D, ready for mailing September 1, 1915, if you wish to see actual cloth samples of our entire line of Women's and Misses' Ready to Wear Tailored Suits. You can order direct from this page, but we will gladly send you Sample Book No. 80D if you will write and ask for it.

Women's Striped Voile Dress. An exceptionally smart dress of fine quality washable cotton voile in a pattern which is a combination of awning and small stripes. Waist made with the new loose hanging jacket. Yoke and collar of fine lawn, both hemstitched in contrasting color, and yoke trimmed with rows of pin tucking and glass buttons. Set-in elbow length sleeves finished with turn-back cuffs of lawn. Belt from each side of waist front to each side of back, and held in place by glass buttons, is an attractive feature. Waist buttons in front with pretty glass buttons. Underwaist of good quality net. Skirt made with long loose hanging overskirt. Women's sizes only. **Give measurements.** Average shipping weight, 1½ pounds.

No. 31V9115 Blue stripe.
No. 31V9116 Black stripe.
EACH **$4.29**

Women's Embroidered Voile Dress. Stunning dress of fine quality washable cotton voile, richly embroidered in heavy Venise design. New jacket effect waist and long loose hanging overskirt with yoke top. Vestee and collar of fine lace; vestee trimmed with small silk covered buttons and collar hemstitched. Three-quarter length set-in sleeves, trimmed with ruffle and band of lace insertion and set off with flaring cuffs of lawn. Jacket at armholes and around vestee is finished with dainty tear drop edging. Rows of corded shirring and hemstitching on shoulders are pleasing features. Wide silk messaline girdle in contrasting color. Rows of corded shirring give popular yoke effect to skirt. Dress fastens in front. Women's sizes only. **Give measurements.** Average shipping wt., 1¾ pounds.

No. 31V9120½ White. EACH **$6.98**

Women's Cotton Jacquard Dress. The material used in this charming wash dress is excellent quality flowered Jacquard. Vestee and laydown collar of fine quality organdy, vestee being trimmed with row of small novelty buttons, and collar with insertion and plaited lace. Silk messaline bow tie. Full length sleeves trimmed with bands of organdy and insertion and finished with plaited frill of lace. Wide silk messaline girdle in contrasting color. The four-tier skirt, over good quality net, is especially attractive. Dress fastens in front of waist and at left side of skirt. Women's sizes only. **Give measurements.** Average shipping weight, 1¾ pounds.

No. 31V9130 Blue flower.
No. 31V9131 Pink flower.
No. 31V9132 Lavender flower.
EACH **$3.48**

Women's Combination Crepe Dress. Made of woven stripe and plain cotton washable crepe in combination effect, the style so popular this spring. Vestee trimmed with novelty glass buttons. Wide revers and attractive turn-back cuffs trimmed with rows of small silk covered buttons. Full length set-in sleeves. Extra wide girdle of good quality silk messaline. Skirt made with yoke top and loose hanging divided overskirt of striped crepe over underskirt of plain crepe. Yoke of skirt is trimmed with large silk covered buttons. Women's sizes only. **Give measurements.** Average shipping wt., 1½ pounds.

No. 31V9110 Blue stripe.
No. 31V9111 Black stripe.
EACH **$3.98**

Women's Dress of Striped Wash Silk. A tub dress made of good quality washable silk, a material that will be extensively used this season. Makes a charming garment. Embroidered vestee and roll collar of fine quality organdy, vestee being trimmed with row of small colored glass buttons. Three-quarter length set-in sleeves finished with turnback cuffs of embroidered organdy. Silk belt with silk braid buckle in front. Attractive yoke top skirt with lap seam running entirely down front. This is a dress sure to give excellent service and one that can be worn for almost any occasion. Women's sizes only. **Give measurements.** Average shipping weight, 1¼ pounds.

No. 31V9125 Black stripe.
No. 31V9126 Blue stripe.
EACH **$4.95**

SIZES Dresses offered on this page are furnished only as illustrated and described and in the following sizes: From 32 up to and including 44 inches bust measure; waist measure up to and including 33 inches, and front skirt length of 39 or 42 inches, with wide basted hem. **When ordering be sure to give bust measure, waist measure and front length of skirt.** See page 732 for simple measuring instructions. Samples of materials furnished on request.

SIZES Dresses offered on this page are furnished only as illustrated and described and in the following sizes: From 32 up to and including 44 inches bust measure; waist measure up to and including 33 inches, and front skirt length of 39 or 42 inches, with wide basted hem. **Be sure to give bust measure, waist measure and front length of skirt when ordering.** See page 732 for simple measuring instructions. Samples of materials furnished on request.

Women's Embroidered Voile Dress. Beautiful dress of excellent quality washable cotton voile, embroidered in an odd and handsome design. Made with the new loose hanging jacket, trimmed with dainty lace edging and tassels, as illustrated. Standing collar of embroidered net. Waist front trimmed with rows of dainty lace insertion and attractive glass buttons. Three-quarter length set-in sleeves of embroidered net, finished in scalloped design. Extra wide silk messaline crushed girdle. Yoke top skirt trimmed around yoke and at bottom with rows of narrow lace insertion. Dress fastens in front. Women's sizes only. **Give measurements.** Av. shpg. wt., 1½ lbs.

	EACH
No. 31V9065½ White.	$5.95

Women's Embroidered Linen Dress. Made of good quality genuine linen with moire trimming. Yoke of embroidered net, trimmed with moire covered buttons. Wide laydown collar, turnback cuffs and piping at waist line of moire in contrasting color. Elbow length set-in sleeves. Collar, cuffs and waist front at waist line trimmed with self covered buttons. Skirt is made with long, loose hanging tunic, divided in front, which is embroidered on each side at bottom. Dress has the popular high waisted effect. Fastens in front. Practical and stylish. Women's sizes only. **Give measurements.** Average shipping weight, 2 pounds.

	EACH
No. 31V9070 Tan.	$3.69

Women's Plisse Crepe Dress. Attractive dress of good quality washable cotton plisse crepe, made with vestee and wide laydown collar of silk messaline. Neck frill of Oriental top embroidered net. Waist trimmed in front, on each side of vestee, with silk covered buttons. Three-quarter length set-in sleeves with turnback cuffs of silk messaline and wide frills of embroidered net. Wide silk messaline girdle. Skirt made in the fashionable Redingote or divided tunic effect, trimmed in front with row of silk covered buttons. Comes in two colors, all black or all white. Dress fastens in front. Women's sizes only. **Give measurements.** Average shpg. wt., 1⅝ lbs.

	EACH
No. 31V9060 Black. No. 31V9061 White.	$3.98

Women's Fancy Crepe Dress. Nobby dress made of good quality washable cotton crepe in a pattern of self and colored woven stripes. Yoke, roll collar and turnback cuffs of sheer lawn, hemstitched in contrasting color. Yoke is trimmed with row of colored glass buttons. Made in the new vest effect with points extending over skirt, giving the fashionable high waisted appearance. Set-in elbow length sleeves. Piping on waist front and covered buttons are of chambray. Attractive yoke in top skirt. Dress buttons in front. Women's sizes only. **Give measurements.** Average shipping weight, 1⅝ pounds.

	EACH
No. 31V9075 Blue stripe. No. 31V9076 Black stripe.	$2.98

Women's Sateen Foulard Dress. The material is high luster floral design French sateen foulard, a material which continues to grow in popular favor. Vestee, roll collar and pretty turnback cuffs of white pique. Full length set-in sleeves. Skirt is made in the new Redingote style, having long loose hanging overskirt divided in front. The wide, loose hanging yoke girdle, trimmed with pique covered buttons, is an attractive feature. Neck is trimmed with popular silk cord, so much in evidence this season. Dress fastens invisibly in front. Women's sizes only. **Give measurements.** Average shipping wt., 1¾ pounds.

	EACH
No. 31V9080 Blue. No. 31V9081 Brown. No. 31V9082 Black.	$3.69

Misses' Embroidered Net Dress. A charming dress, made of excellent quality washable net, richly embroidered. Waist made with the new and popular jacket effect and has three-quarter length sleeves, trimmed with plaited net frills. Attractive round laydown collar, trimmed with Cluny lace and finished off in scalloped design. Waist front trimmed with row of three small artificial rosebuds. Wide crushed girdle of silk messaline. Skirt made with loose hanging overskirt, bottom of both overskirt and underskirt being finished in scalloped design. Dress fastens in front. Misses' sizes only. **Give measurements.** Average shipping weight, 1¾ pounds.

No. 31V8985½ White. EACH **$6.45**

Misses' Embroidered Voile Dress. Made of excellent quality washable cotton voile in modified basque effect, a style especially attractive in a misses' dress. Roll collar and turnback cuffs of sheer lawn. Elbow length set-in sleeves which are prettily set off by band of lace insertion running from neck along top of shoulders and down sleeves to cuffs. Two lace ruffles, one at waist line and the other at top of skirt, modify the severeness of the basque effect. Waist is trimmed in front with lace insertion, running from neck to ruffle on skirt. Dress fastens in front. Misses' sizes only. **Give measurements.** Average shipping weight, 1½ pounds.

No. 31V8990 White. EACH **$2.98**

Misses' Dress of Embroidered Voile. A dainty white dress, handsome enough for any occasion. An excellent dress for confirmation purposes. Made of extra fine quality cotton voile, handsomely embroidered, and will launder beautifully. Wide yoke and cuffs on sleeves are made of rows of pretty lace insertion. Three little bows on front of yoke are of white silk messaline. Elbow length sleeves. Extra wide girdle of white silk messaline. Four-tier skirt, as illustrated, finished in scalloped design, is especially pretty and stylish. Dress fastens in back. Misses' sizes only. **Give measurements.** Average shipping weight, 1¾ pounds.

No. 31V8995½ White. EACH **$5.95**

Misses' Embroidered Voile Dress. Good quality washable cotton voile, handsomely embroidered. Made with the new jacket effect waist and three-tier effect skirt. Elbow length sleeves joined to waist by neat band of lace insertion. Insertion around neck, girdle and on skirt is of Cluny lace. Jacket, sleeves and bottom of tunics on skirt are finished in scalloped design. Dress fastens in back. A most attractive white dress and at a remarkably low price. Misses' sizes only. **Give measurements.** Average shipping weight, 1½ pounds.

No. 31V8980 White. EACH **$2.29**

SIZES Dresses offered on this page are furnished only as illustrated and described and in the following sizes: 14, 16, 18 and 20 years, or 32, 34, 36 and 38 inches bust measure with average skirt lengths of 34, 35, 37 and 38 inches, with wide basted hem. **In ordering be sure to give bust measure, waist measure and front length of skirt.** See page 732 for simple measuring instructions. Samples of materials sent on request.

Misses' Embroidered Voile Dress. An exceptionally pretty dress, made in one of this spring's most popular styles. The material is excellent quality washable cotton voile. Richly embroidered yoke effect shoulders, with elbow length sleeves. Attractive frill around neck and on sleeves of fine quality shadow lace. The waist is handsomely embroidered and set off by a girdle and large bow of self material. Yoke top skirt with wide ruffle of Swiss embroidery. Dress buttons in front with self covered buttons. Misses' sizes only. **Give measurements.** Average shpg. wt., 1¼ lbs.

No. 31V9000 White. EACH **$2.49**

Misses' Linen Dress. Stylish dress made of genuine linen in natural color. A material always in popular favor, not only because it looks good and washes well, but also on account of its wearing qualities. Laydown collar, turnback cuffs and girdle, with long sash, of percale in dark green color make an exceptionally pretty combination. Neck is ornamented with bow tie which, together with the cuffs and collar, is finished off with neat lace edging. Three-quarter length set-in sleeves. Skirt made in long divided overskirt effect and has wide cross tab near bottom, trimmed with percale covered buttons and loops. Dress buttons in front. Misses' sizes only. **Give measurements.** Average shipping weight, 1½ pounds.

No. 31V8970 Tan. EACH **$2.48**

Misses' Fancy Crepe Dress. The material is excellent quality washable cotton crepe with colored woven stripes. Laydown collar, turnback cuffs and piping are of mercerized crepe. Waist made in vestee effect with wide lapels trimmed with velvet loops and novelty glass buttons. Wide yoke girdle, as illustrated. Three-quarter length set-in sleeves. Skirt made in long double overskirt effect. Dress buttons in front with attractive glass buttons. An exceedingly nobby dress in a popular material. Misses' sizes only. **Give measurements.** Average shpg. wt., 1½ lbs.

No. 31V8975 Blue stripe.
No. 31V8976 Black stripe. EACH **$2.89**

SIZES Dresses offered on this page are furnished only as illustrated and described, and in the following sizes: 14, 16, 18 and 20 years, or 32, 34, 36 and 38 inches bust measure, with average skirt lengths of 34, 35, 37 and 38 inches, with wide basted hem. **In ordering be sure to give bust measure, waist measure and front length of skirt.** See page 732 for simple measuring instructions. Samples of materials sent on request.

Misses' Percale Dress. Attractive dress of washable percale in which good quality is combined with low price. Round laydown collar, turnback cuffs, vestee and piping of white cotton poplin, collar and cuffs being richly embroidered. Popular raglan shoulders with three-quarter length sleeves. Skirt made in long tunic effect. Dress closes in front. You will be delighted with the style and workmanship of this dress. Misses' sizes only. **Give measurements.** Average shipping weight, 1¼ lbs.

No. 31V8955 Blue.
No. 31V8956 Tan. EACH **$1.09**

Misses' Checked Gingham Dress. Material is excellent quality washable checked gingham. Wide laydown collar and all piping of percale in contrasting color, collar being daintily embroidered. Yoke effect shoulders with elbow length sleeves finished with neat turnback cuffs. Attractive skirt made with loose hanging divided overskirt and yoke top. Front of waist and yoke of skirt trimmed with large mother of pearl buttons. Dress fastens in front. An exceptionally neat wash dress at a price that is sure to appeal to you. Misses' sizes only. **Give measurements.** Average shipping weight, 1½ pounds.

No. 31V8960 Blue check.
No. 31V8961 Lavender check. EACH **$1.29**

Misses' Sailor Middy Dress. Two-piece dress made of good quality washable cotton suiting with contrasting trimming. A sailor dress is always stylish, and at our price every girl can easily afford one. Braid trimmed collar of self material in contrasting color and turnback cuffs to match. Full length sleeves. Neat pocket on left side of waist front below shoulder, and silk lace at bottom of collar. Skirt has wide plait running entirely down front, and pocket on right side in front. Skirt fastens in front. Misses' sizes only. **Give measurements.** Average shipping weight, 2 lbs.

No. 31V8965 White, blue trimming.
No. 31V8966 Blue, white trimming. EACH **$1.79**

BABIES' LONG AND SHORT CLOAKS

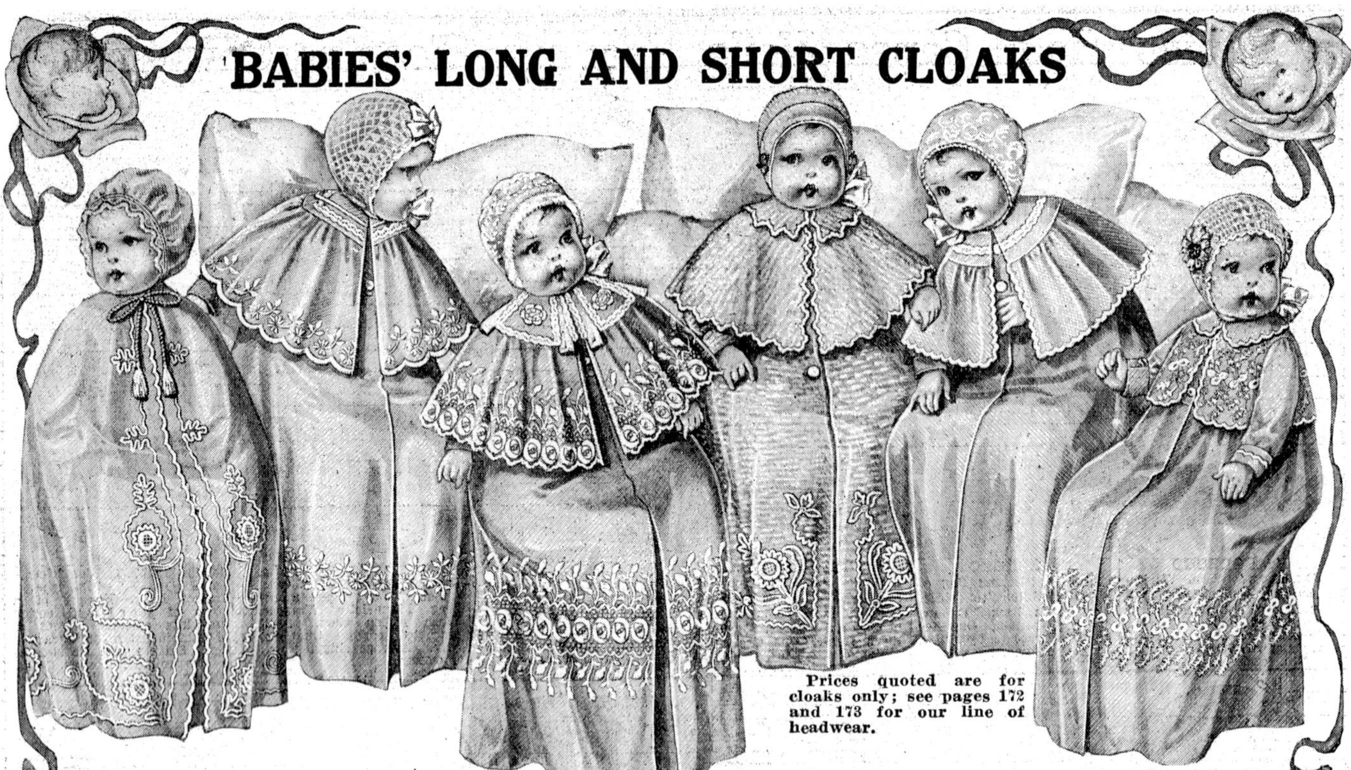

Prices quoted are for cloaks only; see pages 172 and 173 for our line of headwear.

No. 29D7915

Babies' Hood Cape of half wool and half cotton cream-white cashmere. Front edges of cape braided in a neat design and finished with embroidered scallops. Silk lined hood, edged with silk braid. Fastens with silk cord. Sateen lined; flannelette interlined. Average shipping weight, 1⅝ pounds.
Price, each...... **$2.48**

No. 29D7903

Babies' Long Cloak of cream-white cotton cashmere. Yoke cape braid trimmed and finished with embroidered scalloped edge. Skirt and cape are silk embroidered. Flannelette lining. Average shipping weight, 1¾ lbs.
Price, each..... **$1.39**

No. 29D7911

Babies' Long Cloak of heavy cream-white cotton cashmere. Yoke cape ribbon trimmed and deeply silk embroidered to match embroidered skirt. Sateen lining; warm interlining. Average shipping weight, 1¾ pounds.
Price, each.... **$2.48**

No. 29D7913

Babies' Long Cloak of cream-white wool faced ripple eiderdown. Fancy embroidered scalloped edges finish shoulder cape and collar. Front of coat braided in a neat design. Sateen lined. Average shipping weight, 1⅞ lbs.
Price, each.... **$2.88**

No. 29D7901

Unusual value in Babies' Plain Long Cream-White Cotton Cashmere Cloak. Shoulder cape neatly finished with embroidered scalloped edge. Yoke of cape trimmed with silk braid. Flannelette lined. Average shipping weight, 1½ pounds.
Price, each.. **$1.22**

No. 29D7910

Babies' Long Cloak of heavy cream-white cotton cashmere. Bolero scalloped and embroidered both front and back. Collar and cuffs finished with scalloped embroidered edges. Skirt silk embroidered in a neat design. Sateen lined; warmly interlined. Average shpg. wt., 1¾ lbs.
Price, each....... **$1.98**

State Age.

No. 29D7984

Nobby Walking Length Coat of black and white check washable plush. Laydown collar, cuffs and tabs on belt of imitation ermine plush. High belted waist line. Flare skirt. Sateen lined; warmly interlined. Ages, 1, 2 and 3 years. **State age.** Average shpg. wt., 1⅞ lbs.
Price, each...... **$2.98**

No. 29D7949

Babies' Walking Length Coat of cream-white cotton cashmere. Skirt and deep shoulder cape silk embroidered. Yoke of cape silk braid trimmed. Flannelette lining. Sizes to fit ages 6 months, 1 and 2 years. **State age.** Average shipping weight, 1⅜ pounds.
Price, each...... **$1.48**

29D7969 Castor
29D7985 Copenhagen Blue

Walking Length Coat of mercerized poplin with cloth trimming to imitate beaver fur. High belted waist line. Full flare tunic skirt. Well lined and interlined. Ages, 1, 2 and 3 years. **State age.** Av. shpg. wt., 2 lbs.
Price, each..... **$2.58**

No. 29D7956

Attractive Walking Length Coat of white Bedford cord, a ribbed cotton material. Silk embroidered scalloped bolero neatly trimmed with silk braid and pearl buttons. Skirt of coat box plaited both front and back. Silk braid and button trimmed cuffs. Sateen lined; warmly interlined. Ages, 1 and 2 years only. **State age.** Av. shpg. wt., 1⅜ lbs.
Price, each.......... **$1.98**

No. 29D7972

Belted Walking Length Coat of white corduroy velvet. Fastens down front with row of pearl buttons. Sateen lining; warm interlining. Ages, 1, 2 and 3 years. **State age.** Average shipping weight, 2 pounds.
Price, each **$2.48**

No. 29D7965

Walking Length Coat of white Bedford cord, a ribbed cotton material. Neatly trimmed down front of coat with silk braid and medallions. Collar and sleeves braid trimmed. Sateen lined; flannelette interlined. Ages, 6 months, 1 and 2 years. **State age.** Average shipping weight, 1¼ pounds.
Price, each........ **$1.63**

Girls' Pretty White Dresses

SIZE SCALE.

Girls' Dresses offered on this page are furnished to fit girls 6 to 14 years old. Be sure to state age when ordering.

Ages	6	8	10	12	14
Av. bust measure, in.	26	28	30	32	34
Av. length, inches	26	28	32	38	42

Girls' Embroidery Dress. This is a substantial dress at a very moderate price. Made of good washable embroidery flouncing in one-piece button back style. Sleeves set in with lace insertion in drop shoulder effect. Back of waist has clusters of pin tucks. Skirt is full plaited. **State age.** Average shipping weight, 1 pound.
No. 31V8500 White. EACH **89c**

Girls' Embroidery Dress. Made of good embroidery flouncing in a one-piece style, buttoning invisibly in back. Has set-in sleeves and two-tier skirt. Underskirt is of sheer lawn trimmed at bottom with pretty lace edging. Belt of good strong embroidery insertion has neat bow of fancy silk ribbon in front. Back of waist has clusters of tucks. A serviceable dress at a moderate price. **State age.** Average shipping weight, 1¼ pounds.
No. 31V8512 White. EACH **$2.19**

Girls' Embroidery Trimmed Organdy Dress. This is a beautiful dress of good quality organdy elaborately embroidered in an attractive floral design. Made in one-piece style buttoning visibly in back with neat pearl buttons. Has wide loose belt of silk ribbon with bow in back. Sleeves are set in with lace insertion, giving it the drop shoulder effect. **State age.** Average shipping wt., 1⅛ lbs.
No. 31V8515 White. EACH **$3.69**

Girls' White Embroidery Dress. Made of good washable embroidery flouncing both in front and back. Has V-neck and wide belt of embroidery insertion with rosette of silk ribbon in front. Full plaited skirt. Buttons invisibly in back with pearl buttons. This is a dress that you will be well satisfied with and would be willing to pay a great deal more for. **State age.** Average shipping weight, 1¼ pounds.
No. 31V8516 White. EACH **$2.57**

Girls' Lace Trimmed Batiste Dress. Made of extra quality sheer batiste, elaborately trimmed with Valenciennes lace. Has latest sleeves and wide belt of exceptionally pretty silk ribbon with large bow at side front. Lace revers form fancy Gibson plait over shoulders and run all the way down back to waist line. One-piece style with two-tier skirt trimmed with lace insertion and edging. **State age.** Average shpg. wt., 1¼ lbs.
No. 31V8518 White. EACH **$4.95**

Girls' White Dress. Made of good quality sheer lawn and strong washable embroidery. Cut in a pretty one-piece style buttoning invisibly in back with pearl buttons. The embroidery on waist forms a fichu effect over shoulders with pointed collar in back. Skirt made in full plaited, two-tier style. Sash of fancy silk ribbon runs through loops of lace and forms large bow in front. **State age.** Average shipping weight, 1¼ pounds.
No. 31V8510 White. EACH **$2.29**

Girls' White Dress. Made of embroidery flouncing and white lawn, prettily trimmed with lace insertion. Made in two-tier skirt style with extra row of lace edging on underskirt, giving it the three-tier effect. Neat belt of silk ribbon with rosette in front. Buttons invisibly in back with pearl buttons and has clusters of pin tucks in back of waist. **State age.** Average shipping weight, 1¼ lbs.
No. 31V8506 White. EACH **$1.79**

Girls' White Embroidery Dress. Made of strong washable embroidery flouncing. Back of waist is just as pretty as the front. Cut in one-piece button back style. Has wide belt now so popular, made of embroidery insertion. Neat rosette of silk ribbon in front. Waist trimmed with lace insertion both in front and back. Skirt is full plaited. An exceptionally good dress for the money. **State age.** Average shipping weight, 1¼ pounds.
No. 31V8514 White. EACH **$2.48**

One of Our Best Embroidery Dresses for Girls. Material is good quality embroidery flouncing in a neat design. Made in one-piece style with two-tier skirt, and buttons invisibly in back. Has imitation collar of embroidery to match. Wide loose belt and small bows in front are of lustrous black velvet. Sleeves are set in with hemstitching. **State age.** Average shipping wt., 1½ lbs.
No. 31V8517 White. EACH **$3.25**

Girls' Embroidery Dress. Not often will you find a dress at this price with so much washable embroidery. Waist cut in the one-sided effect and trimmed with pin tucks in back. Sleeves set in with lace insertion giving it the drop shoulder effect. Belt of wide embroidery insertion with neat silk ribbon drawn through beading. Buttons invisibly in back. Skirt full plaited. **State age.** Average shipping wt., 1¼ lbs.
No. 31V8503 White. EACH **$1.29**

Remarkable Values
in Young Fellows' Hot Weather Suits of Khaki, Panama and Palm Beach Cloths

We realize the great popularity of these garments and have therefore made special efforts to produce them to sell at very reasonable prices.

Sizes to fit average size young men from 17 to 21 years of age or measuring from 33 to 37 inches breast measure. Take measurements the same as for other young men's suits, as described on page 732.

No. 40V5075 $5.00
DARK BLUE PENCIL STRIPED PALM BEACH COAT AND PANTS in a splendid linen and cotton mixed fabric. A very desirable hot weather suit. Single breasted coat with three outside patch pockets, one inside pocket, deep facings and piped seams. Peg top pants with tunnel belt loops, three small belt loops, side pockets, hip pockets made to button, watch pocket and cuff bottoms. **Sizes—33 to 37 inches breast measure. Give measurements.** Average shipping weight, 4 pounds.

No. 40V5071 $3.50
VERY STYLISH NORFOLK EFFECT OLIVE TAN SATEEN FINISHED KHAKI CLOTH COAT AND PANTS. Made with three outside patch pockets; lower ones made to button. Stitched on belt all around, yoke effect, plaits to the waist line in the back. Peg top pants with belt loops, side buckle straps, side pockets, two hip pockets with tab and button, watch pocket, closed welt seams and cuff bottoms. **Sizes—33 to 37 inches breast measure. Give measurements.** Average shipping weight, 4 pounds.

No. 40V5077 $5.50
GRAY PINCHECKED PANAMA CLOTH COAT AND PANTS in Bulgarian Norfolk style. A very dressy hot weather suit. Easily kept clean. Yoke effect, stitched down plaits front and back, stitched on belt all around, patch pockets, one inside pocket. Peg top pants with tunnel belt loops, side pockets, hip pockets made to button, watch pocket and permanent cuff bottoms. **Sizes—33 to 37 inches breast measure. Give measurements.** Average shipping weight, 4 pounds.

No. 40V5079 $5.75
STYLISH BULGARIAN NORFOLK COAT AND PANTS in linen color Palm Beach cloth with a raised white silk striped effect. Very popular material for hot weather suits. Plaits front and back, yoke effect, patch pockets, stitched on belt all around. The latest peg shape pants with side pockets, hip pockets made to button, watch pocket, tunnel belt loops, three small belt loops, closed welt seams and cuff bottoms. **SIZES—33 to 37 inches breast measure. Give measurements.** Average shipping weight, 4 pounds.

No. 40V5073 $4.75
HOT WEATHER COAT AND PANTS IN SUMATEX BEACH CLOTH. Plain linen color. A splendid fabric, linen and cotton mixed. Single breasted coat with three outside patch pockets. Unlined, but made with broad facings. Inside pocket. Perfectly tailored. Peg top pants with tunnel belt loops, three small belt loops, side pockets, two hip pockets made to button, watch pocket, closed welt seams and stylish cuff bottoms. **Sizes—33 to 37 inches breast measure. Give measurements.** Average shipping weight, 4 pounds.

White Khaki and Duck Pants

FOR TENNIS, GOLF AND AS GENERAL OUTING PANTS there is nothing that excels our white khaki and duck pants. They are strongly made, all seams are well sewed. Will launder perfectly. You will doubly enjoy your outdoor sports this summer if you have a pair or more of these outing pants.

SIZES All outing pants are furnished in sizes from 30 to 42 inches waist measure and 30 to 36 inches inseam measure. Give WAIST and INSEAM measures when ordering. See page 732 for simple measuring instructions.

95c WELL MADE WHITE DUCK OUTING PANTS.

The illustrations on this page show the style of these pants. Made to fit comfortably through the hips and hang correctly. Nicely finished. Fitted with belt loops, usual pockets and cuff bottoms. Closed welt seams. Will launder perfectly. Average shipping wt., 2 lbs.

No. 45V6238

Price for outing pants......**95c**

$1.35 FINE QUALITY WHITE DUCK OUTING PANTS.

Higher grade duck pants than No. 45V6238. The illustration to the left shows these pants. Fitted with belt loops, cuff bottoms, two side pockets, a watch pocket and hip pockets with tab to button. Will launder perfectly. Average shipping wt., 2 lbs.

No. 45V6240

Price for outing pants....**$1.35**

$1.65 STRONG AND DURABLE WHITE KHAKI OUTING PANTS.

For the man who prefers a softer material than duck here are pants made of finely woven white khaki cloth that are very strong and durable. The illustration to the right shows the style of these pants. Fitted with belt loops, usual pockets and cuff bottoms. Average shpg. wt., 2 lbs.

No. 45V6242

Price for outing pants..**$1.65**

Men's Straw Hats

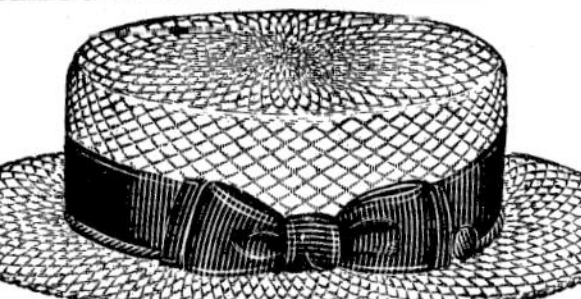

$1.50 EACH

No. 33V4876 Our Special Sennit Straw Hat will please you. Has latest style side bow and patent sweatband which conforms to your head shape. Crown, 3 inches high. Brim, 2½ inches wide. Sizes, 6¾ to 7½. **State size.** Shipping weight, 1⅞ pounds.

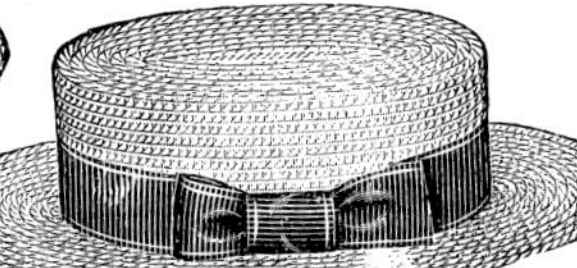

$1.65 EACH

No. 33V4874 Split Straw. Extra fine quality of split straw used in making this hat. Has patent sweatband which conforms to your head shape. Crown, 2¾ inches high. Brim, 2⅝ inches wide. Sizes, 6¾ to 7½. **State size.** Shipping weight, 1⅞ pounds.

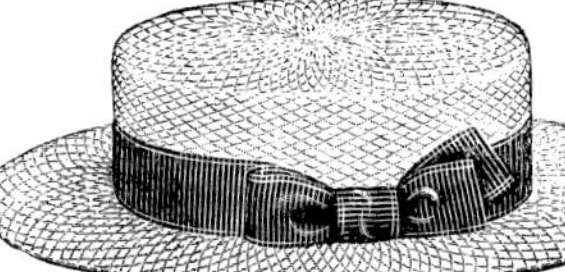

$1.65 EACH

No. 33V4880 Fancy Sennit Straw. Fine quality straw sailor. Has a patent sweatband which conforms to your head shape. Crown, 2¾ inches high. Brim, 2⅝ inches wide. Sizes, 6¾ to 7½. **State size.** Shipping weight, 1 pound 13 ounces.

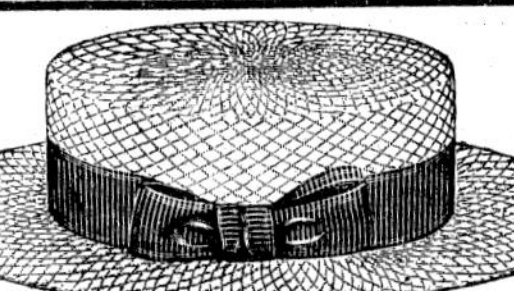

$1.00 EACH

No. 33V4870 Fancy Sennit Straw. A very nobby straw hat. Crown, 2¾ inches high. Brim, 2⅝ inches wide. Sizes, 6¾ to 7½. **State size.** Shipping weight, 1⅞ lbs.

$1.50 EACH

No. 33V4872 Genuine Milan Straw Brim. One of the best shapes to be had today. Has no superior for genuine comfort. Crown, 3⅜ inches high. Brim, 2½ inches wide. Sizes, 6¾ to 7½. **State size.** Shipping weight, 1¾ pounds.

$1.75 EACH

No. 33V4882 Genuine Porto Rican Telescope. Made from fine quality of Porto Rico straw. Crown, 3⅜ inches high, silk bound brim, 2½ inches wide. Sizes, 6¾ to 7½. **State size.** Shpg. wt., 1¾ lbs.

$1.75 EACH

No. 33V4884 Porto Rican Straw. Optimo shape is a very popular style with men of all ages. Crown, 3½ inches high. Brim, 2½ inches wide. Sizes, 6¾ to 7½. **State size.** Shipping weight, 1¾ pounds.

Stylish New Belts and Girdles

98c No. **18V1160** **A Beautiful Sash Girdle.** Made of soft lustrous messaline silk of exceptional quality. Prettily shirred and supported by strong stays. Double faced sash has two ends, one 10 and one 15 inches long. Black only. Even sizes, 24 to 32 inches waist measure. **State size.** Shipping weight, 8 ounces.

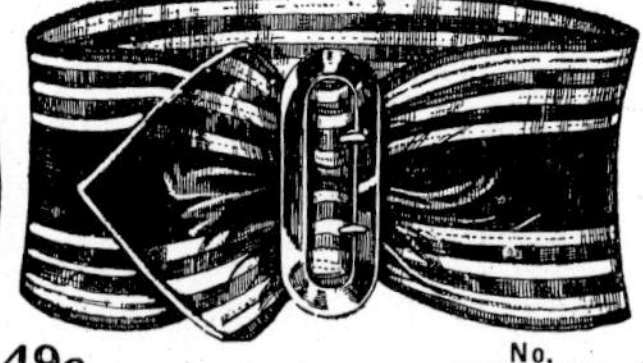

49c No. **18V1162** **The Popular Roman Stripe Belt.** Made of wood fiber silk woven in a splendid pattern. These striped belts harmonize with almost any color costume. Belt, 5½ inches wide. Large gilt metal buckle. Colors, dark red or navy blue as the predominating shade. Even sizes, 24 to 32 inches waist measure. **State size and color wanted.** Shipping weight, 5 oun·es.

98c No. **18V1164** **A Handsome Wide Belt** of fine quality messaline shirred over wide elastic. Splendid workmanship throughout. Large bow conceals the hook and eye fasteners. Belt is full 6½ inches wide. Colors, black, navy blue or emerald green. Even sizes, 24 to 32 inches waist measure. **State size and color wanted.** Shipping weight, 4 ounces.

98c No. **18V1166** **The Stylish Basque Girdle** which is worn over the hips. Made of black messaline silk in graceful folds, shaped on strong flexible stays. About 10 inches wide. Five silk covered buttons down the front. Black only. Even sizes, 24 to 32 inches waist measure. **State size.** Shipping weight, 8 ounces.

23c No. **18V1168** **For misses and children.** To be worn loose. A splendid imitation patent leather belt, about 2½ inches wide. An excellent value at our low price. Colors, black, red or white, with large enameled buckle to match. Even sizes, 26 to 36 inches waist measure. **State size and color wanted.** Shipping weight, 6 ounces.

49c No. **18V1194** **Good Quality Belt** made of black messaline silk. Shirred on flexible stays. Width, about 5½ inches. Ornamented with pretty artificial rose with natural looking green foliage. Color, black only, with choice of pink or American beauty red rose. Even sizes, 24 to 32 inches waist measure. **State color of rose and size.** Shipping wt., 6 oz.

49c No. **18V1184** **An Amazing Value in a Silk Girdle** of good quality messaline, about 5 inches wide. Shirred over strong elastic webbing. Closes with strong hook fasteners covered by a wide bow in the front. Well made. Colors, black, navy blue, emerald green or white. Even sizes, 24 to 34 inches waist measure. **State size and color wanted.** Shipping weight, 3 ounces.

49c No. **18V1170** **A Very Stylish Tailored Belt** of good quality lustrous grosgrain silk. Closes with large silk covered buckle set in bow at front. Very neatly lined. Width, 4¾ inches. Black only. Even sizes, 24 to 32 inches waist measure. **State size.** Shpg. wt., 6 oz.

49c No. **18V1174** **A Dainty Belt** of satin striped and flowered silk taffeta ribbon, shirred over a fine elastic band. Expertly made and a splendid value. Closes with strong fasteners and finished with two self covered buttons. Comes in pink or light blue. Even sizes, 24 to 32, inches waist measure. **Give size and color wanted.** Shipping weight, 3 ounces.

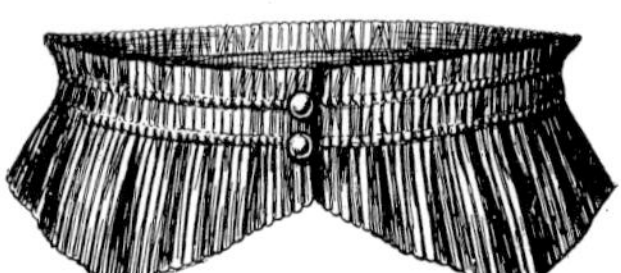

49c No. **18V1172** **New Military Belt.** Made of messaline silk, neatly accordion plaited and shirred over elastic webbing. A very graceful design. Finished in front with two gilt buttons. Width from top of belt to points in front, 6 inches. Colors, black or navy blue. Even sizes, 24 to 32 inches waist measure. **State size and color wanted.** Shipping wt., 5 oz.

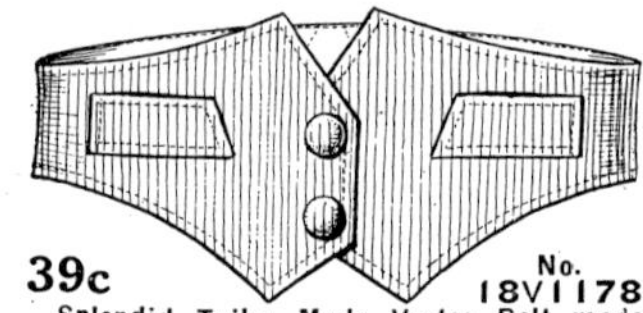

39c No. **18V1178** **Splendid Tailor Made Vestee Belt** made of washable white pique. Neat outside pockets and covered buttons. Closes with snap fasteners. Well lined and interlined. Extreme width in front, 6 inches. Sizes, 24 to 32 inches waist measure. **State size.**

39c No. **18V1192** **Same style as above, but made of** black mercerized moire. **State size.** Shipping weight of these belts, 5 ounces.

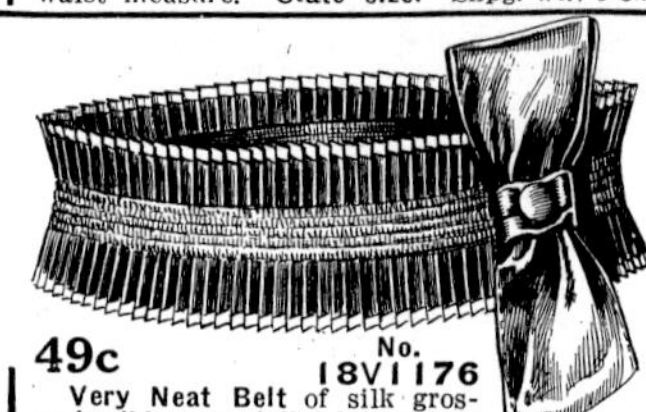

49c No. **18V1176** **Very Neat Belt** of silk grosgrain ribbon carefully plaited and shirred over elastic webbing. Draped bow of silk messaline to match. Ribbon edged with narrow folded gold color cloth. Width of belt, 4 inches. Colors, black or navy blue, both with gold color edges. Even sizes, 24 to 32 inches waist measure. **State size and color wanted.** Shipping weight, 5 ounces.

89c No. **18D806** Good quality leather with new crossgrain finish. Pretty curved silver finished metal frame with imitation jeweled catch. All tan leather lining. Coin purse and hanging mirror. Strong leather strap handle. A rare bargain in a finely made bag. Size, 8½x6½ inches.

98c No. **18D870** A Fine Appearing Genuine Leather Bag in pin seal finish with plaited front. Fitted on bright platinum finished metal frame with new automatic safety lock. Lining of gray leather. Fitted with purse, mirror and powder box. Strong leather strap handle. Size, 7¼x6⅝ inches.

98c No. **18D889** Beautifully Plaited Soft Leather Bag in pin seal finish. Bright platinum finished metal frame. Partly leather covered. Practical Duplex safety lock. Silk poplin lining. Coin purse and mirror. Strong leather strap handle. Size 7x6¾ inches.

89c No. **18D804** Beautifully Fitted Bag, containing purse, mirror, powder box, perfume bottle and hairpin holder. Bag is made of good quality leather, seal grained. Bright silver finished metal frame. Poplin lining and double strap handle. A bargain value. Size, 8¾x5⅝ inches.

98c No. **18D858** Wonderful Value Genuine Leather Bag in walrus graining. Plaited front. Tan leather lined throughout. Coin purse and hanging mirror. Popular stirrup style leather handle. Neatly etched metal frame fitted with the very practical Simplex safety lock. Size, 7x7 inches.

98c No. **18D842** A Popular Shape Genuine Leather Bag in fine walrus grain. Engraved platinum finished German silver frame with the new automatic safety lock. Full gray leather lining. Fitted with purse, mirror, powder box and hairpin holder. Stirrup style leather handle. Size, 7¼x7¼ inches.

98c No. **18D821** Popular double strap leather handles strongly sewed on to bag. Good quality genuine leather with seal grain finish. Leather covered overlapping metal frame. All black leather lining. Large coin purse. Size, 12x8 inches.

98c No. **18D811** Stylish Roomy Bag with new patented automatic safety lock. Good quality genuine leather, fine walrus grained. All gray leather lined. Inside purse on frame. Hanging mirror. Strong strap handle. Size, 9x7 inches.

$1.98 No. **18D772** Beautiful Imported Beaded Bag. Design of gold and steel colored beads on jet black bead background. Gold finish metal frame and chain handle. Good quality lining. 2¾-inch bead fringe. Size, without fringe, 7¾x7¼ inches.

$1.25 No. **18D774** Imported Beaded Bag with design worked out in gold and steel colored beads on black bead background. Gold finish frame and chain. Beaded tassel. Size, without tassel, 6x7½ inches.

98c No. **18D802** Wide opening German silver frame in gold finish. Bag is of good quality leather with pin seal graining. All tan leather lined. Purse and hanging mirror. Strong leather strap handle. Size, 7¼x7 inches.

98c No. **18D850** Large Genuine Leather Bag in seal grain finish. French gray finish metal frame with beautiful grape and vine design. Practical Duplex safety lock. Black leather lined throughout. Fitted with good coin purse. Size, 8¾x7½ inches.

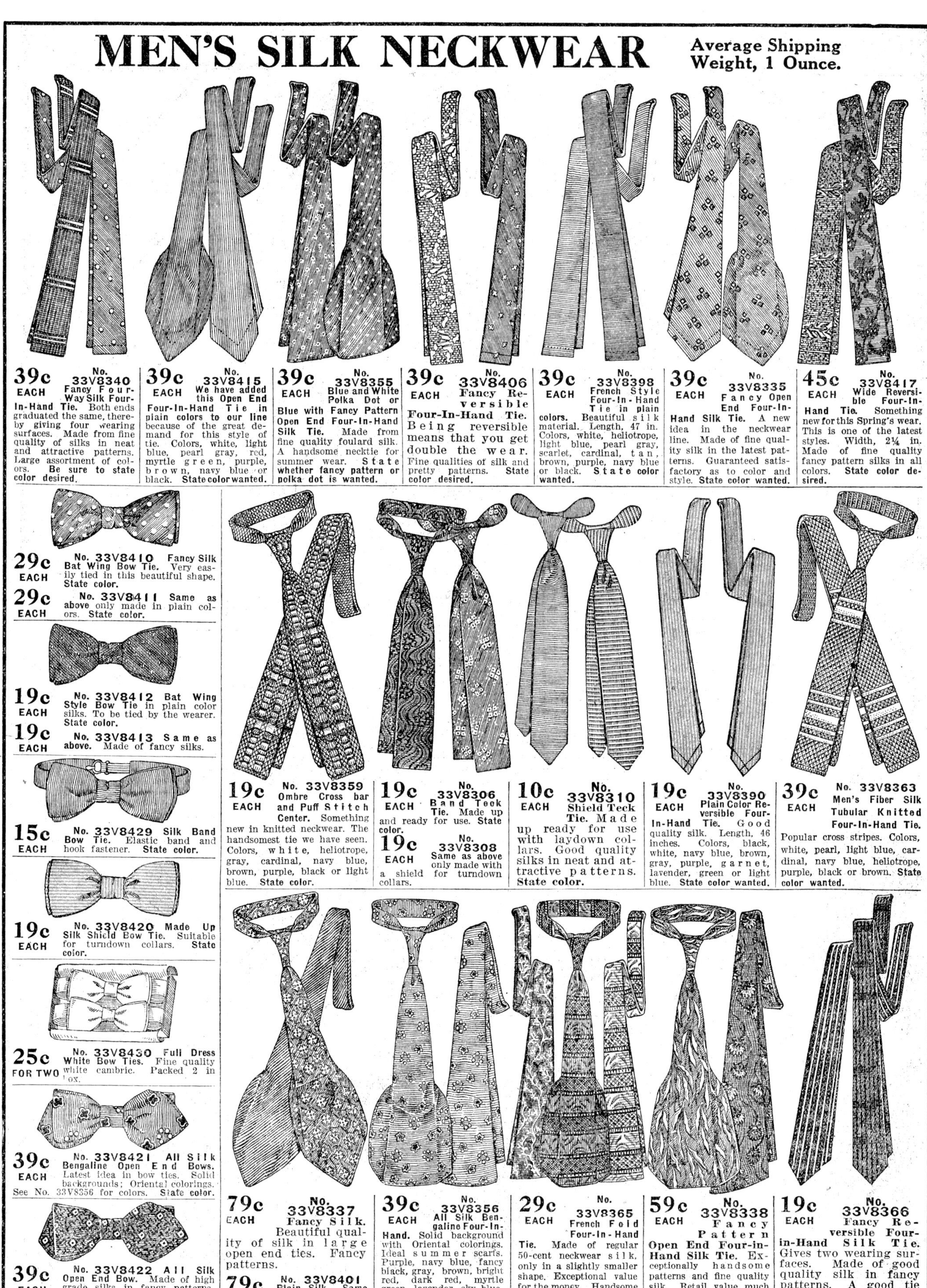
MEN'S SILK NECKWEAR
Average Shipping Weight, 1 Ounce.
39c EACH No. 33V8340 Fancy Four-Way Silk Four-In-Hand Tie. Both ends graduated the same, thereby giving four wearing surfaces. Made from fine quality of silks in neat and attractive patterns. Large assortment of colors. Be sure to state color desired.
39c EACH No. 33V8415 We have added this Open End Four-In-Hand Tie in plain colors to our line because of the great demand for this style of tie. Colors, white, light blue, pearl gray, red, myrtle green, purple, brown, navy blue or black. State color wanted.
39c EACH No. 33V8355 Blue and White Polka Dot or Blue with Fancy Pattern Open End Four-In-Hand Silk Tie. Made from fine quality foulard silk. A handsome necktie for summer wear. State whether fancy pattern or polka dot is wanted.
39c EACH No. 33V8406 Fancy Reversible Four-In-Hand Tie. Being reversible means that you get double the wear. Fine qualities of silk and pretty patterns. State color desired.
39c EACH No. 33V8398 French Style Four-In-Hand Tie in plain colors. Beautiful silk material. Length, 47 in. Colors, white, heliotrope, light blue, pearl gray, scarlet, cardinal, tan, brown, purple, navy blue or black. State color wanted.
39c EACH No. 33V8335 Fancy Open End Four-In-Hand Silk Tie. A new idea in the neckwear line. Made of fine quality silk in the latest patterns. Guaranteed satisfactory as to color and style. State color wanted.
45c EACH No. 33V8417 Wide Reversible Four-In-Hand Tie. Something new for this Spring's wear. This is one of the latest styles. Width, 2¼ in. Made of fine quality fancy pattern silks in all colors. State color desired.
29c EACH No. 33V8410 Fancy Silk Bat Wing Bow Tie. Very easily tied in this beautiful shape. State color.
29c EACH No. 33V8411 Same as above only made in plain colors. State color.
19c EACH No. 33V8412 Bat Wing Style Bow Tie in plain color silks. To be tied by the wearer. State color.
19c EACH No. 33V8413 Same as above. Made of fancy silks.
15c EACH No. 33V8429 Silk Band Bow Tie. Elastic band and hook fastener. State color.
19c EACH No. 33V8420 Made Up Silk Shield Bow Tie. Suitable for turndown collars. State color.
25c FOR TWO No. 33V8430 Full Dress White Bow Ties. Fine quality white cambric. Packed 2 in box.
39c EACH No. 33V8421 All Silk Bengaline Open End Bows. Latest idea in bow ties. Solid backgrounds; Oriental colorings. See No. 33V8356 for colors. State color.
39c EACH No. 33V8422 All Silk Open End Bow. Made of high grade silks in fancy patterns. worth much more than our price. State color wanted.
19c EACH No. 33V8359 Ombre Cross bar and Puff Stitch Center. Something new in knitted neckwear. The handsomest tie we have seen. Colors, white, heliotrope, gray, cardinal, navy blue, brown, purple, black or light blue. State color.
19c EACH No. 33V8306 Band Teck Tie. Made up and ready for use. State color.
19c EACH No. 33V8308 Same as above only made with a shield for turndown collars.
10c EACH No. 33V8310 Shield Teck Tie. Made up ready for use with laydown collars. Good quality silks in neat and attractive patterns. State color.
19c EACH No. 33V8390 Plain Color Reversible Four-In-Hand Tie. Good quality silk. Length, 46 inches. Colors, black, white, navy blue, brown, gray, purple, garnet, lavender, green or light blue. State color wanted.
39c EACH No. 33V8363 Men's Fiber Silk Tubular Knitted Four-In-Hand Tie. Popular cross stripes. Colors, white, pearl, light blue, cardinal, navy blue, heliotrope, purple, black or brown. State color wanted.
79c EACH No. 33V8337 Fancy Silk. Beautiful quality of silk in large open end ties. Fancy patterns.
79c EACH No. 33V8401 Plain Silk. Same quality as above only in plain colors.
39c EACH No. 33V8356 All Silk Bengaline Four-In-Hand. Solid background with Oriental colorings. Ideal summer scarfs. Purple, navy blue, fancy black, gray, brown, bright red, dark red, myrtle green, lavender, sky blue, old rose, navy blue or polka dots. State color.
29c EACH No. 33V8365 French Fold Four-In-Hand Tie. Made of regular 50-cent neckwear silk, only in a slightly smaller shape. Exceptional value for the money. Handsome colorings and patterns. State color desired.
59c EACH No. 33V8338 Fancy Pattern Open End Four-in-Hand Silk Tie. Exceptionally handsome patterns and fine quality silk. Retail value much more than we ask. State color desired.
19c EACH No. 33V8366 Fancy Reversible Four-in-Hand Silk Tie. Gives two wearing surfaces. Made of good quality silk in fancy patterns. A good tie for the money. State color wanted.

Ladies' Silver Plated Party Boxes

An absolutely new item. An article of real practical value for the ladies. Holds all the necessary toilet accessories. Illustrations show the outside as well as the inside view of the boxes.

No. 4V842 Our Highest Grade Party Box. Silver plated on German silver. Gray finish design. Perfect in its entire construction. Length, 4⅛ inches; height, 3⅛ inches; width, 1¼ inches. Contains powder box and puff, box for face cream, rouge stick case, place for cards, mirror and change purse. One of the handsomest boxes on the market. Has flexible metal handle. Shipping weight, 1 pound.
Price, complete..........................**$4.50**

No. 4V844 This Party Box is silver plated on German silver. Gray finished floral design. Length, 4½ inches; height, 3¼ inches; depth, about 1¼ inches. Contains comb, nail file, orange wood stick, scent bottle, powder box, rouge stick case, mirror, writing pad and pencil, receptacle for cards and change. Beautifully finished. Soldered lin' carrying chain. Shipping weight, 1 pound.
Price, complete..........................**$3.80**

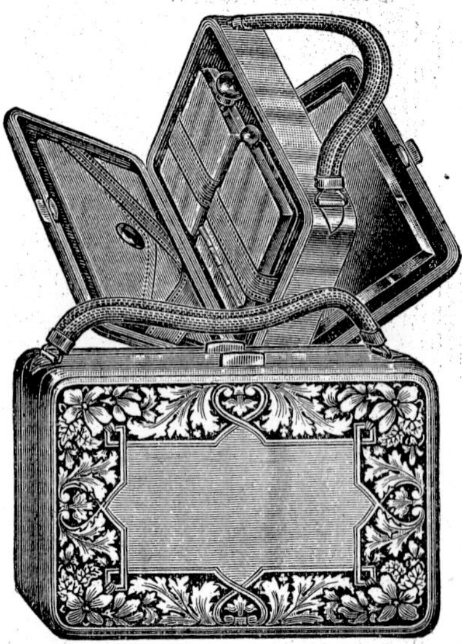

No. 4V850 Party Box, silver plated, gray finish design. High grade in every detail. One of the finest boxes we illustrate. Length, 4⅛ inches; height, 2¾ inches; width, 1¼ inches. Contains hand mirror, box for face cream, lip stick case, powder box and puff, scent flask, writing tablet, pencil and change purse. A box we recommend. Has flexible metal handle. Shipping weight, 1 pound.
Price, complete..........................**$3.75**

No. 4V854 Vanity Case, silver plated. Length, 4¾ inches; height, 3 inches. Gray oxidized design. Leather handle. Contains powder box, perfume flask, mirror, glove buttoner and change purse. Shipping weight, 8 ounces.
Price, complete..........................**$1.10**

No. 4V858 Party Box, silver plated. Length, 3½ inches; height, 2⅜ inches; width, 1¼ inches. Contains powder receptacle and puff, mirror, coin holders for nickels and dimes, place for cards, nail file, scent flask and rouge case. Soldered link carrying chain. Shipping weight, 12 ounces.
Price, complete..........................**$2.35**

No. 4V862 Vanity Case, silver plated, oxidized gray finish. Length, 5 inches; height, 3¼ inches. Contains mirror, receptacle for pins, place for powder and puff, coin holders for small change, and place for cards. Leather handle. Shipping weight, 12 ounces.
Price, complete..........................**$1.10**

No. 4V866 Vanity Case, silver plated, oxidized gray design. Height, 4½ inches; width, 3¼ inches, with carrying chain. Contains receptacle for cards, spring coin holders for small change, place for powder and puff, also mirror. Shipping weight, 12 ounces.
Price, complete...............**65c**

No. 4V870 Vanity Case, silver plated. Height, 3¼ inches; width, 2¼ inches. Contains place for cards, spring coin holders for small change, receptacle for powder and puff. Shipping weight, 6 ounces.
Price, complete...............**23c**

No. 4V874 Vanity Case, silver plated. Height, 4⅛ inches; width, 2½ inches. Contains place for powder and puff, also for pins, spring coin holders for small change, card receptacle and mirror. Shipping weight, 8 ounces.
Price, complete...............**45c**

No. 4V878 Party Box, silver plated, oxidized gray finish design. An attractive case for little money. Length, 3½ inches; height, 2½ inches; thickness, 1 1/16 inches. Contains mirror, comb, powder box and puff, case for lip stick, box for face cream, and receptacle for cards. Metal carrying chain. Shipping weight, 12 ounees.
Price, complete............**$1.15**

Give your corset size if you know it. If in doubt, take your waist measure tight over your corset and subtract 2 inches (for the spread of the lacing). Example: If your waist measures 23 inches over your corset, order size 21. Average shipping weight of corsets, 2 pounds.

No. 18F126 48c

Popular Bust Form.

Made of strong batiste, well boned like the top part of Perfect Form No. 18F127. For slender or narrow chested women. Is also a good confiner for a full bust. Neat braid trimming. Even sizes from 34 to 40. **Give the ideal bust size you desire.**

Popular Corsets for Medium to Slender Figures

No. 18F268 $1.50

Brocaded corset cloths are rich looking and very popular. They give good wear, too. This corset is really a wonderful value. Comfortable skirt. Flexible stays throughout. Pretty lace trimming. Four good hose supporters, 1¼ inches wide. Medium low bust, 4¼ inches above waistline. Clasp, 11 inches long, with strong hook below. Length of back below waistline, 14¼ inches. Sizes, 19 to 28. **Be sure to state corset size.**

No. 18F219 $1.50

Very low bust elastic top corset, especially designed for dancing and athletic wear. Allows ease and comfort with proper support. Made of strong coutil with correctly placed stays stitched in pockets. Extra heavy elastic webbing at the top, and in the bottom of skirt. Short 8-inch front clasp, with hook and elastic lacing below. Four strong hose supporters, 1⅜ inches wide. Low bust, only 2 inches above waistline. Length of back, 13½ inches below waistline. Choice of white or shell pink color. Sizes, 19 to 28. **Give corset size and state color wanted.**

No. 18F264 $1.50

Great freedom of movement is permitted by this remarkably well liked low bust style. High back gives splendid support. Made of good coutil. Elastic gores in bust and hips hold corset to the figure. Narrow lace trimming. Pliable duplex stays arranged to leave the hip bones free. Six good quality hose supporters, 1⅜ inches wide. Bust, 2½ inches above waistline. Clasp, 9 inches long, with two strong hooks below. Length of back below waistline, 12¼ inches. Sizes, 19 to 26. **Give corset size.**

No. 18F135 98c

Truly comfortable low bust model, exceptionally popular with young women. Splendid wearing strong garment. Made of good quality coutil. Pretty silk embroidery trimming. Four extra fine 1¼-inch hose supporters. Bust height, 3½ inches above waistline. Clasp, 10 inches long, with two strong hooks below. Length of back below waistline, 12½ inches. Sizes, 19 to 26. **Give corset size.**

No. 18F127 98c

Trade Mark Registered in U. S. Patent Office.

QUALITY GUARANTEED CHS TRADE MARK

Perfect Form and Corset Combined. This stylish figure builder has perfectly shaped built-out bust and gives the slender, flat chested woman the correct proportions. Shoulder straps are easily adjusted. They hold shoulders back and induce correct breathing. Made of strong batiste, well boned and stayed. Neat braid trimming. Four good 1⅛-inch hose supporters. Corset sizes run from 19 to 28. **Give your corset size.** See instructions to get your corset size. Also give length from armpit to waistline.

No. 18F132 $1.35

This corset and bust form is different from our popular No. 18F127, because the bust is soft and is fitted with a removable washable lawn pad or ruffle that can be gathered to any desired fullness, giving a most natural soft appearance. Just the corset that the slender or flat chested woman has been looking for. It gives all the support of a corset from the waist down, as it is strongly but flexibly boned. Made of strong batiste with neat trimming. Fastens in back with straps and buckles. Shoulder straps easily adjusted. Four 1⅛-inch hose supporters. Corset sizes, 19 to 28. **State corset size wanted.**

31F5120
WOMEN'S WOOL MIXED
SHADOW CHECK
31F5125
WOMEN'S SILK
TAFFETA
31F5130
WOMEN'S WOOL
MIXED SERGE

31E4160
Mens Wear Serge
31E4165
Suiting
31E4170
Serge
For Prices and Description See Page 268

Women's Chin-Chin Fur Collars and Collarettes

No. 41F5077
Brown...**$2.98**
Brown Blended Northern Winter Muskrat Collar. Straight Chin-Chin style with guaranteed satin lining. Average shipping weight, 14 oz.

No. 41F5070
Tan and Black...........................**$1.65**
Chin-Chin Style Collar of natural coney striped black to imitate tiger. Skinner's guaranteed satin lining. Average shipping weight, 12 ounces.

No. 41F5093
Black.............**$6.50**
No. 41F5094
Natural..............**$6.25**
Blended Black or Natural Gray Opossum Collarette. Fur is first quality, the black very much resembling black marten. A very practical as well as serviceable neck piece. Silk lining. Average shipping weight, 1 pound.

No. 41F5091
Brown.
$3.95
Very Attractive Mink Brown Blended Marmot Collarette. Fur known as Russian mink. Silk lining. Average shipping weight, 1 pound.

No. 41F5072 Black...........**$1.98**
No. 41F5073 Brown.......... **1.98**
Black or Brown Imported French Coney Collar in straight Chin-Chin effect. Guaranteed satin lining. Average shipping weight, 14 ounces.

No. 41F5086
White...**$1.39**
White Iceland Fox (Combed Thibet) Neck Piece. Fur on all sides. Fastens with silk ribbon. Average shipping weight, 12 ounces.

No. 41F5081 Natural...**$3.25** **No. 41F5082 Black**.....**$3.50**
Natural Gray or Blended Black First Grade Opossum Collar, in shaped Chin-Chin style. Silk lining. Average shipping weight, 12 ounces.

No. 41F5088 Black............**$2.98**
No. 41F5089 Brown........... **2.98**
Fine Grade Imported French Coney Collar. Made in the new large shape Chin-Chin collarette style, with guaranteed satin lining. Average shipping weight, 1⅛ pounds.

No. 41F5075
Black...**$2.95**
Glossy Black Newchwang Dog Fur Collar. Made in the new large straight Chin Chin effect, with Skinner's guaranteed satin lining. Average shipping weight, 1 pound.

No. 41F5079
Brown...**$3.00**
Mink Blended Weasel Chin-Chin Collar. Usually sold as Jap mink, and has the color and appearance of real mink. Silk lining. Average shipping weight, 12 ounces.

No. 41F5096
Brown...**$7.50**
Natural Brown Plucked Nutria Collarette. Similar to beaver and is often sold as such. New collarette style, which protects the neck. Lined with a good quality of silk. Average shipping weight, 12 ounces.

No. 41F5084
Black...**$4.35**
Fine Grade Hudson Seal Collar. Made of plucked, clipped and dyed Winter muskrat. Has the appearance and wearing qualities of genuine sealskin. Made in the new Chin-Chin style. Guaranteed silk lining. Average shpg. wt., 12 oz.

Women's Fur Coats—New York Models

No. 41F5008 Length, 36 Inches.. $57.50
No. 41F5009 Length, 45 Inches.. 67.50

Dark Brown Blended Northern Spring Muskrat Coat. Skins are of good quality, heavily furred. Cut in the late semi-fitted style with full flare skirt. Pointed effect striped collar and wide striped border and cuffs of the same fur. Entire coat worked in dropped skin effect, thus making the striping and blending very attractive. Sizes, 32 to 42 inches bust measure. **State size.** Average shipping weight of the 36-inch length, 7 pounds; 45-inch length, 7½ pounds.

ALWAYS STATE SIZE.

No. 41F5000 Length, 40 Inches.......... $37.50
No. 41F5001 Length, 45 Inches.......... 42.50
No. 41F5002 Length, 50 Inches.......... 47.50

Women's Beautiful Imported Black Russian Ponyskin Fur Coat with natural markings, and first grade black opossum collar. Coat is cut semi-fitted with the new style wide flare skirt. Lined throughout with Skinner's guaranteed satin. Furnished in three lengths. Sizes, 32 to 42 inches bust measure. **State size.** Average shipping weight of 40-inch length, 6 pounds; 45-inch length, 6½ pounds; 50-inch length, 7½ lbs.

BE SURE TO MENTION SIZE.

No. 41F5004 Length, 36 Inches......... $47.50
No. 41F5005 Length, 45 Inches......... 57.50
No. 41F5006 Length, 52 Inches......... 67.50

Natural Northern Muskrat Fur Coat. The fur used in this coat is of choice selection. Cuffs and collar of the same material. Coat is cut in the new full loose fitting style; suitable for driving or dress wear. Lined throughout with Skinner's satin. Sizes, 32 to 42 inches bust measure. **State size.** Average shipping weight of the 36-inch length, 6⅝ pounds; 45-inch length, 8⅝ pounds; 52-inch length, 9½ pounds.

No. 41F5011 Hudson seal........ $89.00

Women's New Model Beautiful High Grade Black Hudson Seal Coat. Made from plucked, clipped and dyed heavily furred muskrat, and has the appearance of genuine sealskin. Average length, 40 inches. Sizes, 32 to 42 inches bust measure. **State size.** Average shipping weight, 6½ pounds.

No. 41F5012 Nearseal.............. $67.50

Women's Imported Black Nearseal Coat. Made from clipped and dyed imported French coney and has the appearance of sealskin. These coats are cut semi-fitted style with the new wide flare skirt. Collar and cuffs of the same material. Lined throughout with Skinner's satin. Average length, 40 inches. Sizes, 32 to 42 inches bust measure. **State size.** Average shipping weight, 6½ pounds.

For Simple Measuring Instructions See Order Blanks in Back of Catalog.

31F5540 Navy blue.
31F5541 Dark brown.
31F5542 Black.
EACH **$15.90**

Misses' or Small Women's Suit at $15.90. Of good wearing quality all wool worsted poplin. COAT in Fall length. Lined with guaranteed satin. Sleeves with tailored tabs of self material. Fancy back, with buttons and arrow heads. SKIRT in plain flared style, closing at left front. Belted and shirred back. Average sweep, 76 inches. Misses' sizes only, from 32 to 38 inches bust measure, 22 to 28 inches waist measure, proportionate hip measure, and from 34 to 38 inches front length. For larger sizes see women's regular size suits. **State bust measure, waist measure and front length of skirt.** Average shpg. wt., 4½ lbs.

31F5530 Navy blue.
31F5531 Dark brown.
31F5532 Dark green.
EACH **$22.50**

Misses' or Small Women's Fur Trimmed Suit at $22.50. Good wearing fine quality velveteen. COAT in belted style, moderately flared. Standing Chin-Chin collar, edged with opossum fur. Button trimmed fancy cuffs. Lined with peau de cygne silk. Belted back. SKIRT closes at left front. Shirred back with frill above belt. Average sweep, 76 inches. Misses' sizes, from 32 to 38 inches bust measure, 22 to 28 inches waist measure, proportionate hip measure, and from 34 to 38 inches front length. **State bust measure, waist measure and front length of skirt.** Average shipping weight, 4½ lbs.

For Samples of Material Send for No. 80F Sample Book. Free on Request. Ready August 1st.

SIZES—Junior Suits furnished in ages 13, 15, 17 and 19 years. Open basted hem. Note the proportionate measurements given below. **When ordering state age.**

Age, years	13	15	17	19
Average bust measure, in.	33	34½	36	38
Average waist measure, in.	25	25½	26	27
Average length, inches	34	36	37	38

No. 31F5535 Navy blue.
No. 31F5536 Black.
No. 31F5537 Dark brown.
No. 31F5538 Dark green.
EACH **$12.95**

Misses' or Small Women's Suit at $12.95. Of fine quality all wool double twisted warp serge. COAT in moderately flared, semi-belted style and popular Fall length. Lined with guaranteed satin. Plain collar and lapels. Opossum fur trimmed cuffs. Slanting pockets. Belted back. SKIRT with raised waist, closing at left front. Full flared style. Belted and shirred back. Average sweep, 78 in. Misses' sizes only, from 32 to 38 inches bust measure, 22 to 28 in. waist measure, proportionate hip measure, and from 34 to 38 inches front length. **State bust measure, waist measure and front length of skirt.** Average shipping weight, 4½ pounds.

No. 31F5545 Navy blue.
No. 31F5546 Dark brown.
No. 31F5547 Dark Copenhagen blue.
No. 31F5548 Dark green.
EACH **$10.98**

Junior or Small Misses' Suit at $10.98. Made of standard all wool double twisted warp serge. Typical girlish model with coat buttoning up to neck as illustrated. Lined throughout with guaranteed satin. Large novelty shape collar, inlaid with fine quality velvet. Fancy shape button trimmed pocket at each side. Set-in sleeves with button trimmed cuffs. See small illustration for belted back, trimmed with loops of self material. SKIRT with raised waist. Full plaited in front and back. Average sweep, 76 inches. Furnished in junior sizes only, ages 13, 15, 17 and 19 years. For larger sizes see misses' suits on this and other pages. **When ordering state age.** Average shipping weight, 4½ pounds.

Attractive Cloth and Fur Fabric Coats

Fur Trimmed Astralama Cloth Coat. A serviceable Fall and Winter coat in 48-inch length, made of Astralama cloth, which is a very good quality astrakhan that has the appearance of real astrakhan fur, being woven of bright lustrous mohair in small close curls. Coat is cut along loose easy fitting lines in full belted style and wide flaring skirt. Large collar is of black coney fur. Lined throughout with mercerized sateen. Sizes, 34 to 46 inches bust measure. **Mention size when ordering.** Average shipping weight, 5¾ lbs.

No. **17F4435** **Black.**
No. **17F4436** **Navy blue.**
No. **17F4437** **Brown.** Price...... **$9.98**

Muff to match. Satin lined. **State color.** Average shipping weight, 2½ pounds.
No. **17F5502** Price.............. **$2.19**

Black and White Check Fall and Winter Coat. Made along the correct loose fitting lines in 45-inch length, of a good winter weight cloth that is practically all wool and has a soft camel hair finish with the appearance of a wool plush. Coat is unlined and shows fancy patch pockets of black silk plush and button trimmed. The sailor collar has inlay of black silk plush. Coat can also be worn in closed front style. Sizes, 34 to 46 inches bust measure. **Mention size when ordering.** Sample of material sent free on request. Av. shpg. wt., 5¾ lbs.

No. **17F4438** **Black and white check.**
Price................................ **$9.45**

Velour Corduroy Coat. The material is a heavy Winter weight durable wearing velour corduroy that has a high lustrous finish, giving it the appearance of silk velvet. Garment is fashioned along loose, easy fitting lines in 48-inch length, full belted style and wide flaring skirt. Collar is of black silk seal plush. Coat fastens with plush buttons and plush loops and is lined with a good wearing mercerized sateen in colors to harmonize. Sizes, 34 to 46 inches bust measure. **State size.** Sample of material sent free on request. Average shipping weight, 6 pounds.

No. **17F4440** **Black.**
No. **17F4441** **Navy blue.**
No. **17F4442** **Brown.**
No. **17F4443** **Dark green.**
Price.............................. **$9.95**

Women's Mercerized Cotton Foulard Dress. This pretty dress is made of excellent quality fine cluster striped mercerized cotton foulard. Stylish collar, yoke and frills on sleeves are of cotton marquisette daintily pin tucked and finished off with lace edging, and small bows on front of collar are of silk messaline trimmed with small mother of pearl buttons. Wide laydown collar extending down waist front on each side to girdle is ornamented with large mother of pearl buckle and edged with sateen in color to match. Skirt has box plait panel down front, and overskirt trimmed with sateen ruffle, which extends from under each side of panel entirely around back. Fastens in front and has skirt sweep of about 87 inches. Women's sizes only. **Give measurements.** Average shipping weight, 1¾ lbs.

No. **31F5055** Black, white stripe.
No. **31F5056** Navy blue, white stripe.
EACH **$4.95**

Women's All Wool French Serge Dress. A smartly tailored dress of fine quality all wool French serge. The panel effect waist is trimmed with narrow silk military braid and silk covered buttons and the roll collar in front with silk Bengaline and small gilt buttons. Neat cord with tassels at neck is of silk. Sleeves are finished off with wide silk military braid and small gilt buttons, and tabs on skirt front below girdle, showing continuation of the panel on waist front, are trimmed with silk braid and silk covered buttons. Dress fastens in front and has skirt sweep of about 81 inches. Women's sizes only. **Give measurements.** Average shipping weight, 1¾ pounds.

No. **31F5060** Navy blue.
No. **31F5061** Black.
EACH **$6.98**

Women's Cotton Gabardine Dress. A neat and serviceable velveteen trimmed dress, made of good quality cotton gabardine, an excellent wearing material. Collar, turnback cuffs, girdle and trimming on waist front are of velveteen. Waist, made with two narrow knife plaits extending from shoulder seams on each side part way down front, is trimmed with novelty buttons. The skirt has wide set-in panel in front and two plaits on each side. Dress fastens in front and has skirt sweep of about 82 inches. Women's sizes only. **Give measurements.** Average shipping weight, 2 pounds.

No. **31F5065** Navy blue.
No. **31F5066** Green.
No. **31F5067** Wine.
EACH **$3.48**

Women's Wool Mixed Serge Dress. An attractive and reasonably priced dress, made of wool serge containing just enough cotton to insure excellent service. Yoke of white silk poplin is trimmed with row of neat glass buttons and self material collar is edged with silk messaline in contrasting color. Plaits on each side of waist front extending from shoulder seams to girdle, also cuffs are trimmed with self covered buttons. Tabs on each side of skirt are faced with silk messaline in contrasting color and with skirt front near bottom are trimmed with self covered buttons. Dress fastens in front and has skirt sweep of about 82 inches. Women's sizes only. **Give measurements.** Average shipping wt., 2¼ lbs.

No. **31F5070** Navy blue.
No. **31F5071** Black.
No. **31F5072** Russian green.
EACH **$5.49**

SIZES Women's Dresses offered on this page can be furnished only as illustrated and described and in the following sizes: From 32 up to and including 44 inches bust measure; waist measure up to and including 33 inches, and front skirt length of 39 or 42 inches, with wide basted hem. **In ordering be sure to give bust measure, waist measure and front length of skirt.** See order blanks in back of catalog for simple measuring instructions.

WOMEN'S ALL SILK CREPE DE CHINE DRESS. Charming gown, made of excellent quality all silk crepe de chine, in the popular jacket style. A dress suitable for any occasion, and one of the handsomest in our line. Waist front and wide loose hanging girdle are trimmed with small gilt buttons, and girdle is prettily embroidered on each side in front. Underwaist is of fine quality silk mull. Full length sleeves are of Georgette crepe, with self material cuffs, trimmed with small gilt buttons. Small Georgette crepe tie at neck is held in place by mother of pearl buckle. The plaited skirt is especially attractive, and has sweep of about 80 inches. Dress fastens in front. Women's sizes only. **Give measurements.** Average shipping wt., 1½ pounds.

No. 31E3650 Navy blue.
No. 31E3651 Russian green.
No. 31E3652 Black.
EACH **$10.95**

WOMEN'S ALL WOOL FRENCH SERGE DRESS. An exceptionally handsome dress made of all wool Botany serge, a cloth needing no recommendation. Collar and cuffs are of white silk poplin and girdle is of satin messaline. Bead ornaments with silk tassels on each side of waist front are a charming feature. Waist in front is piped with satin messaline. Skirt is made with wide box plait panel extending entirely down both front and back, and has yoke top with knife plaits below yoke, extending on each side from front panel to back panel. Dress fastens in front and has skirt sweep of about 86 inches. Women's sizes only. **Give measurements.** Average shipping weight, 2 pounds.

No. 31E3655 Navy blue.
No. 31E3656 Black.
EACH **$6.98**

When Ordering Be Sure to Give All Measurements Asked For.

MISSES' CREPE DE CHINE AND ORIENTAL LACE PARTY DRESS. This delightful misses' dancing or party frock is made of excellent quality all silk crepe de chine over net, with yoke and sleeves of richly embroidered heavy Oriental lace. Ruching on waist and skirt, both front and back, is of silk messaline. Yoke and waist front are ornamented with small silk rosebuds, and velvet ribbon girdle is held in place on each side in front with dainty rhinestone buckles. Skirt is made with long tunic over net drop, with accordion plaited silk crepe de chine bottom. Without doubt one of the daintiest party dresses we have ever cataloged. Dress fastens in back and has full skirt sweep of about 80 inches. Misses' sizes only. **Give measurements.** Average shipping weight, 1½ pounds.

No. 31E3660 Light blue.
No. 31E3661 Pink.
No. 31E3662 White.
EACH **$11.95**

WOMEN'S SILK TAFFETA DRESS. The material used in this stylish dress is extra good quality all silk chiffon taffeta. Yoke and wide laydown hemstitched collar are of white silk chiffon. Sleeves and underarm sections, which are attached to net underwaist, are of silk chiffon with fancy taffeta cuffs trimmed with small self covered buttons. Wide self material girdle. Skirt is made with four ruffles, each set on with heavy self material covered cord. Fastens in front and has skirt sweep of about 2¼ yards. You will be well pleased with the style and material of this dress. Women's sizes only. **Give measurements.** Average shipping weight, 1¾ pounds.

No. 31E3665 Navy blue.
No. 31E3666 Taupe gray.
No. 31E3667 Black.
EACH **$11.95**

SIZES WOMEN'S Dresses offered on this page can be furnished in the following sizes only: From 32 up to and including 44 inches bust measure, waist measure up to and including 33 inches and front skirt length of 39 or 42 inches, with wide basted hem. MISSES' Dress can be furnished to fit ages 14, 16, 18 and 20 years, or 32, 34, 36 and 38 inches bust measure, with average skirt lengths of 34, 35, 37 and 38 inches, with basted hem. **When ordering be sure to give bust measure, waist measure and front length of skirt.** See page 771 for measuring instructions.

Hats for Motor and Sports Wear

Wear the Right Hat at the Right Time.

Average Shipping Weight, 2 Pounds.

No. 18E7020
$2.48
Smart toque with brim of pretty satin finished straw braid. Shirred and draped crown of good quality satin. Four tiny satin rosettes across front. The 1¼-yard veil is of open silk mesh with beautiful embroidered pattern at edge. **COLORS:** Black brim with royal blue, white or Kelly green crown; navy blue brim with Copenhagen blue crown, or Russian green brim with emerald green crown. **State color.** Veils are black only.

No. 18E7024 Hat, without veil. **$1.88**
No. 18E9113 Veil only. Price. **.60**

No. 18E7028
$1.48
Soft finished hat with pliable double brim, made of genuine hemp braid in two contrasting colors. Facing always matches the crown. Trimming band and bow of pretty silk grosgrain ribbon. **COLORS:** Cardinal, green, navy blue or black; all with white upper brim and white trimming, or green with burnt crown and tan trimming.

No. 18E7032
$1.98
Beautiful motor cap with pliable brim of fancy silk. Binding and trimming band of imitation patent leather. Full gathered crown of fine quality messaline silk. Shirred elastic at back of cap. Veil is of very fine quality soft silk chiffon, 42 inches wide, 68 inches long, hemstitched across both ends. Cap comes in Copenhagen blue, navy blue, sand color or emerald green. Veil comes in white, navy blue, light blue, brown or emerald green. **State color.**

No. 18E7036 Cap, without veil. Price **$1.00**
No. 18E7037 Veil only. Price. **.98**

No. 18E7040
$1.35
Soft finished hat with pliable double brim, made of very fine quality chip straw braid. Trimming band and bow of velvetta ribbon in colors to match facing of hat. **COLORS:** White with green, navy blue or black facing; or solid white with black band. **State color.**

No. 18E7044
$1.98
A motor hat of lustrous silk, which is dressy enough for street wear. This hat is so perfectly made that it can be rolled up into pocket size without the least damage. Brim can be turned and stays in any desired position. Band, bow and buckle trimming of silk. Invisible tape in lining to adjust head size. **COLORS:** Navy blue, Copenhagen blue, sand color, emerald green or black hat with white, green or Copenhagen blue band and bow. **State color.**

No. 18E7048
89c
Soft finished hat of fine quality Panama cloth, a closely woven cotton material which makes a good, low priced hat. Trimming band and bow of good quality velvetta. **COLORS:** Natural cream-white with black, royal blue, green or cardinal velvetta trimming band. **State color.**

No. 18E7052
$1.98
A beautifully made motor hat with close rolling brim, which can be turned and stays in any desired position. The brim and sides of crown are of fine quality messaline satin; top of crown and trimming band of beautiful fancy silk in colors to harmonize with brim. Perfectly lined and has invisible tape to adjust head size. A very stylish, high grade hat. **COLORS:** Navy blue, Copenhagen blue, sand color or emerald green. **State color.**

No. 18E7056
$1.75
A really smart toque of fine quality satin finished straw braid, laid in folds around the crown and draped over the trimming ears, which are of good quality silk faced velvet. A fold of this velvet encircles the crown. **COLORS:** Burnt color, navy blue, green or white; all with black velvet wings; navy blue with Copenhagen blue velvet, or solid black. **State color.**

No. 18E7060
45c
Good quality, pliable felt hat, which can be rolled up and put into a pocket or any small hand bag. A wonderful hat for all kinds of outing wear and a great bargain at our price. Trimmed with a narrow band and bow of mercerized grosgrain ribbon. **COLORS:** White, pearl gray, sand color, old rose, royal blue or emerald green. **State color.**

No. 18E7064
$1.10
For misses and young women this charming saucer brim sailor with its low rounded crown is most becoming. The shape is a good quality imported Java body hat with folded band and facing of flowered cretonne. A nickel plated buckle finishes the hat. Hat comes in natural cream-white only, with facing and band of rose pink. Copenhagen blue, cream-yellow or tan cretonne.

No. 18E7070
$1.10
The facing of this genuine imported body hat is of good quality fine ribbed grosgrain silk, the band and bow of striped hemp braid in colors to match the facing. **COLORS:** Natural cream-white with either emerald green, Copenhagen blue, sand color or cardinal facing.

No. 18E7074
$1.25
Genuine imported Java body hat with narrow pliable brim, bound on edge with a novelty silk stripe trimming. 1½-inch band and bow to match. **COLORS:** Natural cream-white hat only, with trimmings in combination colors as follows—green and white, navy blue and white, cardinal and white or black and white. **State color.**

Stylish Middy Blouses

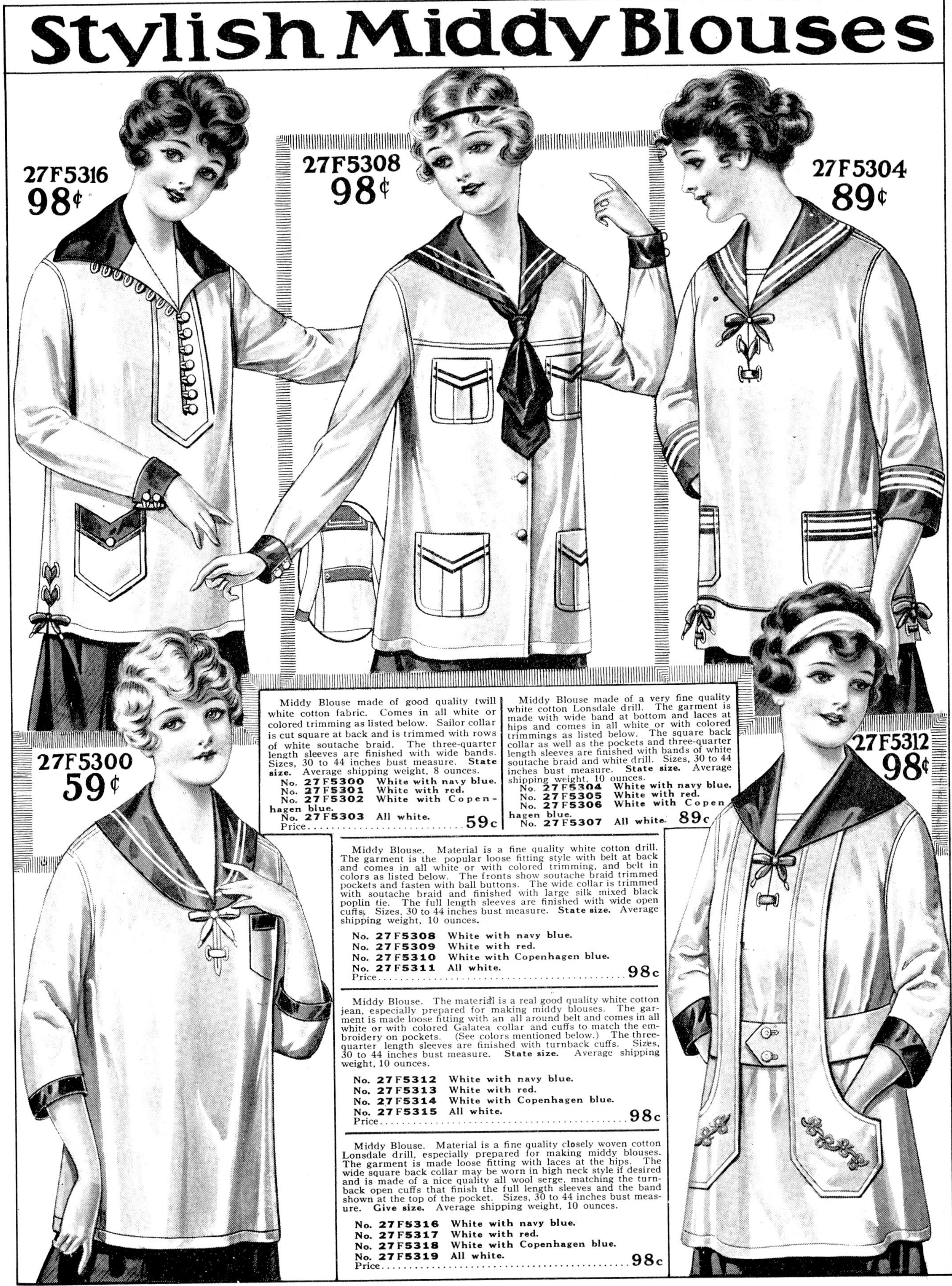

Middy Blouse made of good quality twill white cotton fabric. Comes in all white or colored trimming as listed below. Sailor collar is cut square at back and is trimmed with rows of white soutache braid. The three-quarter length sleeves are finished with wide bands. Sizes, 30 to 44 inches bust measure. **State size.** Average shipping weight, 8 ounces.

No. **27F5300** White with navy blue.
No. **27F5301** White with red.
No. **27F5302** White with Copenhagen blue.
No. **27F5303** All white.
Price.......... 59c

Middy Blouse made of a very fine quality white cotton Lonsdale drill. The garment is made with wide band at bottom and laces at hips and comes in all white or with colored trimmings as listed below. The square back collar as well as the pockets and three-quarter length sleeves are finished with bands of white soutache braid and white drill. Sizes, 30 to 44 inches bust measure. **State size.** Average shipping weight, 10 ounces.

No. **27F5304** White with navy blue.
No. **27F5305** White with red.
No. **27F5306** White with Copenhagen blue.
No. **27F5307** All white. 89c

Middy Blouse. Material is a fine quality white cotton drill. The garment is the popular loose fitting style with belt at back and comes in all white or with colored trimming, and belt in colors as listed below. The fronts show soutache braid trimmed pockets and fasten with ball buttons. The wide collar is trimmed with soutache braid and finished with large silk mixed black poplin tie. The full length sleeves are finished with wide open cuffs. Sizes, 30 to 44 inches bust measure. **State size.** Average shipping weight, 10 ounces.

No. **27F5308** White with navy blue.
No. **27F5309** White with red.
No. **27F5310** White with Copenhagen blue.
No. **27F5311** All white.
Price.......... 98c

Middy Blouse. The material is a real good quality white cotton jean, especially prepared for making middy blouses. The garment is made loose fitting with an all around belt and comes in all white or with colored Galatea collar and cuffs to match the embroidery on pockets. (See colors mentioned below.) The three-quarter length sleeves are finished with turnback cuffs. Sizes, 30 to 44 inches bust measure. **State size.** Average shipping weight, 10 ounces.

No. **27F5312** White with navy blue.
No. **27F5313** White with red.
No. **27F5314** White with Copenhagen blue.
No. **27F5315** All white.
Price.......... 98c

Middy Blouse. Material is a fine quality closely woven cotton Lonsdale drill, especially prepared for making middy blouses. The garment is made loose fitting with laces at the hips. The wide square back collar may be worn in high neck style if desired and is made of a nice quality all wool serge, matching the turnback open cuffs that finish the full length sleeves and the band shown at the top of the pocket. Sizes, 30 to 44 inches bust measure. **Give size.** Average shipping weight, 10 ounces.

No. **27F5316** White with navy blue.
No. **27F5317** White with red.
No. **27F5318** White with Copenhagen blue.
No. **27F5319** All white.
Price.......... 98c

Fall and Winter Dresses for Girls of 6 to 14 Years

GIRLS' ONE-PIECE WOOL MIXED SERGE SAILOR DRESS. Made of wool mixed serge. Neat sailor collar and fancy cuffs trimmed with red braid, and collar is finished with red cord tie. Buttons visibly in front with fancy buttons. Has middy effect belt, stitched at top only, with red silk lacing at sides. Skirt is full plaited. **State age.** Av. shpg. wt., 1½ lbs.

No. 31F4455 Navy blue. EACH
No. 31F4456 Wine. **$2.98**

GIRLS' PLAID COTTON SUITING DRESS. Made in one-piece button front style. Has neat collar and cuffs of solid color suiting, and loose belt of velveteen, finished with buckle in front. Full plaited skirt. A serviceable school dress. **State age.** Average shipping weight, 1½ pounds.

No. 31F4450 Wine. EACH
No. 31F4451 Green. **$1.00**

GIRLS' COMBINATION DRESS. Waist of cotton serge in either blue or wine color with full plaited skirt and trimmings of woven black and white shepherd check cotton suiting. Has neat lacing in front and trimming buttons of red. A pleasing combination as well as serviceable. Average shpg. wt., 1¼ lbs.

EACH
No. 31F4460 Blue.
No. 31F4461 Wine. **$1.33**

GIRLS' TWO-PIECE SAILOR DRESS. Made of a woven black and white shepherd check cotton suiting. Blouse buttons visibly in front with fancy buttons, and has elastic at belt. Has good size sailor collar and cuffs of red rep, trimmed with rows of black soutache braid. Black bow tie. The underwaist, to which the full plaited skirt is attached, is of cambric, and has sewed on embroidered dickey of shepherd check, with high neck collar of red rep to match sailor collar. **State age.** Average shipping wt., 1½ lbs.

EACH
No. 31F4440 Shepherd check. **$1.48**

GIRLS' CASHMERE DRESS. Made in one-piece button back style, of wool mixed cashmere. Has collar of embroidered and hemstitched lawn, finished with neat velveteen tie. Fancy waist and turnback cuffs trimmed with straps of velveteen. Wide belt is stitched at top only. Skirt is full plaited. **State age.** Average shipping weight, 1¼ lbs.

No. 31F4465 Navy blue.
No. 31F4466 Wine. EACH
No. 31F4467 Brown. **$2.98**

GIRLS' ONE-PIECE SUITING DRESS. Made of fancy cotton suiting, neatly embroidered in two-tone silk. Has up to date cuffs. Collar of hemstitched pique, finished with cord tie and tassels. Skirt full plaited. Blue dress has belt and piping of tan. Wine color dress is trimmed with green. Buttons invisibly in front. **State age.** Average shipping wt., 1¾ lbs.

No. 31F4445 Blue. EACH
No. 31F4446 Wine. **$1.55**

GIRLS' WOOL SERGE DRESS. Made in one-piece button front style, of wool serge. Waist is neatly embroidered in front and trimmed with fancy buttons. Collar and turnback cuffs piped in red. Has loose belt. Buttons invisibly in front. Skirt is full plaited. **State age.** Average shipping weight, 1¾ pounds.

No. 31F4470 Navy blue. EACH
No. 31F4471 Brown. **$3.79**

GIRLS COTTON SERGE DRESS. Made of good cotton serge with the standard sailor style, buttoning invisibly in front. The sailor collar, also the high neck collar and cuffs are trimmed with two rows of red braid. Has large bow tie of rep. Belt stitched at top only giving it the middy effect. Skirt full plaited. **State age.** Average shipping wt., 1½ pounds.

EACH
No. 31F4435 Navy blue. **$1.29**

GIRLS' CRASH DRESS. Made of strong fancy cotton crash, in one-piece button front style. Waist is cut in coat effect, giving it the appearance of a two-piece dress. Has loose belt of plaid, fastening in front with buckle. Skirt of neat pattern plaid, full plaited. **State age.** Average shipping weight, 1½ pounds.

EACH
No. 31F4475 Blue.
No. 31F4476 Tan. **$1.76**

Girls' dresses on this page are furnished in sizes 6 to 14 years. Be sure to state SIZE when ordering.

Age	6	8	10	12	14
Average bust measure, in.	28	29	30	32	34
Average length, in.	26	28	32	38	42

SIZES

Dresses offered on this page can be furnished in junior sizes only.

Ages	13	15	17	19
Average bust measure, inches	32	34	36	38
Average waist measure, inches	25½	26	26½	27
Average skirt length, inches	32	34	36	38

When ordering state age. We do not furnish in larger sizes. See order blanks in back of catalog for simple measuring instructions.

Junior Cotton Serge Dress. Good wearing cotton serge in plaid pattern. The style is new and attractive. Waist in front and girdle are trimmed with attractive metal buttons and sateen, and collar and turnback cuffs are of pique finished off with neat Venise lace edging. The large cape effect collar is trimmed with self material ruffle. The skirt, made in overtunic effect, has box plaited panel extending to bottom of tunic and tunic is finished off with ruffle of self material. Dress fastens in front. Junior sizes only. **State age.** Average shipping weight, 1¾ pounds.
No. 31F4860 Navy blue, white plaid. EACH
No. 31F4861 Brown, white plaid. **$3.39**

Junior Wool Mixed Serge Dress. A neat and becoming dress for school or general wear, made of good quality wool mixed serge. Waist, made with yoke both front and back, has two straps extending from yoke in front to girdle. Sailor collar and turnback cuffs are trimmed with two rows of wide silk military braid in contrasting color, and neck is set off with two-color silk cord. Trimmed on waist front with novelty shape bone buttons. Pocket on each side of skirt is an attractive feature. Dress fastens in front. Junior sizes only. **State age.** Average shipping weight, 1¾ pounds.
No. 31F4865 Navy blue. EACH
No. 31F4866 Wine. **$3.98**

Junior All Wool Serge Dress. An unusually attractive dress, made of excellent quality all wool serge. Waist, front and back, is made in panel effect, trimmed in front with plaid silk covered buttons and has stylish cape effect shoulders. Collar is of self material and neck frill of dainty shadow lace. Combination girdle is of plaid silk taffeta in front and self material in back. Skirt is made with yoke top in front, and has inverted panel extending from yoke to bottom. Dress fastens in front. Junior sizes only. **State age.** Average shipping weight, 2 pounds. EACH
No. 31F4870 Navy blue. **$6.59**

Junior Cotton Black and White Check Dress. An inexpensive and serviceable school dress, made in sailor style, of cotton black and white woven check suiting. Collar and turnback cuffs are of white pique, edged with rep in contrasting color. Sailor tie is of rep and belt with metal buckle is of patent leather. Pockets on left side of waist and on each side of skirt are attractive features. Dress is trimmed on waist front and on pockets with small mother of pearl buttons, and on skirt front below belt, with large buttons of the same kind. Dress fastens in front. Junior sizes only. **State age.** Average shipping weight, 1½ pounds. EACH
No. 31F4875 Black and white check. **$2.89**

Misses' and Children's High and Low Shoes of Worth

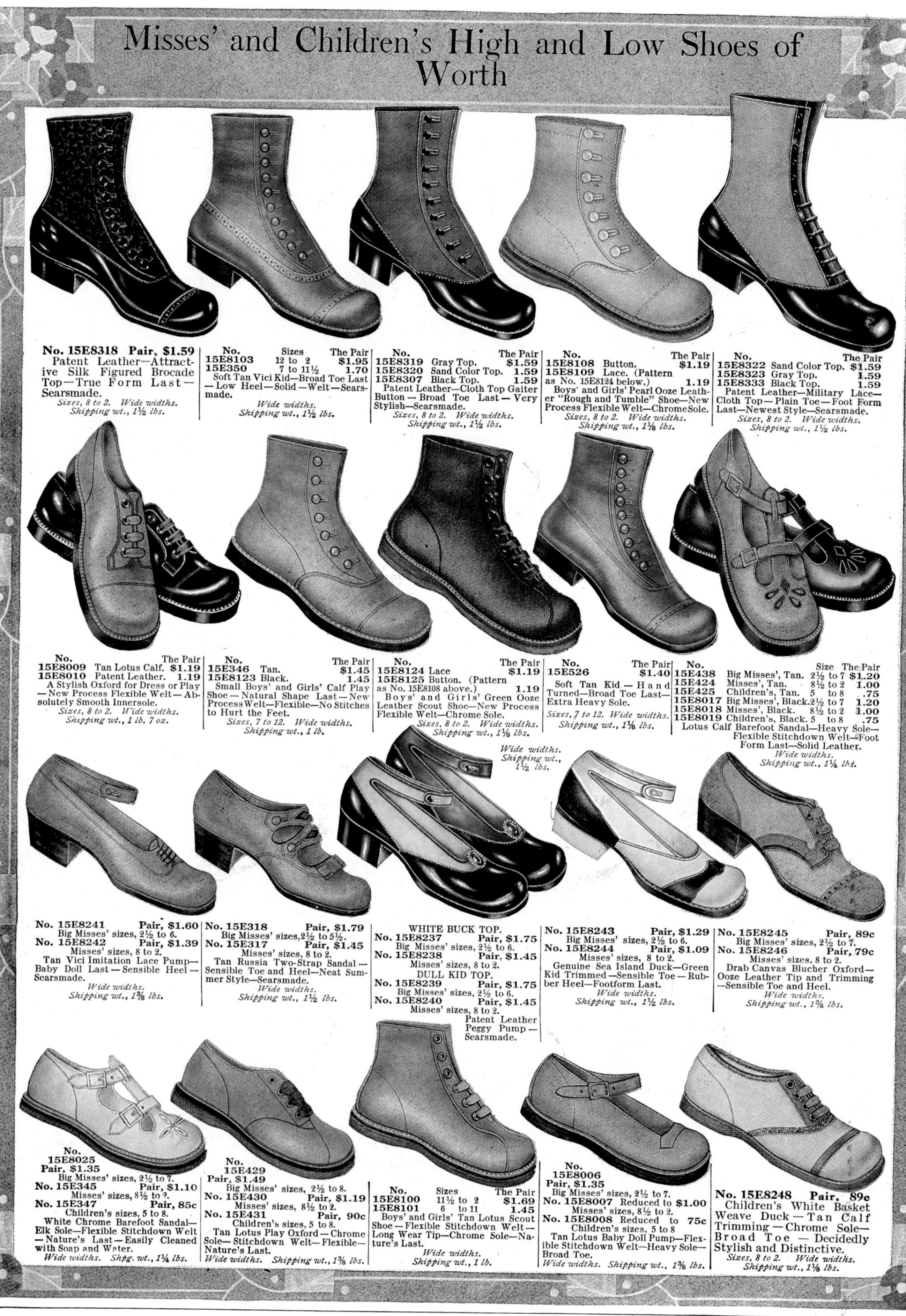

No. 15E8318 Pair, $1.59
Patent Leather—Attractive Silk Figured Brocade Top—True Form Last—Searsmade.
Sizes, 8 to 2. Wide widths.
Shipping wt., 1½ lbs.

No.	Sizes	The Pair
15E8103	12 to 2	$1.95
15E350	7 to 11½	1.70

Soft Tan Vici Kid—Broad Toe Last—Low Heel—Solid—Welt—Searsmade.
Wide widths.
Shipping wt., 1½ lbs.

No.		The Pair
15E8319	Gray Top.	$1.59
15E8320	Sand Color Top.	1.59
15E8307	Black Top.	1.59

Patent Leather—Cloth Top Gaiter Button—Broad Toe Last—Very Stylish—Searsmade.
Sizes, 8 to 2. Wide widths.
Shipping wt., 1½ lbs.

No.		The Pair
15E8108	Button.	$1.19
15E8109	Lace. (Pattern as No. 15E8124 below.)	1.19

Boys' and Girls' Pearl Ooze Leather "Rough and Tumble" Shoe—New Process Flexible Welt—Chrome Sole.
Sizes, 8 to 2. Wide widths.
Shipping wt., 1⅛ lbs.

No.		The Pair
15E8322	Sand Color Top.	$1.59
15E8323	Gray Top.	1.59
15E8333	Black Top.	1.59

Patent Leather—Military Lace—Cloth Top—Plain Toe—Foot Form Last—Newest Style—Searsmade.
Sizes, 8 to 2. Wide widths.
Shipping wt., 1½ lbs.

No.		The Pair
15E8009	Tan Lotus Calf.	$1.19
15E8010	Patent Leather.	1.19

A Stylish Oxford for Dress or Play—New Process Flexible Welt—Absolutely Smooth Innersole.
Sizes, 8 to 2. Wide widths.
Shipping wt., 1 lb. 7 oz.

No.		The Pair
15E346	Tan.	$1.45
15E8123	Black.	1.45

Small Boys' and Girls' Calf Play Shoe—Natural Shape Last—New Process Welt—Flexible—No Stitches to Hurt the Feet.
Sizes, 7 to 12. Wide widths.
Shipping wt., 1 lb.

No.		The Pair
15E8124	Lace	$1.19
15E8125	Button. (Pattern as No. 15E8108 above.)	1.19

Boys' and Girls' Green Ooze Leather Scout Shoe—New Process Flexible Welt—Chrome Sole.
Sizes, 8 to 2. Wide widths.
Shipping wt., 1⅛ lbs.

No.	The Pair
15E526	$1.40

Soft Tan Kid—Hand Turned—Broad Toe Last—Extra Heavy Sole.
Sizes, 7 to 12. Wide widths.
Shipping wt., 1⅛ lbs.

No.		Size	The Pair
15E438	Big Misses', Tan.	2½ to 7	$1.20
15E424	Misses', Tan.	8½ to 2	1.00
15E425	Children's, Tan.	5 to 8	.75
15E8017	Big Misses', Black.	2½ to 7	1.20
15E8018	Misses', Black.	8½ to 2	1.00
15E8019	Children's, Black.	5 to 8	.75

Lotus Calf Barefoot Sandal—Heavy Sole—Flexible Stitchdown Welt—Foot Form Last—Solid Leather.
Wide widths.
Shipping wt., 1¼ lbs.

No. 15E8241 Pair, $1.60
Big Misses' sizes, 2½ to 6.
No. 15E8242 Pair, $1.39
Misses' sizes, 8 to 2.
Tan Vici Imitation Lace Pump—Baby Doll Last—Sensible Heel—Searsmade.
Wide widths.
Shipping wt., 1⅜ lbs.

No. 15E318 Pair, $1.79
Big Misses' sizes, 2½ to 5½.
No. 15E317 Pair, $1.45
Misses' sizes, 8 to 2.
Tan Russia Two-Strap Sandal—Sensible Toe and Heel—Neat Summer Style—Searsmade.
Wide widths.
Shipping wt., 1½ lbs.

WHITE BUCK TOP.
No. 15E8237 Pair, $1.75
Big Misses' sizes, 2½ to 6.
No. 15E8238 Pair, $1.45
Misses' sizes, 8 to 2.
DULL KID TOP.
No. 15E8239 Pair, $1.75
Big Misses' sizes, 2½ to 6.
No. 15E8240 Pair, $1.45
Misses' sizes, 8 to 2.
Patent Leather Peggy Pump—Searsmade.
Wide widths.
Shipping wt., 1½ lbs.

No. 15E8243 Pair, $1.29
Big Misses' sizes, 2½ to 6.
No. 15E8244 Pair, $1.09
Misses' sizes, 8 to 2.
Genuine Sea Island Duck—Green Kid Trimmed—Sensible Toe—Rubber Heel—Footform Last.
Wide widths.
Shipping wt., 1½ lbs.

No. 15E8245 Pair, 89c
Big Misses' sizes, 2½ to 7.
No. 15E8246 Pair, 79c
Misses' sizes, 8 to 2.
Drab Canvas Blucher Oxford—Ooze Leather Tip and Trimming—Sensible Toe and Heel.
Wide widths.
Shipping wt., 1⅜ lbs.

No. 15E8025
Pair, $1.35
Big Misses' sizes, 2½ to 7.
No. 15E345 Pair, $1.10
Misses' sizes, 8½ to 2.
No. 15E347 Pair, 85c
Children's sizes, 5 to 8.
White Chrome Barefoot Sandal—Elk Sole—Flexible Stitchdown Welt—Nature's Last—Easily Cleaned with Soap and Water.
Wide widths. Shpg. wt., 1¼ lbs.

No. 15E429
Pair, $1.49
Big Misses' sizes, 2½ to 8.
No. 15E430 Pair, $1.19
Misses' sizes, 8½ to 2.
No. 15E431 Pair, 90c
Children's sizes, 5 to 8.
Tan Lotus Play Oxford—Chrome Sole—Stitchdown Welt—Flexible—Nature's Last.
Wide widths. Shipping wt., 1⅜ lbs.

No.	Sizes	The Pair
15E8100	11½ to 2	$1.69
15E8101	6 to 11	1.45

Boys' and Girls' Tan Lotus Scout Shoe—Flexible Stitchdown Welt—Long Wear Tip—Chrome Sole—Nature's Last.
Wide widths.
Shipping wt., 1 lb.

No. 15E8006
Pair, $1.35
Big Misses' sizes, 2½ to 7.
No. 15E8007 Reduced to **$1.00**
Misses' sizes, 8½ to 2.
No. 15E8008 Reduced to **75c**
Children's sizes, 5 to 8
Tan Lotus Baby Doll Pump—Flexible Stitchdown Welt—Heavy Sole—Broad Toe.
Wide widths. Shipping wt., 1⅜ lbs.

No. 15E8248 Pair, 89c
Children's White Basket Weave Duck—Tan Calf Trimming—Chrome Sole—Broad Toe—Decidedly Stylish and Distinctive.
Sizes, 8 to 2. Wide widths.
Shipping wt., 1⅛ lbs.

Stylish Knitted Garments for the Little Tots

See Pages 198 and 199 for Long and Short Coats, Also Muff and Scarf Sets.

Remember to State Age or We Cannot Fill Your Order.

29K8875 Gray, assorted stripes. Girls' Combination Underwaist and Skirt. Closely knit of soft cotton yarn. Neatly finished shell crocheted edge. Assorted fancy stripes at bottom of skirt. Ages, 2, 4 and 6 years. **State age.** Average shipping weight, 5 oz. Price, each..........**48c**

29K9108 White, blue trim. **29K9109** White, pink trim. Little Tots' Practical Two-Piece Set. Consisting of one-piece sweater and leggings and attractive toque, knit in fancy design of soft pure wool yarn. Ages, 1, 2 and 3 yrs. Av. shpg. wt., 1⅛ lbs. Price, each set....**$2.33**

29K9155 Copenhagen, gray trim. Children's Stylish Three-Piece Set. Knit of a mixture of one-third wool and two-thirds cotton yarn with a brushed surface. Semi-belt and V shaped pocket. Ages, 1, 2, 3 and 4 yrs. **State age.** Average shipping wt., 1½ pounds. Price, each set....**$3.18**

No. **29K9127** Gray. No. **29K9143** Red. No. **29K9144** Copenhagen. Children's Belted Style Cardigan Three-Piece Set. Knit of a mixture of cotton and a small quantity of wool. Double fabric hockey cap. Ages, 1, 2, 3 and 4 years. **State age.** Average shipping weight, 1 pound 9 ounces. Price, each set......**$1.98**

29K9146 Navy blue, gold stripes. **29K9147** Maroon, white stripes. **29K9167** Gray, red stripes. Children's Two-Piece Jersey Athletic Suit. Knit of pure wool worsted yarn. Snap fasteners at shoulder. Full size bloomers; elastic waist and knees. Ages, 2 to 6 yrs. **State age.** Average shpg. wt., 1 lb. Each suit..**$1.98**

29K9137 Oxford gray. Our Finest Quality Brushed Four-Piece Set. Knit of selected pure wool yarn. Sailor collar, semi-belt and top of pockets of contrasting color. Pearl button trimmed. Fancy sport cap. Full size drawer leggings; double seams. Ages, 1 to 6 yrs. **State age.** Av. shpg. wt., 2 lbs. 5 oz. Price.....**$5.95**

29K9125 Copenhagen blue. **29K9124** Golden brown. **29K9123** Red. Three-Piece Set. Knit from a mixture of one-third wool and two-thirds cotton. Sweater has a round belt. Double fabric toque. Full size drawer leggings. Ages, 1 to 4 yrs. **State age.** Av. shpg. wt., 1 lb. 13 oz..**$2.63**

Children's Sweaters.

29K9092 Rose, white trim. **29K9093** Copenhagen, white trim. Babies' Warm Sweater Coat. Knit of pure wool zephyr yarn. Interwoven stripe of contrasting color forms belt effect. Ages, 1, 2 and 3 yrs. **State age.** Av. shpg. wt., 7 oz. Price, each......**$1.98**

29K9042 Blue trim. 29K9043 Pink trim. Pure Wool Sweater with detachable belt. Stripe on collar and cuffs. Ages, 1 to 4 yrs. **State age.** Av. shpg. wt., 7 oz. Each....**$1.48**
29K8120 Blue trim. 29K8119 Pink trim. Pure Wool Sport Cap to match. Av. shpg. wt., 3 oz. **49c**

Average shpg. wt., These Sets, 9 oz.

29K9217 Copenhagen, white trim. **29K9216** Rose, white trim. **29K9218** White. Brushed Toque and Scarf Set. Toque knit of ⅔ wool and ⅓ cotton. Scarf knit of ⅓ wool and ⅔ cotton. Ages 2 to 6 yrs. Price, set...**$1.08**

29K9228 Gray, rose trim. 29K9229 Copenhagen blue, white trim. 29K9230 Plain white. Combination brushed toque and scarf. Knit of ⅓ wool and ⅔ cotton; Av. length, 40 in. For ages 2 to 6 yrs. Price........**98c**

29K9224 Gold, white trim. 29K9225 Copenhagen blue, white trim. Toque and Scarf Set. Knit of ⅓ wool and ⅔ cotton. Fancy sport cap with pompons. Heavy tubular scarf about 44 in. long. Ages 2 to 6 yrs. Each set...**$1.33**

Children's Knit Middies.

29K9057 Copenhagen blue, white trim. 29K9056 Red, white trim. Girls' Middy Style Sweater. Knit in cardigan stitch of pure wool yarn. Sailor collar attractively trimmed in contrasting color. Ages, 2, 3, 4, 5 and 6 years. **State age.** Av. shpg. wt., 10 oz. Each....**$1.55**

29K9054 Navy blue, gold trim. 29K9055 Red, navy blue trim. Girls' Jersey Middy. Knit of pure wool worsted yarn. Sailor collar, detachable guimpe. Stripes of contrasting color. Ages, 2, 3, 4, 5 and 6 years. **State age.** Shipping weight, 7 oz. Price, each.......**$1.73**

No. **29K9051** Light blue. No. **29K9052** Pink. No. **29K9053** White. SAXONY BRAND. Babies' Sweater. Knit of very soft pure wool yarn. Satin ribbon draw string at neck and on cuffs. Ages, 6 months, 1 and 2 years. **State age.** Av. shpg. wt., 4 oz. Price, each.........**$1.65**
No. **29K8124** Pink and white. No. **29K8125** Light blue and white. No. **29K8133** Plain white. Cap to match. Av. shpg. wt., 3 oz. Each..**55c**

29K8144 Gold, white trim. **29K8145** Rose, white trim. **29K8147** Copenhagen, white trim. Sport Cap of double crown, fancy stitch of two-thirds wool and one-third cotton, artificial silk stripes. Cotton lining. Brushed half wool and half cotton band with artificial silk pompon. Ages, 2 to 6 years. Av. shpg. wt., 4 oz......**83c**

No. **29K9074** White, blue trim. No. **29K9075** White, pink trim. Sweater. Knit of pure wool zephyr yarn. Hand crocheted edge. Trimmed with large hand crocheted buttons. Ages 1, 2 and 3 years. **State age.** Average shpg. wt., 8 oz. Price, each......**$2.18**
No. **29K8134** White, blue trim. No. **29K8135** White, pink trim. Sport Cap to match. Knit of pure wool. Hand crocheted edge and buttons. One size. For ages up to 3 yrs. Av. shpg. wt., 4 oz. Price, each...**72c**

No. 31K8320 **Navy blue.**
No. 31K8321 **Black.** EACH
No. 31K8322 **Dark brown.** **$21.75**

Misses' or Small Women's Suit in tailored style at $21.75. Made of heavy fine quality all wool men's wear serge. Coat in appropriate length, lined throughout with yarn dye construction satin. Convertible collar and lapels can be worn as shown in large and small illustrations. Belt in front. Tailored panels at sides with tailored plaits below. Set-in sleeves, button trimmed. Skirt with raised waist, closing at left front. Belted and shirred back. Average sweep, 72 inches. Furnished in misses' or small women's sizes only, from 32 to 38 inches bust measure, 22 to 28 inches waist measure, proportionate hip measure, and from 34 to 38 inches front length of skirt. For larger sizes see women's regular size suits. **State bust, chest, waist and hip measures, also front length of skirt.** Average shpg. weight, 4½ pounds.

Sample Book No. 580K, ready about **August 1, 1917**, contains actual cloth samples of these four suits, as well as samples of our complete line of Women's and Misses' Ready to Wear Tailored Suits.

31K8315
Junior
Serge

31K8320
Misses'
Men's Wear Serge

31K8325
Misses'
Serge

31K8330
Misses'
Poplin

No. 31K8315 **Navy blue.**
No. 31K8316 **Black.** EACH
No. 31K8317 **Dark green.** **$14.50**

Junior or Small Misses' Suit at $14.50. Popular military style of our standard all wool double twisted warp serge. Coat lined throughout with guaranteed satin. Large serge collar. Military patch pocket. (See small illustration for belted back.) Skirt with raised waist, closing at left front. Military pockets to match pockets on coat. Belted and shirred back. Average sweep, 72 inches. Junior sizes only, ages 13, 15, 17 and 19 years only. For larger sizes see misses' suits on this and the opposite page. **State age.** Average shipping weight, 3 pounds.

SIZES Junior Suits furnished in ages 13, 15, 17 and 19 years. Open basted hem. Note the proportionate measurements given below. **When ordering state age.**

Age, years	13	15	17	19
Av. bust measure, in.	33	34½	36	38
Av. waist measure, in.	25	25½	26	27
Average length, in.	34	36	37	38

No. 31K8325 **Navy blue.**
No. 31K8326 **Black.** EACH
No. 31K8327 **Dark green.** **$15.95**

Misses' or Small Women's Suit. Made of our standard all wool double twisted warp serge. Coat in double breasted style in appropriate Fall length. Lined with guaranteed satin. Mannish collar and lapels. Inverted welt pockets. Set-in sleeves with imitation cuffs. (See small illustration for back.) Skirt closes at left front. Detachable tailored all around belt. Wide panel in front, ending in open plaits toward bottom. Shirred back. Average sweep, 72 inches. Misses' or small women's sizes only, 32 to 38 inches bust measure, 22 to 28 inches waist measure, proportionate hip measure, and 34 to 38 inches front length of skirt. **State bust, chest, waist and hip measures, also front length of skirt.** Average shipping weight, 4½ pounds.

No. 31K8330 **Navy blue.**
No. 31K8331 **Dark green.** EACH
No. 31K8332 **Dark brown.** **$19.95**

Misses' or Small Women's Suit at $19.95. Very stylish model, made of good quality all wool worsted poplin. Coat in semi-Norfolk style in appropriate Fall length. Lined with guaranteed satin. Convertible collar can be worn buttoned up to neck, as shown in large illustration, or with lapels turned down, as shown in small illustration. Belted all around, with novelty shape pouch pocket at sides. Set-in sleeves with fancy cut cuffs. (See small illustration for belted back in semi-Norfolk style.) Skirt with raised waist, closing at left front. Detachable belt all around. Shirred back. Average sweep, 72 inches. Misses' or small women's sizes, from 32 to 38 inches bust measure, 22 to 28 inches waist measure, proportionate hip measure, and from 34 to 38 inches front length of skirt. For larger sizes see women's suits. **State bust, chest, waist and hip measures, also front length of skirt.** Average shipping weight, 4½ pounds.

New 1917 Models for Women and Misses

Women's and Misses' Sizes, 34, 36, 38, 40, 42, 44 and 46 Inches Bust Measure.

Fall and Winter Coat of Chase Pannette cloth. This material is one of the new fabrics this season and is very popular. It has a short hairy surface of bright glossy mohair which is very rich and silky in appearance. The coat is cut full and loose along straight lines, and is lined throughout with a splendid quality mercerized sateen. Coat is 48 inches long and fastens with silk plush buttons and elastic loops. The extra large cape collar is of kit coney fur (color gray). Women's and misses' sizes, 34 to 46 inches bust measure. **State bust measure.** Samples of material sent free on request. Average shipping weight, 6¼ pounds.

No. **17K7191** **Black.**
No. **17K7192** **Navy blue.**
No. **17K7193** **Burgundy.**
No. **17K7194** **Green.**
Price, each.......... **$12.98**

Kersey Velour Cloth Coat for Fall and Winter wear. Made in 48-inch length in full belted style along straight loose fitting lines. The material is all wool, has a smooth silky finish and is a nice Winter weight. It is one of the new and popular fabrics this season, of good warmth and will give splendid wear and satisfaction. The large cape collar is of black silk seal plush and may be worn with lapels buttoned across, fitting close around the neck. The fancy patch pockets have lapels of silk plush to match collar. Coat is unlined and fastens with fancy buttons. Women's and misses' sizes, 34 to 46 inches bust measure. **State bust measure when ordering.** Samples of material sent free on request. Average shipping weight, 5¾ pounds.

No. **17K7182** **Black.**
No. **17K7183** **Navy blue.**
No. **17K7184** **Brown.**
No. **17K7185** **Green.**
No. **17K7186** **Burgundy.**
Price, each................. **$14.98**

Shetland Velour Cloth Coat for Fall and Winter wear. The style is a copy of the new military trench coats. It makes an ideal warm Winter coat and the style will be very popular. The material, which is 90 per cent wool, has a slightly roughed surface, it is very thick and soft and of great warmth and serviceability. Coat is 48 inches long, unlined, and fastens in double breasted style with large fancy buttons. Belt all around has gunmetal buckle and eyelets. Collar may be worn open at the front in regular coat style. Women's and misses' sizes, 34 to 46 inches bust measure. **State size.** Samples of material sent free on request. Average shipping weight, 6¼ pounds.

No. **17K7187** **Brown.**
No. **17K7188** **Navy blue.**
No. **17K7189** **Green.**
No. **17K7190** **Oxford gray.**
Price, each................ **$15.00**

31K7750
Misses' and Women's
Silk Taffeta
31K7755
Misses' and Women's
Silk Crepe de Chine
31K7760
Women's Crepe de Chine
or Satin

See Descriptions on Page 17.
31K7800
Women's
Half-Wool Challis
31K7805
Misses' and Women's
Wool Serge
31K7810
Women's
Wool-Mixed Shepherd Check

31K7705 Navy blue.

31K7706 Black. Each.........**$5.25**

WOMEN'S COTTON POPLIN DRESS. An inexpensive and remarkably attractive dress of good weight mercerized cotton poplin. The extra large collar is of fine quality white rep. Waist front, cuffs and skirt, both front and back, are trimmed with gold color stitching, making an unusually pretty effect, and the wide girdle, both front and back, with extra large poplin covered buttons stitched with gold thread. Waist is made with wide panel in front and the extra full skirt is box plaited both front and back. Fastens in front and has full skirt sweep of about 106 inches. One of the neatest dresses in our line. Women's regular sizes only. **Give measurements.** Average shipping weight, 1¾ pounds.

31K7710 Copenhagen blue.

31K7711 Navy blue.

31K7712 Black. Each.........**$10.89**

MISSES' AND WOMEN'S ALL SILK SATIN DRESS. A becoming prettily embroidered dress, made of good quality all silk satin. Yoke and hemstitched collar are of Georgette crepe. Waist front is trimmed with row of very small gilt buttons and both waist and skirt in front are prettily embroidered with silk and tinsel. The girdle has three tucks, and sleeves are finished off with flared cuffs. Fastens in front and has skirt sweep of about 81 inches. You will be agreeably surprised at the quality of this dress. Misses' and women's sizes, 14 to 20 years and 32 to 44 inches bust measure. **Give measurements.** Average shipping weight, 1½ pounds.

31K7715 Navy blue.

31K7716 Black. Each.........**$10.95**

MISSES' AND WOMEN'S ALL WOOL SERGE DRESS. A charming example of the straight plaited style so much in vogue this season. The material is excellent quality all wool worsted serge. The collar and turnback cuffs are of white satin and the cord and tassels at neck are of silk, trimmed with small ornaments. Waist front and girdle are prettily trimmed with select quality smoked pearl buttons. Dress is straight plaited from yoke to bottom of skirt, both front and back. Fastens in front and has skirt sweep of about 82 inches. Misses' and women's sizes, 14 to 20 years and 32 to 44 inches bust measure. **Give measurements.** Average shipping weight, 2 pounds.

SIZES All Dresses offered on this page can be furnished in women's regular sizes, from 32 up to and including 44 inches bust measure; waist measure up to and including 35 inches and front skirt length of 38 or 41 inches, with basted hem. Nos. 31K7710 and 31K7715 can also be furnished in misses' sizes. See below. **Be sure to give bust and chest measures, waist measure and front length of skirt.** See order blanks in back of catalog for simple measuring instructions.

31K7705
Cotton Poplin

31K7710
Satin

31K7715
Wool Serge

Misses' sizes, to fit ages 14, 16, 18 and 20 years, or 32, 34 36 and 38 inches bust measure. Average skirt lengths of 34, 35, 37 and 38 inches, with basted hem. **Be sure to give bust and chest measures, waist measure and front length of skirt.**

For your convenience we have placed in the back of this catalog—just inside the back cover page—order blanks containing simple measuring instructions. If you have used all the order blanks we will gladly send you a supply on request.

No. 31K8260 Navy blue.
No. 31K8261 Black.

EACH
$30.00

Women's Fur Trimmed Suit at $30.00. Made of a better quality all wool men's wear serge. Coat in appropriate Fall length, lined throughout with guaranteed yarn dye construction satin. Extra large convertible collar of fine grade opossum fur, which can be worn down, or buttoned up to neck. Set-in sleeves with wide opossum fur cuffs. Tailored double belt at waist, gathered above and trimmed below in front and back with handmade silk arrow heads. Skirt in flared style, closing at left front. Detachable belt at waistline. Shirred back. Average sweep, 76 inches. Furnished in women's regular sizes only, from 32 to 44 inches bust measure, 22 to 32 inches waist measure, proportionate hip measure, and from 36 to 44 inches front length. For larger sizes see page 46. **State chest, bust, waist and hip measures, also front length of skirt.** Average shipping weight, 4½ pounds.

No. 31K8255 Navy blue.
No. 31K8256 Black.
No. 31K8257 Dark gray.

EACH
$10.98

Women's Suit at $10.98. Made of cotton warp broadcloth, 60 per cent wool. Coat in appropriate Fall length, lined with good wearing quality sateen. Collar inlaid with velvet. Stitched-down belt effect at waistline. Deep slash pockets. Set-in sleeves with imitation cuffs. See small illustration for back. Skirt closes at left front. Belted and shirred back. Average sweep, 76 inches. Women's regular sizes, 32 to 44 inches bust measure, 22 to 32 inches waist measure, proportionate hip measure, and 36 to 44 inches front length. **State chest, bust, waist and hip measures, also front length of skirt.** Average shipping weight, 4½ pounds.

No. 31K8265 Navy blue.
No. 31K8266 Dark brown.
No. 31K8267 Black.

EACH
$16.50

Women's Suit at $16.50. Made of our standard all wool double twisted warp serge. Coat in Fall length, satin lined. Large convertible collar inlaid with velvet, as shown in large and small illustrations. Belted at waistline. Tailored pockets at sides. Set-in sleeves with imitation cuffs. See small illustration for fancy back. Skirt closes at left front. Wide panel in center, ending toward bottom in open plaits. Plain back. Average sweep, 76 in. Women's regular sizes, 32 to 44 in. bust measure, 22 to 32 inches waist measure, proportionate hip measure, and 36 to 44 in. front length. **State chest, bust, waist and hip measures, also front length of skirt.** Av. shpg. wt., 4½ lbs.

CORSET COVERS-BRASSIERES

The Brassieres shown on this page are some of our most popular styles and are much in demand this season. We feel sure you will be pleased with any selection you may make.

Our line of Corset Covers contains many new and pleasing styles. Especially note the combination Corset Cover and Brassiere, Nos. 38K3131 and 38K3132, listed below on the left side of this page.

Price, 23c Each
No. 38K3149
Women's Front Closing Cambric Brassiere. Yoke of eyelet embroidery insertion. Arm openings and neck lace edged. Has rustproof boning and arm shields. Sizes, 34 to 48 bust measure. **State size.** Shipping weight, 4 ounces.

Price, 78c Each
No. 38K3145
Women's Good Quality Nainsook Corset Cover. Made with four pretty ribbon run set-in embroidery panels. Arm openings and yoke lace edged. Ribbon drawn. A very neat and attractive cover. Sizes, 34 to 44 bust measure. **State size.** Shipping wt., 4 oz.

Price, 49c Each
No. 38K3152
Women's Good Quality Allover Embroidery Front and Back Corset Cover. Ribbon drawn. Arm openings embroidery edged. Sizes, 34 to 44 bust measure. **State size.** Shipping weight, 4 ounces.
STOUT SIZES.
Price, 59c Each
No. 38K3191
Same as above. Bust measure, 46 to 50. **State size.** Shipping weight, 5 ounces.

Price, 44c Each
No. 38K3130
Women's Good Quality Nainsook Corset Cover. Yoke made of lace and embroidery insertion with two ribbon bows. Ribbon drawn. A very neat and attractive cover. Full sizes. Sizes, 34 to 44 bust measure. **State size.** Shipping weight, 4 ounces.

Price, 76c Each
No. 38K3153
Women's Fine Quality Allover Embroidery Front and Back Corset Cover. Short embroidered sleeves. Ribbon drawn. Sizes, 34 to 44 bust measure. **State size.** Shipping weight, 4 ounces.
STOUT SIZES.
Price, 86c Each
No. 38K3190
Same as above. Bust measure, 46 to 50. **State size.** Shipping weight, 5 ounces.

Price, 29c Each
No. 38K3150
Women's Front Closing Good Quality Cambric Brassiere. Yoke, front and back of eyelet embroidery. Scalloped embroidery trim. Rustproof boning. Arm shields. Sizes, 34 to 48 bust measure. **State size.** Shipping weight, 4 ounces.

98c Each
No. 38K3131
Women's Fine Quality Cambric Combination Corset Cover and Brassiere. Arm openings and yoke trimmed with neat embroidery edging. An ideal cover for large women, as it eliminates wearing a separate brassiere. Sizes, 34 to 44 bust measure. **State size.** Shpg. wt., 6 oz.

98c Each
No. 38K3132
Women's Fine Quality Nainsook Combination Bust Ruffle and Corset Cover. Trimmed with a neat lace edging. This is an ideal cover for the flat chested woman, as it eliminates wearing a separate bust ruffle. Sizes, 34 to 44 bust measure. **State size.** Shpg. wt., 4 oz.

39c Each
No. 38K3173 Open.
No. 38K3174 Closed.
Women's Embroidery Ruffle Cambric Drawers. Length, 23 to 29 in. **State length.** Shpg. wt., 7 oz.
STOUT SIZES.
44c Each
No. 38K3175 Open. Lengths, 23 to 29 in. **State length.** Shipping weight, 8 ounces.

59c Each
No. 38K3177 Open.
No. 38K3178 Closed.
Women's Good Quality Cambric Drawers. Embroidery ruffle. Lengths, 23 to 29 in. **State length.** Shipping weight, 7 oz.
STOUT SIZES.
67c Each
No. 38K3179 Open. Length, 23 to 29 in. **State length.** Shipping weight, 8 ounces.

79c Each
No. 38K3169
Women's Nainsook Corset Cover. Yoke, back and sleeves of fine quality strong net lace. Ribbon draw at neck. A very dainty and pretty cover. Sizes, 34 to 44 bust measure. **State size.** Shipping wt., 5 ounces.

68c Each
No. 38K3133
Women's Muslin Fluffy Ruffle Corset Cover. Made with three embroidery ruffles. Neck and arm openings trimmed with a neat lace edging. Ribbon draw. Sizes, 34 to 44 bust measure. **State size.** Shpg. wt., 5 oz.

29c Each
No. 38K3170 Open.
No. 38K3171 Closed.
Women's Cambric Drawers. Ruffle trimmed with hemstitched pin tucks. Length, 23 to 29 inches. **State length.** Shipping weight, 8 ounces.
STOUT SIZES.
34c Each
No. 38K3172 Open. Lengths, 23 to 29 inches. **State length.** Shpg. wt., 9 oz.

Price, 39c Each
No. 38K3165
Women's Good Quality Front Closing Cambric Brassiere. Eyelet embroidery yoke. Arm openings and back lace trimmed. Rustproof boning. Sizes, 34 to 48 bust measure. **State size.** Shipping wt., 4 ounces.

Price, 48c Each
No. 38K3166
Plaited Style Good Quality Cambric Bust Confiner. Closes in front, laces in back. Durable rustproof boning. Ventilated front. Cambric shoulder straps. Sizes, 34 to 48 bust measure. **State size.** Shipping wt., 4 oz.

Price, 59c Each
No. 38K3168
Women's Good Quality Cambric Brassiere. Closes in front with hooks and eyes. Dainty pattern embroidery yoke. New style lace trimmed arm shields. Rustproof boning. Sizes, 34 to 48 bust measure. **State size.** Shipping wt., 5 oz.

56c Each
No. 38K3139 Open.
No. 38K3140 Closed.
Women's Good Quality Cambric Drawers. Bottoms trimmed with rows of pin tucks and pretty embroidery ruffle with scalloped edging. Lengths, 23 to 29 inches. **State length.** Shipping weight, 7 ounces.

PETTICOATS

Price, $1.38 Each

No. 38K7773 Black with flowered pattern.

Women's Fine Quality Cotton Taffeta Petticoat in flowered pattern. A very attractive garment which will be popular this fall. Has wide corded flounce. String top. Lengths, 36 to 44 inches. **State length.** Shipping weight, about 9 ounces.

Price, $1.48 Each

No. 38K7795 Black.
No. 38K7796 Navy.

Women's Attractive Petticoat of our standard Rusleen cloth. Plaited flounce. Beautiful scalloped embroidery ruffle gives this skirt a very stylish appearance. String top. Lengths, 34 to 44 inches. **State length.** Shpg. wt., about 1 lb. 3 oz.

Price, $1.87 Each

38K7722 Black.
38K7723 Russian green.
38K7724 Navy.

Women's High Grade Petticoat. Material used in this garment is our standard Rusleen cloth, which has the appearance of silk and wears much better. Top of flounce is trimmed with shirring and bottom with two small scalloped ruffles in neat gathered effect. Elastic waistband. Lengths, 34 to 42 in. **State length.** Shipping wt., abt. 1 lb. 3 oz.

Price, $1.98 Each

38K7731 Black.
38K7732 Emerald.
38K7733 Navy.
38K7734 Purple.

Lengths, 34 to 42 in. **State length.**

Women's Petticoat. Made of our standard Rusleen cloth. Flounce trimmed with five small gathered ruffles. Elastic waistband. Shpg. wt., 1¼ lbs.

STOUT SIZES.

Price, $2.18 Each

38K7797 Black.
38K7798 Emerald.
38K7799 Navy.
38K7800 Purple.

Lengths, 38 to 42 in. **State length.** Shipping weight, about 1⅜ lbs.

Price, $4.98 Each

38K7785 Black.
38K7786 Navy.
38K7787 Blue and green changeable.
38K7788 Red and green changeable.
38K7789 Copenhagen blue.

Women's Petticoat. Made of excellent quality silk taffeta. Deep flounce trimmed with ruffle in scalloped effect and two small gathered ruffles at bottom. Silk dust ruffle. Elastic waistband. Lengths, 34 to 42 in. **State length.** Shpg. wt., about 1 lb. 3 oz.

Price, $4.98 Each

38K7780 Black.
38K7781 Navy.
38K7782 Blue and green changeable.
38K7783 Red and green changeable.
38K7784 Emerald.

Women's Fine Quality Silk Taffeta Petticoat. Flounce trimmed with shirring, headings, machine stitching and scalloped pin plaited ruffle. Silk dust ruffle. Elastic waistband. Lengths, 34 to 42 in. **State length.** Shpg. wt., abt. 1 lb. 3 oz.

STOUT SIZES.

Price, $5.78 Each

38K7804 Black.
38K7805 Navy blue.
38K7806 Blue and green changeable.
38K7807 Red and green changeable.
38K7808 Emerald.

Lengths, 38 to 42 inches. **State length.** Shpg. wt., abt. 1 lb. 5 oz.

Price, $4.98 Each

No. 38K7790 Black.
No. 38K7791 Navy.
No. 38K7792 Blue and green changeable.
No. 38K7793 Red and green changeable.
No. 38K7794 Wistaria.

Women's High Grade Petticoat. Made of fine quality silk taffeta. Deep attractive flounce, trimmed with shirring, headings and machine stitching and finished at bottom with heavy cording. Has silk dust ruffle. This is one of the latest patterns and will be much in demand this Fall. Elastic waistband with snap fasteners. Lengths, 34 to 42 in. **State length.** Shpg. wt., about 1 lb. 3 oz.

Price, $1.88 Each

38K7769 Black.
38K7770 Navy.
38K7771 Russian green.

Women's Rusleen Petticoat. Made of our standard Rusleen cloth that has the rustle of silk. Flounce is corded and trimmed with three plaited ruffles. Has dust frill. Self adjusting elastic waistband. Lengths, 34 to 42 in. **State length.** Shipping weight, about 1 lb. 5 oz.

Rusleen is our own trade mark, registered in U. S. Patent Office, and is a cotton material made exclusively for us. It is light in weight and has the rustle and appearance of silk, but wears much better.

Our Silk Petticoats are the latest designs of a leading manufacturer.

Every Silk and Rusleen Petticoat comes neatly packed in a box.

Price, $1.68 Each

38K7741 Black.
38K7742 Russian green.
38K7743 Purple.

Women's Petticoat. Made of our standard Rusleen cloth. Flounce trimmed with rows of cording and diagonal pointed ruffle. Elastic waistband. Lengths, 34 to 42 inches. **State length.** Shpg. wt., about 1¼ lbs.

STOUT SIZES. **Price, $1.88 Each**

38K7801 Black.
38K7802 Russian green.
38K7803 Purple.

Lengths, 38 to 42 in. **State length.** Shpg. wt., abt. 1 lb. 5 oz.

17L7839
$6.98
Fancy Mixture

17L7842
$7.98
All Wool Serge

17L7841
$5.98
Black & White Check

17L7845
$4.98
Black & White
Check

17L7846
$6.48
All Wool Serge

New 1918 Styles at Popular Prices

Women's and Misses' Sizes, 34, 36, 38, 40, 42, 44 and 46 Inches Bust Measure.

Fancy Mixture Cloth Coat. A very stylish model for Spring and Fall wear in the new 48-inch length. The material is about one-fourth wool and three-fourths cotton, has good appearance and weight and will give splendid wear. The design is a gray and black stripe with overplaid in a contrasting color. The fronts have wide belt and attractive patch pockets, which are trimmed with bright faille silk, matching trimming on collar and belt in back. Coat is unlined and fastens with large fancy buttons. Sizes, 34 to 46 in. bust measure. **State size when you order.** Sample of material sent free on request. Av. shpg. wt., 3½ lbs.

No. **17L7839** Tan overplaid.
No. **17L7840** Green overplaid.
Price, each............**$6.98**

Women's and Misses' Spring and Fall Coat. This style comes in 45-inch length. Made of an all wool double warp serge of good wearing qualities, or a splendid quality of black and white check cloaking, about one-third wool and two-thirds cotton. (See numbers and colors below.) Has plaited back, large button trimmed patch pockets, is unlined and fastens with large fancy buttons and belt with buckle. Collar has deep inlay of silk mixed pongee in Persian design. Sizes, 34 to 46 inches bust measure. **State size wanted.** Average shipping weight, 3½ pounds.

Wool Mixed Check.
No. **17L7841** Black and white.
Price, each............**$5.98**

All Wool Serge.
No. **17L7842** Black.
No. **17L7843** Navy blue.
No. **17L7844** Copenhagen blue. Price, each...**$7.98**

Women's and Misses' Spring and Fall Coat. This style comes in 34-inch length and makes an ideal sport coat. May be ordered as illustrated in a black and white check, about one-third wool and two-thirds cotton, or an all wool serge. (See numbers and colors below.) The convertible collar has trimming of silk mixed pongee in a Persian design. Coat is unlined and fastens with fancy buttons; belt shows a large metal buckle. Sizes, 34 to 46 in. bust measure. **Be sure to mention size.** Av. shpg. wt., 2½ lbs.

Wool Mixed Check.
No. **17L7845** Black and white. Price, each...**$4.98**

All Wool Serge.
No. **17L7846** Black.
No. **17L7847** Navy blue.
No. **17L7848** Copenhagen blue.
Price, each............**$6.48**

No. 31L9880 EACH
Black and white check. **$7.98**
MISSES' OR SMALL WOMEN'S SUIT in black and white cotton check. Extremely smart and bright looking. Lined throughout with sateen. Coat in proper Spring length and has pretty collar with overcollar of white cotton rep. Braid bound belt runs all around to sides of front. Set-in sleeves trimmed with braid to match belt. Back has knife plait on each side below belt and plenty of fullness between. Skirt in plain style, closing invisibly at side. Belted and shirred back. Average sweep, 72 inches. Misses' or small women's sizes only. For cloth samples of suits illustrated in this catalog send for our 480L Suit Sample Book, ready February 1, 1918. **State bust, chest, waist and hip measures, also front length of skirt.** Average shipping wt., 3½ lbs.

No. 31L9875 Navy blue.
No. 31L9876 Black.
No. 31L9877 Copenhagen blue. EACH **$16.66**
MISSES' SUIT in our standard all wool double twisted warp serge. Lined throughout with guaranteed satin. This charming suit in proper Spring length is appropriate for street or dress wear, and is designed with large collar and overcollar of white silk faille. Coat has belt all around and is trimmed in front with rows of buttons and silk chain stitching. Set-in sleeves trimmed with buttons and silk chain stitching. Back slightly gathered above belt, trimmed with buttons and stitching to match front and sleeves. Plaits in back below belt and rows of buttons and stitching at each side. Skirt in plain style, closing invisibly at side. Belted and shirred back. Average sweep, 74 inches. Misses' or small women's sizes only, 32 to 38 inches bust measure, 22 to 28 inches waist measure, proportionate hip measure and 34 to 38 in. front length of skirt. **State bust, chest, waist and hip measures, also front length of skirt.** Av. shpg. wt., 3¾ lbs.

No. 31L9885 Navy blue.
No. 31L9886 Black. EACH **$25.00**
MISSES' SUIT in excellent quality all wool men's wear serge. Very smart semi-Norfolk style. Lined with peau de cygne silk. The appropriate collar is set off by an overcollar of silk faille, trimmed with stitching, and can be buttoned up to neck as shown in small illustration. Pockets with button trimmed flap. Double belt in front. Set-in sleeves trimmed with strap of self material. Yoked and belted back with two box plaits and row of buttons on each side. Skirt has a detachable belt and slash pockets. Closes invisibly at side. Average sweep, 76 inches. Misses' or small women's sizes only, 32 to 38 inches bust measure, 22 to 28 inches waist measure, proportionate hip measure and 34 to 38 inches front length of skirt. For cloth samples of suits illustrated on this page, send for our Suit Sample Book No. 480L, ready February 1, 1918. **State bust, chest, waist and hip measures, also front length of skirt.** Average shipping weight, 3¾ pounds.

No. 31L9890 Rose.
No. 31L9891 Green.
No. 31L9892 Copenhagen blue. EACH **$17.95**
MISSES' OR SMALL WOMEN'S SUIT of all wool jersey, the popular sport material, close knit and smooth finish. This suit is unlined and is the proper weight for Spring and Summer. New collar with overcollar of same material in contrasting color. Belt all around, forming sash in front. Patch pockets at sides trimmed with flaps to match overcollar. Back is gathered at waist above and below belt. Sleeves have cuffs trimmed with buttons. Overcollar, back of belt, cuffs on sleeves and pocket flaps on skirt and coat are made of self material in contrasting color. Skirt has handy patch pockets with flap. Closes invisibly at side. Belted and shirred back. Average sweep, 72 inches. Misses' or small women's sizes only, 32 to 38 inches bust measure, 22 to 28 inches waist measure, proportionate hip measure and 34 to 38 inches front length of skirt. **State bust, chest, waist and hip measures, also front length of skirt.** Average shipping weight, 3½ pounds.

27N3215
Silk Georgette
Crepe
$5.95
27N3240
Silk Crepe
de Chine
$5.00
27N3235
Silk Georgette Crepe
$6.50
27N3220
Silk Crepe
de Chine
$5.98
27N3245
Silk
Georgette
Crepe
$6.95
27N3225
Silk Georgette Crepe
$5.00
27N3230
Silk Georgette Crepe
$3.98
27N3250
Silk Georgette Crepe
$5.95
See Opposite Page For Descriptions
And Other Colors

For descriptions and prices see opposite page

Especially Designed for Stout Women

No. 31N5490 Navy blue. EACH
No. 31N5491 Dark green.
No. 31N5492 Black. **$27.75**

STOUT WOMEN'S SILK CREPE DE CHINE AND GEORGETTE CREPE DRESS. A beautiful dress, made of splendid quality all silk crepe de chine and silk Georgette crepe. Designed especially for women of full figure, and without doubt one of the most attractive we have ever listed. The Georgette crepe waist, with sleeves attached to underwaist of silk mull, is charmingly draped with crepe de chine from wide girdle on each side of front over shoulders and down each side of back. The vestee and waist front on each side are beautifully **hand embroidered** with jet beads and silk in color to match dress. Girdle is trimmed with jet ornaments and has long sash finished with silk fringe. Skirt, with long graceful one sided tunic, has sweep of about 76 inches. Fastens in front. **Stout women's sizes only. Give measurements.** Average shipping weight, 1¾ pounds.

No. 31N5480 Navy blue.
No. 31N5481 Dark brown. EACH
No. 31N5482 Black. **$25.50**

STOUT WOMEN'S WOOL FRENCH SERGE AND SATIN DRESS. A most attractive dress, designed along lines especially appropriate for women of full figure, and made of excellent quality all wool French serge and all silk satin. The sleeves are of satin. The satin vestee, with narrow strip of contrasting color set in center, is trimmed with rows of small good quality buttons and the serge collar is beautifully **hand embroidered** with silk. The serge cuffs, lined with contrasting color satin, are trimmed with small buttons and belt is set off with pretty black buckles. Serge panels on waist front extend into long straight hanging drapery on each side of skirt. Skirt has wide box plait panel in back and sweep of about 80 inches. Fastens in front. **Stout women's sizes only. Give measurements.** Average shipping weight, 2½ pounds.

No. 31N5485 Navy blue. EACH
No. 31N5486 Black. **$15.89**

STOUT WOMEN'S ALL WOOL POPLIN DRESS. Straight plaited styles, having a tendency to give height and slenderness, are especially desirable for stout women. The material used in this becoming dress is excellent quality medium weight all wool poplin, and in addition to giving excellent service makes a splendid appearance. The collar is of white silk poplin and dress is prettily trimmed on waist and skirt, both front and back, with wide silk military braid and small composition buttons. Skirt has full sweep of about 82 inches and dress fastens in front. Reasonably priced and excellent value. **Stout women's sizes only. Give measurements.** Average shipping weight, 2¼ pounds.

EACH
No. 31N5495 Navy blue.
No. 31N5496 Black. **$16.95**

STOUT WOMEN'S WOOL SERGE DRESS. This becoming dress, made of excellent quality all wool double warp serge, has all the lines so necessary for stout women and is one with which you will be well pleased. Made in vestee effect with vestee of serge in soft folds and yoke, collar and cuffs of gray color silk poplin, yoke being trimmed with small glass buttons. The skirt, made with wide box plait panel both front and back and side drapery, is especially appropriate for stout women. Wide lapels on waist front, panels on back and front of skirt and side drapery are prettily trimmed with good quality black composition buttons. Fastens in front and has skirt sweep of about 78 inches. **Stout women's sizes only. Give measurements.** Average shipping weight, 2½ pounds.

For Sizes in Which Stout Women's Dresses on This Page Can Be Furnished, See Page 73, Opposite.

Distinctive Styles in Popular Materials

No. 31N5400 Navy blue. EACH
No. 31N5401 Green.
No. 31N5402 Black. **$13.75**

WOMEN'S SILK BRAID TRIMMED VELVETEEN DRESS. A stunning dress, made of good quality velveteen and handsomely trimmed with silk military braid and select quality buttons. The high turnover collar is lined with white satin and the pretty vestee effect and narrow cuffs are of the same material. Vestee and dress in front from shoulder seam down left side and across bottom of tunic effect are trimmed with good quality silk military braid, making a most becoming effect. Belt is set off with neat buckle and dress closes in front. Skirt sweep is about 70 inches. Women's regular sizes only. **Give measurements.** Average shipping weight, 2¼ pounds.

No. 31N5405 Navy blue. EACH
No. 31N5406 Black. **$14.50**

MISSES' AND WOMEN'S WOOL FRENCH SERGE AND SILK FOULARD DRESS. A most charming combination dress, made of excellent quality all wool French serge and lustrous all silk foulard. The serge part of the waist, extending into the girdle in front, with bow and sash in back, is attached at neck only, the foulard extending underneath. Collar is of white satin and waist front and sash are trimmed with large ball shaped serge covered buttons. Dress fastens in front and has skirt sweep of about 70 inches. Misses' sizes, 14 to 20, and women's sizes, 32 to 44 inches bust measure. **When ordering give measurements.** Average shipping weight, 2 pounds.

SIZES Women's sizes, 32 to 44 inches bust measure, with waist measure up to and including 35 inches and skirt lengths of 36, 38 or 41 inches, with basted hem. Those dresses listed in misses' sizes can be furnished in sizes 14, 16, 18 and 20, with skirt lengths of 34 to 38 inches. **When ordering a women's dress give bust, chest and waist measures and front length of skirt; for misses' dress give size.**

No. 31N5410 Navy blue. EACH
No. 31N5411 Black. **$16.38**

MISSES' AND WOMEN'S BRAID TRIMMED WOOL SERGE DRESS. A charming example of the tunic skirt style so much in vogue this season. Made of excellent quality all wool worsted serge. The collar and turnback cuffs are of fine quality filet lace. Dress is handsomely trimmed on loose hanging panel waist front and on tunic with silk military braid and self material covered buttons edged with silk poplin in contrasting color. Closes in front and has skirt sweep of about 70 inches. This dress is extra well made throughout and is splendid value. Misses' sizes, 14 to 20, and women's sizes, 32 to 44 inches bust measure. **Give measurements.** Average shipping weight, 2¼ pounds.

Dresses for Mourning and General Wear

No. **31N5440** All black. EACH **$14.85**

MISSES' AND WOMEN'S BLACK SILK SATIN MESSALINE DRESS. An exeptionally attractive mourning dress, made of extra good quality lustrous all silk satin messaline. The yoke, collar and sleeves are of Georgette crepe, collar being prettily **hand embroidered** with silk. Trimming buttons on waist front are silk covered. The skirt is made with fashionable pointed tunic and has sweep of about 75 inches. The belt is set off with long sash in front, trimmed with large silk tassel. Dress fastens at left side. Furnished in black only and an excellent value at $14.85. Misses' and women's sizes. **Give measurements.** Average shipping weight, 1¾ pounds.

FOR SIZES See Size Paragraph on Page 69

31N5435
Misses' and Women's
Wool Serge

31N5440
Misses' and Women's
Satin Messaline

31N5445
Misses' and Women's
Wool Mixed
Serge

31N5450
Women's
Cotton
Foulard

No. **31N5435** All black.
No. **31N5436** Navy blue. EACH **$14.75**

MISSES' AND WOMEN'S ALL WOOL SERGE DRESS. For women in mourning, or those who prefer black, we can recommend this reasonably priced dress of excellent quality all wool double warp serge. The large collar and turnback cuffs are of silk poplin, collar being trimmed with dainty self material covered buttons. The waist front, made in panel effect, is trimmed with rows of good quality vegetable ivory buttons. Loose hanging tabs, extending from belt part way down each side of skirt, are beautifully embroidered with soutache braid and belt is finished off in back with long sash. Can also be furnished in navy blue with white collar and cuffs. Dress fastens in front and has skirt sweep of about 76 inches. Misses' and women's sizes. **Give measurements.** Average shipping weight, 2¼ pounds.

No. **31N5445** Navy blue.
No. **31N5446** Brown.
No. **31N5447** Black. EACH **$11.98**

MISSES' AND WOMEN'S WOOL MIXED SERGE DRESS. Vest effects in dresses are extremely popular and we know you will be well pleased with this one. The material is our best quality wool and cotton mixed serge, containing about 50 per cent of each. The vest, collar and turnback cuffs are of white satin, the vest being trimmed with a row of dainty extra quality pearl buttons. Long lapels, extending over skirt, and bottom of jacket, entirely around, are trimmed with silk military braid. The skirt, with yoke top and plaits below, has sweep of about 70 in. and buttons through at left side on yoke with large composition buttons. Fastens in front. Misses' and women's sizes. **Give measurements.** Average shipping weight, 2 pounds.

No. **31N5450** Navy blue.
No. **31N5451** Green.
No. **31N5452** Black. EACH **$5.48**

WOMEN'S COTTON FOULARD DRESS. A neat and becoming dress, made of good quality semi-lustrous cotton foulard, a material that wears well and increases in popularity each season. Collar, cuffs and piping on waist front and pockets of skirt are of good quality rep. The arrangement of the waist front, with its wide lapels, piping and small rep covered buttons, is decidedly attractive. The skirt, plaited in front and trimmed with large patch pockets, has sweep of about 72 inches. Dress fastens in front. Women's sizes only. **Give measurements.** Average shipping weight, 1¾ pounds.

Stylish Silk Dresses for All Occasions

No. **31N5345** White. EACH **$24.95**

WOMEN'S SATIN WEDDING DRESS. A most dainty wedding gown, made of splendid quality all silk satin with underwaist and sleeves of fine quality silk net. The waist is beautifully trimmed with satin ruching and narrow satin ribbon, and the corsage bouquet is of imitation orange blossoms and long streamers of narrow satin ribbon. The gracefully draped skirt has sweep of about 78 inches and dress fastens in front. A charming dress for the bride. Cap and veil are not included. Women's sizes only. **Give measurements.** Average shipping weight, 1¾ pounds.

31N5340 Misses' *and* Women's Satin Messaline

31N5350 Misses' *and* Women's Silk Taffeta

31N5355 Misses' *and* Women's Georgette Crepe

31N5345 Women's Satin

No. 31N5340 Navy blue.
No. 31N5341 Dark brown.
No. 31N5342 Black. EACH **$13.98**

MISSES' AND WOMEN'S EMBROIDERED SATIN MESSALINE DRESS. A decidedly attractive low priced dress, made of good quality lustrous all silk satin messaline. The sleeves and the softly gathered vestee are of Georgette crepe and the large collar is of white satin. The cuffs and pretty divided tunic of skirt are beautifully embroidered with silk and tinsel and the belt is set off with large celluloid buckle. Dress fastens in front and has skirt sweep of about 72 inches. Splendid value for the price asked. Misses' sizes, 14 to 20, and women's sizes, 32 to 44 inches bust measure. **Give measurements.** Average shipping weight, 1¾ pounds.

No. **31N5350** Navy blue.
No. **31N5351** Copenhagen blue.
No. **31N5352** Brown. EACH **$19.95**

MISSES' AND WOMEN'S SILK TAFFETA DRESS. An unusually smart vest effect dress, made of excellent quality lustrous all silk taffeta. The combination of colors, with the vest, collar and cuffs of contrasting colored silk taffeta, is remarkably pretty. Vest and cuffs are trimmed with silk military braid and waist front and top of plaited tunic on each side of vest are trimmed with large taffeta and tinsel covered buttons, and sleeves with small buttons of the same kind. The girdle in front is set off with extra large buckle and sleeves are attached to silk mull underwaist. Fastens in front and has skirt sweep of about 70 inches. A most beautiful dress. Misses' sizes, 14 to 20, and women's sizes, 32 to 44 inches bust measure. **When ordering give measurements.** Average shpg. wt., 1¾ pounds.

No. **31N5355** Pearl gray, turquoise blue beads.
No. **31N5356** Navy blue, navy blue beads.
No. **31N5357** Black, black beads. EACH **$22.50**

MISSES' AND WOMEN'S BEAD TRIMMED GEORGETTE CREPE DRESS. It would be hard to select a more dainty dress than this one, made of excellent quality silk Georgette crepe and handsomely trimmed throughout with bead embroidery in soft harmonizing color. The collar and the girdle with long sash are of satin and cuffs are piped with same. The arrangement of the waist front, which is loose hanging and extends to a point over each side of girdle, is most attractive. The skirt is made with a wide panel in front, giving an overtunic effect, and has sweep of about 65 inches. Dress fastens in front. Misses' sizes, 14 to 20, and women's sizes, 32 to 44 inches bust measure. **Give measurements.** Average shipping weight, 1¾ pounds.

SIZES Women's sizes, 32 to 44 inches bust measure, with waist measure up to and including 35 inches and skirt lengths of 36, 38 or 41 inches. Misses' sizes, 14 to 20, with skirt lengths of 34 to 38 inches. **When ordering women's size give bust, chest and waist measures and front length of skirt; for misses' dress give size.** See order blanks in back of catalog for simple measuring instructions.

No. 31L9975 Olive tan khaki, with Hat No. 31L9997.
Outfit.......... **$9.75**

No. 31L9976 Olive tan khaki, with Hat No. 31L9998.
Outfit........ **$13.75**

FOUR-PIECE RIDING HABIT. Made of good quality guaranteed fast color khaki. Consists of coat, riding breeches leggings, Hat Nos. 31L9997 or 31L9998. Coat in semi-fitted style with full flare. Plain collar and lapels. Set-in sleeves with cuffs. Patch pocket at each side. Breast pocket. Separate breeches, buttoning at both sides at hips. Leggings as illustrated. **When ordering state bust and waist measures, also calf measure for leggings.** Average shipping weight, 5 pounds.

No. 31L9997 Olive tan khaki.
Each.............. **63c**

HAT, as illustrated, made of khaki. Average shpg. wt., 1 lb.

No. 31L9998 Black.
Each.......... **$5.00**

HAT, as illustrated. Average shipping weight, 1 pound.

No. 31L9980 Olive tan khaki
Each........... **$4.75**

ONE-PIECE RIDING OR CYCLING DRESS. Fast color khaki. Opens all the way down front. **State bust measure.** Shpg. wt., 4½ lbs.

No. 31L9981 Olive tan khaki.
Outfit.......... **$6.60**

THREE-PIECE OUTFIT. Consists of riding dress, leggings and Hat No. 31L9997 to match. **Give bust measure, also calf measure for leggings.** Shipping weight, 5 lbs.

No. 31L9982 Navy blue.
No. 31L9983 Brown.
Each.......... **$7.90**

RIDING DRESS of velveteen corduroy. Shpg. wt., 4 lbs.

Riding Skirts.

No. 31L9985 Olive tan khaki.
Each............ **$3.19**

No. 31L9986 Tan cotton covert.
Each............ **$2.93**

No. 31L9987 Oxford gray cotton covert.
Each............ **$2.93**

No. 31L9988 Brown corduroy.
Each............ **$6.48**

No. 31L9989 Tan corduroy.
Each............ **$6.48**

DIVIDED RIDING SKIRT Furnished in materials as described. Opens all the way down front with buttons and buttonholes. Large patch pocket at side. **State waist measure and front length of skirt.** Av. shpg. wt., 2¾ lbs.

No. 31L9990 Olive tan khaki.
Suit.............. **$6.35**

TWO-PIECE RIDING OR CYCLING SUIT. Norfolk coat and divided skirt of khaki. **Give bust and waist measures, also front length of skirt.** Shpg. wt., 4½ lbs.

No. 31L9991 Olive tan khaki
Outfit........... **$8.20**

FOUR-PIECE OUTFIT. Norfolk coat, divided skirt, leggings and Hat No. 31L9997 to match. **Give bust and waist measures, also front length of skirt and calf measure for leggings.** Shipping weight, 5½ pounds.

No. 31L9992 Brown.
No. 31L9993 Tan. Suit.... **$11.75**

TWO-PIECE RIDING SUIT. Norfolk coat and divided skirt of velvet finish corduroy. **State bust and waist measures, also front length of skirt.** Shpg.wt., 4¾ lbs.

No. 31L9995 Olive tan khaki.
Habit....... **$5.80**

TWO-PIECE RIDING HABIT. Middy blouse and divided skirt. Guaranteed fast color khaki. **Give bust and waist measures, also front length of skirt.** Shipping weight, 4 pounds.

No. 31L9996 Olive tan khaki.
Outfit.......... **$7.65**

FOUR-PIECE OUTFIT. Middy blouse, divided skirt. leggings and Hat No. 31L9997 to match. **Give bust and waist measures, also front length of skirt and calf measure for leggings.** Shipping weight, 5½ pounds.

No. 31L9999 Olive tan khaki.
Per pair....... **$1.29**

LEGGINGS, as illustrated. See size paragraph. Shipping weight, 1¼ pounds.

Women's Overalls have met with such popular favor and are now worn so commonly that further recommendation is scarcely necessary. Those shown here are designed on practical lines. They are made for appearance, for comfort and for service. The materials are all strong and closely woven, which will not easily tear, and are not transparent. Furnished in sizes from 34 to 44 inches bust measure and 24 to 34 inches waist measure in women's sizes, and girls' sizes from 6 years to 14 years. **Be sure to read the descriptions given below carefully, also make sure that your order mentions the size wanted.**

Women's and Girls' Overalls With or Without Blouse.

No. **31L8910** Girls' strong khaki colored cotton material, with bib. Price, each **$1.26**
No. **31L8911** Girls' heavy chambray, with bib. Price, each .... **.92**
Average shipping weight for the above, ¼ pounds.

No. **31L8912** Girls' strong khaki colored cotton material, with blouse. Price, suit **$1.98**
No. **31L8913** Girls' heavy chambray with blouse., Price, suit **1.53**
Average shipping weight for the above, 1¾ pounds.

No. **31L8907** Women's plain blue heavy weight chambray.
No. **31L8908** Women's blue with red stripe heavy weight chambray.
No. **31L8909** Women's tan with white stripe heavy weight chambray. Price, each **$1.59**
Average shipping weight for the above, 1¼ pounds.

No. **31L8919** Women's tan khaki cloth, with blouse Price, suit ....
No. **31L8920** Women's strong cotton blue hickory striped material, with blouse. Price, suit .... } **$3.15**
Average shipping weight for the above, 2½ pounds.

No. **31L8921** Women's tan khaki cloth, without blouse. Price, each ....
No. **31L8922** Women's strong cotton blue hickory striped material, without blouse. Price, each .... } **$2.10**
Average shipping weight for the above, 1⅞ pounds.

No. **31L8923** Women's strong cotton suiting in black and white checks, without blouse. Price, each **$1.29**
Average shipping weight for the above, 1¼ pounds.

No. **31L8924** Women's strong cotton suiting in black and white checks with blouse. Price, suit **2.09**
Average shipping weight for the above, 1¾ pounds.

No. **31L8925** Women's cotton Ladlassie blue stripe, without blouse. Price, each ....
No. **31L8926** Women's cotton beach cloth, without blouse. Price, each .... } **$1.43**

No. **31L8915** Women's tan khaki, without blouse. Price, each ....
No. **31L8916** Women's blue cotton hickory stripe, without blouse. Price, each .... } **$1.55**
Average shipping weight for the above, 1¼ pounds.

No. **31L8927** Women's cotton Ladlassie blue stripe, with blouse. Price, suit ....
No. **31L8928** Women's cotton beach cloth, with blouse. Price, suit .... } **$2.26**

No. **31L8917** Women's tan khaki, with blouse. Price, suit ....
No. **31L8918** Women's blue cotton hickory stripe, with blouse. Price, suit .... } **$2.55**
Average shipping weight for the above, 1¾ pounds.

A Middy Coat of a closely woven cotton fabric with a new smock design. The deep, square back collar is made of beach cloth, which is also used to trim the sleeves and pockets in colors mentioned below. Smocking in harmonizing shades. Sizes, 32 to 44 inches bust measure. **State size.** Average shipping weight, 10 ounces.

No. **27L2512** **White with blue.**
No. **27L2513** **White with rose.**
No. **27L2514** **White with green**
No. **27L2515** **All white.**
Price, each **95c**

Middy Coat of serviceable quality white poplin with colored stripes as mentioned below. The shapely collar is square in back and has colored embroidery on front. Cuffs and trimming on large patch pockets in plain color to match collar. Sizes, 32 to 44 inches bust measure. **State size.** Average shipping weight, 10 ounces.

No. **27L2516** **White with blue.**
No. **27L2517** **White with rose.**
No. **27L2518** **White with green.**
Price, each **$1.29**

Stylish Middy of Lonsdale jean, a medium weight fine cotton fabric which will give excellent service. The novelty collar is square in back and made of beach cloth in colors mentioned below. Pockets are made with turnback flaps with colored embroidery. Cuffs match collar. Sizes, 32 to 44 inches bust measure. **State size.** Average shipping weight, 10 ounces.

No. **27L2504** **White with blue.**
No. **27L2505** **White with rose.**
No. **27L2506** **White with green.**
No. **27L2507** **All White.**
Price, each **$1.48**

Novelty Smock. Something new in style and material. Made of a highly mercerized cotton fabric which looks like silk rajah. Comes in colors mentioned below, with smocking in contrasting colors. The front has side plaits trimming panel down the center. Pockets, cuffs and collar trimmed with same material in contrasting shades. Deep, square back collar. Length of garment, about 30 inches. Sizes, 32 to 44 inches bust measure. **State size.** Average shipping weight, 11 ounces.

No. **27L2520** **Blue with tan.**
No **27L2521** **Green with tan.**
No. **27L2522** **Rose with tan.**
No. **27L2523** **Tan with green.**
Price, each **$2.98**

A Middy Coat of Lonsdale jean, a very serviceable cotton material of medium weight. Garment has a deep, pointed back collar of beach cloth in shades mentioned below, and is attractively trimmed with embroidery in harmonizing colors. Novelty pockets are trimmed to match. Sizes, 32 to 44 inches bust measure. **State size.** Average shipping weight, 10 ounces.

No. **27L2500** **White with blue.**
No. **27L2501** **White with rose.**
No. **27L2502** **White with green.**
No. **27L2503** **All white.**
Price, each **$1.39**

New Coat Smock. A very attractive middy coat smock made of a fine quality Lonsdale jean, a cotton material which will give excellent service. Garment has attractive colored smocking at yoke, and the novelty collar, frilled pockets and turnback cuffs are of beach cloth in colors mentioned below and harmonize with the smocking. Sizes, 32 to 44 inches bust measure. **State size.** Average shipping weight, 11 ounces.

No. **27L2508** **White with blue.**
No. **27L2509** **White with rose.**
No. **27L2510** **White with green.**
No. **27L2511** **All white.**
Price, each **$1.69**

No. 31L9450 Navy blue.
No. 31L9451 Black.
No. 31L9452 Brown.
No. 31L9453 Green.

EACH **$3.65**

A SPLENDID MISSES' SKIRT for school or general wear. Made of half wool and half cotton serge. Convenient novelty pockets with overhanging flap. Detachable belt all around is run through tab loops trimmed with buttons. Back is slightly shirred under belt. Closes invisibly at side. Average sweep, 75 inches. Furnished in misses' sizes only, from 22 to 28 inches waist measure, proportionate hip measure, and from 34 to 38 inches front length of skirt. When taking your waist measure do not make any allowance for high girdle; measure at natural waistline. For larger sizes see women's skirts. **When ordering state waist measure, hip measure and front length of skirt.** Average shipping weight, 1½ pounds.

No. 31L9500 Navy blue.
No. 31L9501 Black.
No. 31L9502 Brown.

EACH **$5.35**

MISSES' OR SMALL WOMEN'S NEATLY TAILORED SKIRT, especially becoming to youthful figures. Made of our standard all wool double twisted warp serge. The cross belt in front is an attractive feature. Fancy and convenient pockets. Back is slightly shirred under belt. Closes invisibly at side. Average sweep, 75 inches. Furnished in misses' sizes only, from 22 to 28 inches waist measure, proportionate hip measure, and from 34 to 38 inches front length of skirt. When taking your waist measure do not make any allowance for high girdle; measure at natural waistline. **When ordering state waist measure, hip measure and front length of skirt.** Average shipping weight, 1½ pounds.

No. 31L9505 Blue plaid.

EACH **$3.59**

THIS MISSES' OR SMALL WOMEN'S SKIRT is made of a stylish cotton plaid suiting which will give very satisfactory wear. A jaunty girlish style with stitched-down girdle effect at waist. The novelty pockets with overhanging flap close with button. Back is slightly shirred under stitched-down belt. Closes invisibly at side. Average sweep, 75 inches. Furnished in misses' sizes only, from 22 to 28 inches waist measure, proportionate hip measure, and from 34 to 38 inches front length of skirt. When taking your waist measure do not make any allowance for high girdle; measure at natural waistline. For larger sizes see women's skirts. **When ordering state waist measure, hip measure and front length of skirt.** Average shipping weight, 1½ pounds.

31N2035
31N2040
31N2050
31N2045
31N2070
31N2055
31N2060
31N2065
31N2080
31N2075

GIRLS' FALL AND WINTER COATS
Ages, years............10 12 14
Length, inches........36 39 42
17N9020
Panné Mohair
$11.48
17N9035
Velour Plush
$10.48
17N9060
Corduroy
$7.98
17N9070
Pannette
$8.48
17N9050
Velour Plush
$11.98
17N9075
Wool Velour
$10.48
17N9030
Velour Plush
$7.98
17N9045
Astrakhan
$8.48
17N9055
Wool Velour
$13.98

"Homestead" House and Garden Wear
Trade Mark Registered in U. S. Patent Office.
No. 31N2460 Blue. No. 31N2461 Pink. EACH $1.59
WOMEN'S PERCALE BUNGALOW HOUSE DRESS. Made of standard quality solid color percale, buttoning visibly all the way down front, making it easy to launder. Has two box plaits in front and one in back. Loose belt running through loops at sides, and is trimmed throughout with rickrack braid. Furnished in sizes 32 to 46 inches bust measure. State size wanted. Average shipping weight, 1½ pounds.
No. 31N2470 Black sateen. EACH $3.19
No. 31N2471 Blue figured flannelette. 2.48
No. 31N2472 Black figured flannelette. 2.48
WOMEN'S WRAPPER. Made in a comfortable roomy style with wide flounce at bottom. Buttons visibly in front with pearl buttons similar to trimming buttons on collar. Has long sleeves with buttoned cuffs and neat patch pocket. Furnished either in mercerized sateen or cotton flannelette in sizes 32 to 46 inches bust measure. State size wanted. Average shipping weight, 1⅞ pounds.
31N2485
31N2470
31N2460
31N2480
No. 31N2465 Blue. No. 31N2466 Black. EACH $2.39
STOUT SIZES. No. 31N2467 Blue. No. 31N2468 Black. 2.78
WOMEN'S STANDARD STYLE MOTHER HUBBARD WRAPPER of cotton flannelette. Has neat collar and button cuff full length sleeves. Regular sizes from 32 to 46 inches bust and in stout sizes from 39 to 53 inches bust. State size. Average shpg. wt., 1¾ lbs.
No. 31N2480 Blue. No. 31N2481 Tan. EACH $2.48
WOMEN'S MILITARY HIGH NECK HOUSE DRESS of standard quality percale, buttoning visibly all the way down front, making it easy to launder. Has four military patch pockets, and button cuff on full length sleeves. The officers' detachable belt and shoulder strap is of tan percale on the blue dress and blue percale on the tan. Furnished in sizes 32 to 46 inches bust measure. State size wanted. Average shipping weight, 1¾ pounds.
No. 31N2475 White. OUTFIT $3.98
NURSES' OUTFIT, consisting of white muslin dress, roomy bib apron fastening in back separate cuffs of white lawn and cap that can be easily laundered, also lawn scarf. An outfit that you are sure to be pleased with. Furnished in sizes 32 to 44 inches bust measure. State size wanted. Average shipping weight, 2 pounds.
WOMEN'S HEAVY WEIGHT CHAMBRAY OVERALLS.
No. 31N2485 Blue, with red stripe.
No. 31N2486 Tan, with white stripe. EACH
No. 31N2487 Plain blue. $2.25
Av. shpg. wt., 1¼ lbs.
31N2465
31N2490
31N2495
31N2475
WOMEN'S TWO-PIECE COTTON OVERALLS.
No. 31N2490 Tan beachcloth. Price, each $2.48
No. 31N2491 Blue hickory stripe suiting. Price, each 2.98
No. 31N2492 Blue stripe ladlassie cloth. Price, each 2.48
No. 31N2494 Black and white check suiting. Price, each 2.37
Average shipping weight, 2½ pounds.
The Women's Overalls illustrated above are well made of durable material that will not rip and is not transparent. Furnished in sizes from 34 to 44 inches bust measure and 24 to 34 inches waist measure. See descriptions for colors and style. Make sure your order mentions size wanted. See order blanks in back of catalog for simple measuring instructions.
WOMEN'S ONE-PIECE COTTON BIB OVERALLS.
No. 31N2495 Black and white check suiting. Price, each $1.48
No. 31N2497 Tan beachcloth. Price, each 1.48
No. 31N2498 Khaki color cotton suiting. Price, each 1.39
No. 31N2499 Blue hickory stripe suiting. Price, each 1.44
Average shipping weight, 1⅞ pounds.

Creepers, Bloomers and Sun Hats

For Other Rompers and Play Suits See Pages 444 and 448.

No. 29L8918 White ground, assorted light figures.
Girls' Coverall Belted Back Style Apron of good quality percale. Neatly trimmed with white piping. Practical apron at a low price. Ages, 2, 4 and 6 years. **State age.** Average shipping weight, 6 oz.
Price, each.......... **40c**

No. 29L8939 Plain blue.
Serviceable and Well Made Rompers or Play Suit of Amoskeag chambray. Collar, yoke, pocket, belt and sleeves finished with white piping. Double stitched seams. Ages, 2, 3, 4, 5 and 6 years. **State age.** Average shipping weight, 6 oz.
Price, each......... **63c**

No. 29L8992 White, blue trim.
Dressy Rompers of good quality white cotton rep. Collar, yoke and belt neatly finished with blue binding. Double stitched crotch seams. An attractive garment and a good value at this price. Ages, 2, 3, 4, 5 and 6 years. **State age.** Average shipping weight, 7 ounces.
Price, each........ **88c**

No. 29L8959 Plain blue, with kindergarten trim.
Children's Attractive Beach Style Rompers. Made of good quality chambray with kindergarten trim on collar, cuffs, belt and bottom of legs, in contrasting colors. Double stitched seams. Patch pockets. A well made garment. Ages, 2, 3, 4, 5 and 6 years. **State age.** Av. shpg. wt., 6 oz. Price, each.. **88c**

No. 29L8969 Medium blue stripe.
Children's Light Weight Percale Rompers for Spring and Summer wear. Neck, belt, sleeves and patch pockets trimmed with white piping. Open leg style. Buttons down front. Ages, 2, 3, 4, 5 and 6 years. **State age.** Average shipping weight, 5 oz.
Price, each...... **53c**

No. 29L8932 White ground with assorted light figures and stripes.
Girls' Good Quality Percale Apron Dress. A neat style. Skirt shirred at back. Pocket and belt in front. Ages, 2, 4 and 6 years. **State age.** Average shipping weight, 5 oz.
Price, each....... **27c**

No. 29L8935 Blue and white check.
Practical Apron Dress of good quality percale. Easy to put on and completely covers skirt, both back and front. Neatly trimmed with white piping. Ages, 2, 4 and 6 years. **State age.** Average shipping wt., 6 oz.
Price, each.......... **37c**

No. 29L8860 White.
High Grade White Sateen Bloomers. Full size. Well made. Finished seams and reinforced plackets. Ages, 2, 4, 6 and 7 years. **State age.** Average shipping wt., 6 ounces.
Price, each......... **50c**

No. 29L8951 White.
Little Tots' Pretty White Embroidered Washable Pique Sun Hat. Adjustable brim embroidered and finished with scalloped edge. Semi-button crown. Easy to launder. Comes in one size, suitable for ages up to 3 years. Average shipping weight, 4 ounces.
Price, each...... **48c**

No. 29L8952 Blue and white check.
No. 29L8953 Pink and white check.
No. 29L8978 Medium light blue.
No. 29L8979 Pink.
Something new in Children's Sunbonnet. Easy to launder, as it is made with a one-piece button back which can be laid out flat and ironed. Made of good quality percale. No bunchy shirring in back. Adjustable tape tie strings on the inside and will fit ages from 3 to 8 years. Av. shpg. wt., 5 oz. Price, each... **29c**

No. 29L8861 Black.
Children's Serviceable Sateen Bloomers. Full size. Finished seams and reinforced plackets. Good value at a low price. Ages, 2, 4, 6 and 7 years. **State age.** Av. shpg. wt., 3 oz.
Price, each...... **35c**

29L8921 Blue; white check gingham.
29L8919 Pink; white check percale.
Girls' Apron in a belted back, kimono sleeve style. Neck, cuffs, belt and pocket finished with white rickrack braid. Ages, 2, 4 and 6 yrs. **State age.** Av. shpg. wt., 4 oz. Each.... **38c**

No. 29L8911 Plain blue.
Babies' Serviceable Overalls or Creepers of good quality chambray. Double stitched seams. Draw string at back. A practical play suit which will stand hard usage. Ages, 1 and 2 years. **State age.** Average shipping weight, 4 ounces.
Price, each......... **35c**

No. 29L8923 Plain blue.
No. 29L8924 Blue and white check.
Popular Style Amoskeag Chambray Creepers. Yoke front and back. Buttons down back and across bottom. Double stitched seams across yoke and arm holes. Ages, 1 and 2 years. **State age.** Av. shpg. wt., 5 oz. Price, each..... **58c**

No. 29L8933 Blue; white check.
No. 29L8934 Pink; white check.
Combination Rompers and Creepers of good quality checked gingham. For creeping babe. Buttons down back and at side of legs. Ages, 1 and 2 yrs. **State age.** Av. shpg. wt., 5 oz. Each.. **68c**

No. 29L8929 White.
Little Tots' Serviceable Cotton Seersucker Creepers. A practical light weight garment for Summer wear. Easily laundered and requires no ironing. Buttons down back and across bottom. Ages, 1 and 2 years. **State age.** Av. shpg. wt., 7 oz. Price, each..... **65c**

No. 29L8927 White.
Serviceable Cotton Poplin Creepers. Neck, sleeves and pocket finished with a neat braid trimming. Buttons down back and at sides. Easy to change diapers. Drop seat. Ages, 1 and 2 years. **State age.** Average shipping weight, 5 oz.
Each............. **69c**

No. 29L8836 Medium blue.
Serviceable Amoskeag Chambray Bloomers. Well made, with finished seams and reinforced plackets. Ages, 2, 4, 6 and 7 years. **State age.** Average shipping weight, 5 oz.
Price, each....... **35c**

Play Suits of Real Wearing Value

No. 40L668 Outfit, $1.65
Wool Mixed Baseball Uniform. Light gray with tan thread stripes. Brown trimmings. Breast pocket. Short sleeves. Bloomers are **full lined.** Hip pocket. Belt loops. Elastic bottoms. Full lined cap with long visor to shade eyes. Belt with patent fastener. Outfit consists of shirt, bloomers, cap and belt. **SIZES—10 to 16 years. State size.** Average shpg. wt., 1¼ lbs.

No. 40L666 Outfit, $1.65
Baseball Uniform of wool mixed stadium uniform cloth. Light gray with black thread stripes. Blue trimmings. Breast pocket. Short sleeves. **Full lined** bloomer pants with hip pocket, belt loops and elastic bottoms. Full lined cap with long visor for shading eyes. Belt with patent fasteners. Outfit consists of shirt, bloomers, cap and belt. **SIZES—10 to 16 years. State size.** Average shipping weight, 1¼ pounds.

No. 40L664 Outfit, $1.45
Light Gray Baseball Uniform of wool and cotton mixed flannel. Maroon trimming. Long sleeves. Breast pocket. Pants with padded front, belt loops and elastic bottoms. Belt with metal fastener. Full lined cap with long visor to shade eyes. Outfit consists of shirt, bloomers, cap and belt. **SIZES—8 to 16 years. State size.** Average shipping weight, 1¼ pounds.

No. 40L662 Outfit, $1.25
Baseball Uniform of wool and cotton mixed gray flannel. Navy blue trimmings. Short sleeves. Bloomer pants with belt loops and elastic bottoms. Belt with metal fastener. Full lined baseball cap with long visor for shading eyes. Outfit consists of shirt, bloomers, cap and belt. **SIZES—6 to 16 years. State size.** Av. shpg. wt., 1¼ lbs.

No. 40L660 Outfit, 95c
Our lowest priced Baseball Uniform. Light gray wool mixed flannel. Blue trimming. Breast pocket, long sleeves. Bloomer pants with elastic bottoms. Full lined baseball cap with long visor for shading eyes. Outfit consists of shirt, bloomers and cap. **SIZES—6 to 12 years. State size.** Average shipping weight, 1¾ pounds.

No. 40L670 Suit, $2.45
Soldier Suit of olive drab cotton fabric. Bronzed buttons. Fancy emblem embroidered on sleeve. Military pockets. Pants with extra broad hips, button snugly just below knees. No leggings required. Pants have front pockets. Coat and pants only. **SIZES—3 to 8 yrs. State size.** Av. shpg. wt., 2 lbs.

No. 40L912 Cap, 65c
Soldier Cap for Suit No. 40L670. **SIZES—6¼ to 6¾. State size.** Average shipping weight, 8 oz.

No. 40L710 Outfit, $2.85
Cadet Suit made of extra strong Galatea. Marine blue with silk braid trimming. Detachable brass buttons. Shoulder straps, slanting side pockets. Breast patch pockets with button flap. Straight style pants with white braid stripes at side. Side pockets. Cap, full lined, with sweatband. Imitation patent leather visor. Outfit consists of coat, pants and cap. **SIZES—3 to 8 years. State size.** Average shipping wt., 2¼ lbs.

No. 40L708 Outfit, $1.50
Military Play Suit made of olive drab cotton drill, trimmed with red. Military collar. Two side pockets. Brass buttons. Long pants have belt loops. Military stripe down side. Military full lined cap. Imitation patent leather visor. Brass emblems on cap and coat collar. Outfit consists of coat, pants and cap. **SIZES—4 to 14 years. State size.** Average shipping weight, 2¼ pounds.

No. 40L706 Outfit, $1.95
Military Outfit of khaki color strong cotton fabric. Military coat has four outside patch pockets with button flap. Pants with wide hips taper to lace below knee. Belt loops. Canvas leggings with strap for spiral wind. Cloth hat with stiff brim, full lined, sweatband. Haversack with shoulder strap. Outfit consists of coat, pants, hat, leggings and haversack. **SIZES—5 to 11 years. State size.** Av. shpg. wt., 2½ lbs.

No. 40L704 Outfit, $1.50
Rancher Cowboy Outfit. Strong khaki color cotton fabric. Shirt with breast pocket and imitation leather trimming. Long pants with belt loops. Imitation leather side trimmings with metal ornaments. Wide brim Western cloth hat, full lined. Outfit consists of shirt, pants, hat, red bandana handkerchief, belt with holster, toy pistol and roping lariat. **SIZES—4 to 14 years. State size.** Average shipping wt., 2¼ lbs.

No. 40L702 Outfit, $1.05
Pocahontas Indian Girl Suit. Blouse and skirt are made of khaki color cotton fabric. Navy blue V shape front, outlined with yellow and red trimmings. Sleeves trimmed in red. Eyelets for lacing front. Full cut skirt with red trimming at bottom. Headdress decorated with a number of large very highly colored feathers. **SIZES—4 to 10 years. State size.** Average shipping wt., 1½ lbs.

No. 40L700 Outfit, $1.05
Powhatan Big Chief Indian Outfit for boys. Made of olive khaki strong cotton drill. Scalloped red trimming. Navy blue V shaped front outlined with red and yellow trimming. Military eyelets for lacing. Long pants with belt loops. Warriors' headdress, trimmed from end to end with big, brightly colored feathers. **SIZES—4 to 10 years. State size.** Average shipping weight, 1¾ pounds.

Our Bathing Suits Are Made Amply Full in Size. To Determine the Proper Size to Order, Draw a Tape Measure Around Breast Next to Undergarment. For Example, if You Measure 38 Inches, Order a Size 38 Garment.

BATHING SUITS

Our Bathing Suits Are Made Amply Full In Size. To Determine the Proper Size to Order, Draw a Tape Measure Around Breast Next to Undergarment. For Example, if You Measure 38 Inches, Order a Size 38 Garment.

Men's One-Piece Suit. Half wool, half cotton. A very durable jersey knitted fabric. Round neck opening. Plain armholes. Sizes, 34 to 44 inches breast measure. **State size wanted.** Shipping weight, 1¼ pounds.

No. 6L7245 **Black with orange stripe.** Price ...$3.25

No. 6L7249 **Oxford gray with green stripe.** Price ...$3.22

Men's Athletic Two-Piece Suit. Navy blue jersey knitted shirt. Half wool, half cotton, with combination supporter attached, like our No. 6L7181 Athletic Shirt, shown on page 875. Pants of khaki color Galatea cloth. White belt, nickel plated buckle. Sizes, 30 to 44 inches breast measure. **State size.** Shipping weight, 1½ lbs.

No. 6L7256 Price..$3.95

Men's Two-Piece Suit. Higher grade than above. All wool shirt, navy blue. All wool jersey knitted navy blue pants. White belt, nickel plated buckle. A very high grade suit. Sizes, 30 to 44 inches breast measure. **State size.** Shipping weight 1¾ pounds.

No. 6L7257 Price.$6.95

Women's One-Piece Jersey Knitted Suit. Half wool, half cotton in a comparatively thin knit. Underpiece sewed to skirt or outer part. V neck, wing sleeves. A very practicable, serviceable suit, also one that has become very popular. Sizes, 32 to 46 inches bust measure. **State size.** Shpg. wt., 1¼ lbs.

No. 6L7261 Navy blue with green trim. Price $4.75

No. 6L7258 Black with orange trim. Price $4.65

Good Weight Knitted Cotton Suit. Style as above. Black with orange trim. Sizes, 34 to 50 inches bust measure. **State size.** Shpg. wt., 1¼ lbs.

No. 6L7260 Price.$1.90

Women's Sailor Style One-Piece Jersey Knitted Suit. Guaranteed all wool. A very high grade attractive suit. Has large sailor collar, belt, laced front. Knitted underpiece sewed to skirt. Sizes, 34 to 46 in. bust measure. **State size.** Shipping weight, 1¾ pounds.

No. 6L7269 **Light green body, gold trim.** Price..$5.85

No. 6L7270 **Navy blue, red trim.** Price $5.75

A Very Stunning Slipover Suit. With collar, belt and two pockets. Made from an unusually good weight strong cotton fabric known as surf satin, possessing a deep, rich luster, that will wear well. The color is black, collar and trim being black and white silk stripes. Separate knitted underpiece. Sizes, 36 to 46 inches, bust measure. **State size wanted.** Shipping weight, 1½ pounds.

No. 6L7250 Price $5.65

Men's One-Piece Heavy All Wool Jersey Knitted Suit. Athletic cut with large armholes. Exceptionally high grade, very attractive garment. Sizes, 34 to 46 inches breast measure. **State size.** Shipping weight, 1½ pounds.

No. 6L7226 **Green body,** gold color trim around armholes and neck. Combination purple and gold chest stripe. Price $5.25

No. 6L7227 **Royal blue body,** white trim around armholes and neck. Combination white and cardinal chest stripe. Price $5.20

Men's One-Piece All Wool Jersey Knitted Suit. Plain armholes, V neck. Good weight, well made garment. Sizes, 34 to 50 inches breast measure. **State size.** Shipping weight, 1¼ pounds.

No. 6L7240 **Navy with white trim.** Price $3.90

No. 6L7246 **Green with red trim.** Price $3.95

No. 6L7251 **Maroon with gold trim.** Price $3.96

Men's One-Piece Knitted Cotton Suit. Trimmed around armholes and bottom of suit. Sizes, 34 to 50 inches breast measure. **State size.** Shpg. wt., 1 lb

No. 6L7228 **Black with white trim.** Price......$1.60

No. 6L7255 **Purple with gold trim.** Price.......$1.65

Same as above, lighter in weight. Sizes, 34 to 44 inches breast measure. **State size.** Shipping weight, 1 pound.

No 6L7239 **Black with white trim.** Price........80c

No. 6L7238 **Oxford with white trim.** Price........85c

Women's Waistline Model Suit. Made of a closely woven cotton fabric. Color black. V neck with white trimming around sleeves, collar and waist, as illustrated. White buttons down front. Knitted underpiece with each suit. Sizes, 32 to 50 inches bust measure. **State size.** Shipping weight, 1¼ pounds.

No. 6L7252 Black. Price $2.80

Juvenile One-Piece Suit. Sweater stitch. Half wool, half cotton. Sizes, 22, 24, 26 and 28 inches breast measure. **State breast measure.** Intended for youngsters up to about five years of age. Shipping weight, 1 pound.

No. 6L7242 **Oxford gray, white trim.** Price..................95c

No. 6L7243 **Navy blue, red trim.** Price................$1.10

Same style as above, all cotton. Oxford gray, blue trim.

No. 6L7241 Price.......63c

Boys' One-Piece Knitted Suit. Half wool, half cotton. Sizes, 26 to 34 inches breast measure. **State size.** Shipping weight, 12 ounces.

No 6L7235 **Oxford gray with white trim.** Price..........$1.96

No. 6L7233 **Maroon with gold trim.** Price...............$1.93

Boys' Medium Weight Cotton Suit. Style as above. Black with white trim. Sizes, 26 to 34 inches breast measure. **State size.** Shipping weight, 12 ounces.

No. 6L7232 Price........65c

Women's One-Piece Close Fitting Knitted Underpiece. Shoulder to knee length, also worn for outdoor swimming and as a tank suit. Color, black only. Made of approximately half cotton and half wool. Sizes, 30 to 44 inches bust measure. **State size wanted.** Shipping weight, 14 ounces.

No. 6L7201 Price.......................................$2.00

Girls' Bathing Suit. Good quality closely woven cotton fabric. Slipover model with belt. Knitted underpiece with each suit. Navy blue with white and red trim. Comes in ages 8 to 16 years. **State age.** Shipping weight, 1 pound.

No. 6L7264

Price $2.55

Men's All Wool Two-Piece Suits. Round neck. Trimmed around armholes and bottom of suit. Sizes, 30 to 44 inches breast measure. **State size.** Shipping weight, 1½ pounds.

No. 6L7236 **Navy blue, white trim.** Price......$3.25

No. 6L7237 **Dark Oxford gray, red trim.** Price...$3.22

Good Weight Cotton Two-Piece Suit. Same style as above. Black with white trim. Sizes, 32 to 46 inches breast measure. **State size.** Shipping weight, 12 ounces.

No. 6L7229 Price.$1.55

Men's Dress Shoes

No. 15N4113 The Pair, $4.95
Dark Brown Calfskin Lace—Invisible Eyelets—Low Heel—Medium Heavy Single Sole—Goodyear Welt—Searsmade.
Sizes, 5 to 11. Wide widths. *Shipping wt., 2⅝ lbs.*

No. 15N4114 The Pair, $3.95
Gunmetal Finish Side Leather Lace—Dull Leather Top—Invisible Eyelets—Low Heel—Medium Heavy Single Sole—Goodyear Welt—Searsmade.
Sizes, 5 to 11. Wide widths. *Shipping wt., 2⅝ lbs.*

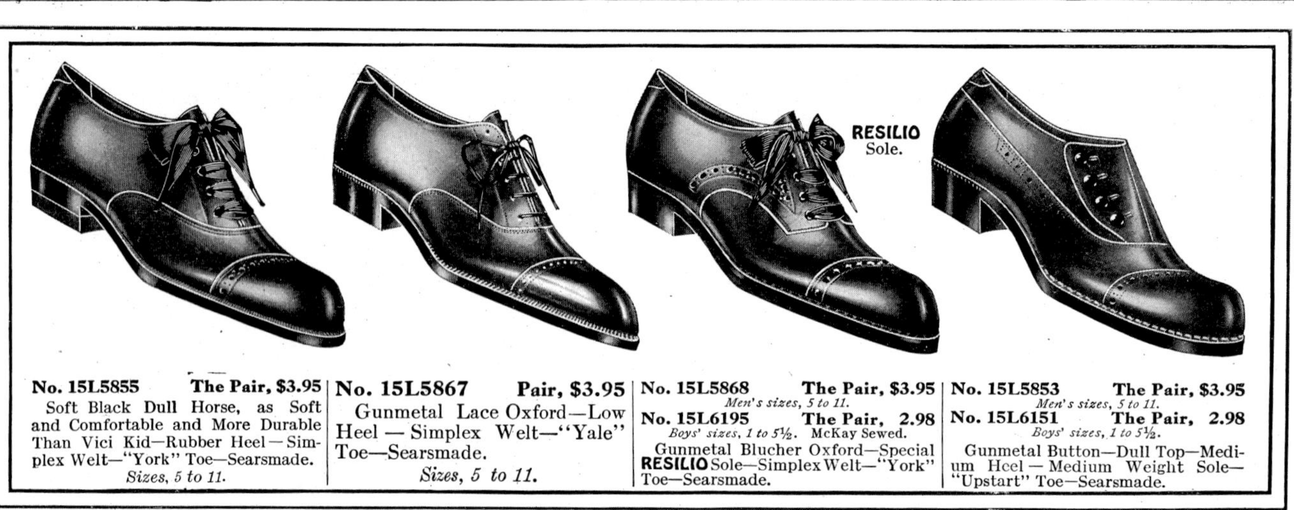

No. 15L5855 The Pair, $3.95
Soft Black Dull Horse, as Soft and Comfortable and More Durable Than Vici Kid—Rubber Heel—Simplex Welt—"York" Toe—Searsmade.
Sizes, 5 to 11.

No. 15L5867 Pair, $3.95
Gunmetal Lace Oxford—Low Heel — Simplex Welt—"Yale" Toe—Searsmade.
Sizes, 5 to 11.

No. 15L5868 The Pair, $3.95
Men's sizes, 5 to 11.
No. 15L6195 The Pair, 2.98
Boys' sizes, 1 to 5½. McKay Sewed.
Gunmetal Blucher Oxford—Special RESILIO Sole—Simplex Welt—"York" Toe—Searsmade.

No. 15L5853 The Pair, $3.95
Men's sizes, 5 to 11.
No. 15L6151 The Pair, 2.98
Boys' sizes, 1 to 5½.
Gunmetal Button—Dull Top—Medium Heel — Medium Weight Sole—"Upstart" Toe—Searsmade.

Seasonable White Shoes for Men

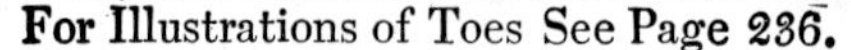

For Illustrations of Toes See Page 236.

When Ordering Shoes Use Size Chart, Page 237.

No. 15L5711 The Pair, $2.95
Men's White Canvas Lace Oxford—Very Durable and Comfortable—Low Heel—Medium Weight Leather Sole—Goodyear Welt—"Yale" Toe.
Sizes, 5 to 11.

No.15L4343 White The Pair, $2.19
No.15L4344 Palm Beach The Pair, 2.19
Men's Canvas Blucher Shoe—A Very Stylish and Cool Shoe for Summer Wear — Medium Weight Leather Sole—Low Heel—"York" Toe.
Sizes, 5 to 11.

No. 15L5710 The Pair, $2.95
Men's White Canvas Lace Oxford—Very Durable and Stylish—Goodyear Welt—White RESILIO Sole and Heel—"Yale" Toe.
Sizes, 5 to 11.

Women's Low Shoes
These Oxfords are popular for late fall wear with wool Stockings
No. The Pair
15N2700 Pat. Leather. $4.45
15N2701 Dull Kid. 4.45
15N2702 Brown Kid. 4.45
15N2703 White Cabaretta. 4.45
Nobby Lace Oxfords for Those Who Want a Neat, Dressy Shoe—Covered Wood French Heel—Leather Top Lift—Aluminum Heel Plate—Flexible McKay Sewed Sole—Very Stylish for Late Summer and Fall Wear.
Sizes, 2½ to 8. Wide widths. Shipping wt., 1½ lbs.
No. The Pair
15N3525 Pat. Leather. $3.75
15N3535 Gunmetal Finish Side Leather. 3.75
15N3536 White Nu-Buck Side Leather. 3.75
15N3545 Brown Side Leather. 3.75
Four Very Smart and Stylish Lace Oxfords With Popular Perforated Wing Tip Effect—Military Heel and Flexible McKay Sewed Sole.
Sizes, 2½ to 8. Wide widths. Shipping wt., 1⅞ lbs.
No. 15N3520 Gunmetal Finish Side Leather. The Pair, $3.65
No. 15N3510 Patent Leather. The Pair, $3.65
Pump—Wing Tip Effect—Military Heel—Flexible McKay Sewed Sole. Sizes, 2½ to 8. Wide widths. Shipping wt., 1½ lbs.
No. 15N3540 White Nu-Buck Side Leather. The Pair, $3.65
No. 15N3530 Brown Side Leather. The Pair, $3.65
Pump—Wing Tip Effect—Military Heel—Flexible McKay Sewed Sole.
Sizes, 2½ to 8. Wide widths. Shipping wt., 1½ lbs.
No. 15N2671 Black. The Pair, $2.25
No. 15N2670 White. The Pair, $2.25
Satin Pump for Afternoon and Evening Wear—Satin Covered Wood French Heel—Leather Top Lift—Flexible Turned Sole. Sizes, 2½ to 8. Wide widths. Shipping wt., 1½ lbs.
No. 15N2673 Black. The Pair, $2.25
No. 15N2672 White. The Pair, 2.25
Satin Ankle Strap Sandal—Satin Covered Wood Military Heel—Leather Top Lift—Flexible Turned Sole.
Sizes, 2½ to 8. Wide widths. Shipping wt., 1½ lbs.
See Page 245 for Size Chart
Unless otherwise specified, the shoes on this page are made with heels having a fiber board base (the part next to the sole). The wearing surface of the heel consists of from two to three lifts of leather, according to the grade of the shoe. These heels are guaranteed to give thoroughly satisfactory wear.
No. 15N3803 Women's sizes, 2½ to 6. The Pair, $2.75
No. 15N7609 Misses' sizes, 12 to 2. The Pair, $2.00
15N7610 Children's sizes, 8 to 11½. Pair, $1.75
15N8546 Infants' spring heel sizes, 5 to 8. 1.25
Patent Leather Ankle Strap Sandal—Low Heel—McKay Sewed Sole. Wide widths. Shpg. wt., 2 lbs.
No. 15N2661 Dull Kid. Pair, $3.95
No. 15N2660 Patent Leather. Pair, $3.95
Pump—Imitation Wing Tip — Covered Wood French Heel—Leather Top Lift—Aluminum Heel Plate—Flexible McKay Sewed Sole. Sizes, 2½ to 8. Wide widths. Shipping wt., 1½ lbs.
No. 15N3800 The Pair, $2.75 Women's sizes, 2½ to 8.
No. 15N7601 Pair, $2.00 Misses' sizes, 12 to 2.
No. 15N7602 Pair, $1.75 Children's sizes, 8 to 11½.
Patent Leather Two-Strap Sandal—McKay Sewed Sole—Low Heel. Wide widths. Shipping wt., 2 lbs.

Men's Hats
MEN'S HAT AND CAP SIZES, 6¾ to 7¾
BOYS' HAT AND CAP SIZES, 6⅜ to 7⅛
Hat Sizes — Measurements Around Head, Inches
6 19
6⅛ 19⅜
6¼ 19¾
6⅜ 20¼
6½ 20¾
6⅝ 21
6¾ 21½
6⅞ 21⅝
Hat Sizes — Measurements Around Head, Inches
7 ....22¼
7⅛ 22½
7¼ 23
7⅜ 23⅜
7½ 23¾
7⅝ 24
7¾ 24½
TO MEASURE FOR HAT SIZE. When you order measure your head as above illustrated and send us either this measurement in inches or compare the number of inches your head measures with this scale of hat sizes and send us the hat size you wear.
$3.15 EACH
93T6197—Black.
93T6198—Brown.
93T6199—Gray.
Pencil Curl Fedora.
The crown is 5¾ inches high. Pencil curl bound brim, 2¼ inches wide. Sizes, 6¾ to 7½. Be sure to mention size wanted. Shipping weight, 2¼ pounds.
$3.95 EACH
93T6230—Black.
93T6231—Gray.
A Nobby Style.
We could not offer a neater and more attractive hat. The crown is 6 inches high. Bound edge brim, 2¾ inches wide. Sizes, 6¾ to 7½. State size desired. Shipping weight, 2 lbs. 5 oz.
$3.00 EACH
93T6119—Navy blue.
93T6120—Gray.
93T6121—Black.
Popular Alpine Style.
This can be worn in several shapes. Illustrations show popular ways of wearing this hat. The crown is 6 inches high. Stitched edge brim, 2¾ inches wide. Sizes, 6¾ to 7½. State size wanted. Shpg. wt., 2 pounds 3 ounces.
$2.89 EACH
93T6104—Black.
93T6105—Brown.
Fedora or Tourist Style.
The crown is 6 inches high. Raw edge brim, 2⅝ inches wide. Illustrations show popular ways of wearing this hat. Sizes, 6¾ to 7½. Be sure to mention size desired. Shipping weight, 2¼ pounds.
$1.25 EACH
93T4850—Gray mixture.
93T4851—Brown mixture.
Alpine Style.
Made of an assortment of wool and cotton mixed cloths in various patterns. Stitched brim and leather sweatband. Good quality cloth lining. Sizes, 6¾ to 7½. State size desired. Shipping weight, 1 pound 5 ounces.
$1.89 EACH
93T4845—Brown mixture.
93T4846—Gray mixture.
Stitched Alpine or Tourist Style.
Attractive and stylish cloth hat. Made from fine quality wool and cotton mixed tweeds. Stitched throughout. Highly lustrous twill lining and sweatband. Sizes, 6¾ to 7½. State size desired. Shipping weight, 1¼ pounds.
$2.98 EACH
93T6117—Gray.
93T6118—Brown.
93T6122—Black.
The Pan Brim Tourist.
One of our best styles that is becoming to men of all ages. The crown is 5⅛ inches high. Raw edge brim, 2¾ inches wide. Sizes, 6¾ to 7½. Be sure to mention size wanted. Shipping weight, 2⅛ lbs.
$4.95 EACH
93T6318—Black.
93T6319—Dark green.
93T6320—Brown.
An Ultra Fashionable Style.
Distinctive for style and quality. One of the season's newest shapes. The crown is 5¾ inches high. Bound edge brim, 2⅝ inches wide. Illustrations show popular ways of wearing this splendid hat. Sizes, 6¾ to 7¾. Do not fail to mention size desired. Shipping weight, 2¼ pounds.
$3.50 EACH
93T6244—Black.
93T6245—Nutria tan.
Graeco Style.
This style hat is generally worn by railroad men. The crown is 4¾ inches high. Raw edge brim, 2⅝ inches wide. Sizes, 6¾ to 7¾. State size desired. Shipping weight, 2 pounds 3 ounces.
$6.00 EACH
93T6304—Black.
93T6305—Nutria tan.
Roelofs Improved Columbia Style.
A well proportioned hat. The crown is 5¾ inches high. Raw edge brim, 3 inches wide. Sizes, 6¾ to 7¾. State size wanted. Shpg. wt., 2 lbs. 1 oz.
$3.95 EACH
93T6165—Gray.
93T6166—Black.
93T6167—Brown.
Fedora or Tourist.
The crown is 6 inches high. Bound edge brim, 2⅝ inches wide. Sizes, 6¾ to 7¾. State size desired. Shipping weight, 2⅛ pounds.

Conservative Serge Suits

$34.50
Blue Serge.

45T2578 Model 3
45T2579 Model 4

Two Splendid All Wool Suits, single or double breasted, semi-conservative and made to give long service. The man who wants a blue serge suit for business or dress will find satisfaction in either of these two numbers. Models 3 and 4 are illustrated on this page. The single breasted coat is the regular three-button style generally worn. The double breasted is a good semi-conservative model any man can wear with satisfaction. Average shipping wt., 5¾ pounds. **Give measurements.**

$18.75

45T2570 Model 1 **Blue Serge**

An Inexpensive Blue Serge Suit, made in Model 1 illustrated to the right. Material is 19 per cent wool, 81 per cent cotton. If you want to get a blue serge suit for a small amount of money this is the suit for you to buy. It will give unusual service. Average shipping weight, 5¼ pounds. **Give measurements.**

$28.50

45T2574 Model 2 **Blue Serge**
Sizes, 34 to 50.

A Semi-Conservative Navy Blue Serge Worsted Suit of good weight all wool material. Illustration of Model 2 above shows the style. A suit made in this model is always in style. At the low price asked it is an exceptional value, offering a great deal of real wear for your money. Average shipping weight, 5¼ lbs. **Give measurements.**

$23.45

45T2572 Model 1 **Blue Serge**
45T2573 Model 4 **Blue Serge**

All Wool Navy Blue Serge Suit. Can be furnished in single breasted Model 1, or double breasted Model 4. See illustrations on this page for style. This suit will give exceptional service for the price—$23.45. Average shipping weight, 5 pounds. **Give measurements.**

$31.50

45T2576 Model 2 **Black Serge**

A Pure Wool Black Serge Suit of good quality. Material is closely woven and will last a long time. For anyone wanting a black suit we believe this Model 2, illustrated above, will be most acceptable. It is a semi-conservative, three-button coat, well made. This suit will hold its shape. Average shipping weight, 5¼ lbs. **Give measurements.**

$38.50

45T2580 **Navy Blue Serge**
Model 3

Very Good Quality All Wool Blue Serge Suit, made in semi-conservative Model 3, illustrated above. The serge is finely woven, of medium weight and will give exceptionally long service and look well. To get a great deal of wear for every dollar you spend for clothes buy this suit. Average shpg. wt., 5¼ lbs. **Give measurements.**

SIZES All suits on this and the opposite page are furnished in sizes 34 to 44 inches breast measure, 30 to 42 inches waist measure and 30 to 36 inches inseam measure. 45T2596 and 45T2574 are furnished from 34 to 50 inches breast measure and 30 to 50 inches waist measure. See order blank in back of catalog for simple measuring instructions.

For Descriptions and Other Colors See Opposite Page
31T6480
Wool Jersey
$25.75
31T6485
Wool Tricotine
$42.50
31T6490
Satin Messaline
$23.95
31T6495
Georgette Crepe
$39.00

For sizes see page 60.

31T6555—Navy blue.
31T6556—Sand.
31T6557—Copenhagen blue.

EACH **$26.95**

FOR SMART STYLE AND SERVICEABLE MATERIAL you can choose no more satisfactory dress than this model of ALL WOOL JERSEY. Made in an attractive style, with square cut neck in front set off with pointed collar HAND embroidered in soft contrasting color. Back of waist is trimmed with jersey covered buttons and sleeves with fine tucks. Waist is lined with fine mull and the stylish tucked skirt has novel shaped patch pockets, HAND embroidered to match collar. Jersey covered buttons trim back of skirt from top of tucks to bottom, where skirt is slit. Fastens at left side and has skirt SWEEP of about 46 inches. Women's sizes only. **Give measurements.** Average shipping weight, 2¼ pounds.

31T6560—Navy blue.
31T6561—Black.

EACH **$29.50**

ARTISTIC HAND EMBROIDERY ADDS A DISTINCTIVE TOUCH to this straight line dress of ALL WOOL POPLIN. Waist, made with round neck in front outlined by self and contrasting color HAND embroidery, has embroidered collar in back. Small silk and poplin covered buttons trim waist front. Stitched cuffs of sleeves are faced with messaline and button trimmed. Fold down back of dress is button trimmed from neck part way down skirt, and waist is lined with Jap silk. Pretty slash pockets of skirt are HAND embroidered and lined with silk messaline. Double sash girdle, lined with messaline, has tassels. Fastens at left side and has skirt SWEEP of about 64 inches. Women's sizes only. **Give measurements.** Average shipping weight, 2 pounds.

31T6565—Taupe.
31T6566—Navy blue.
31T6567—Black.

EACH **$33.50**

AN EXCEPTIONALLY ATTRACTIVE BEADED SILK GEORGETTE CREPE DRESS. The beautiful jet and contrasting color beaded design on front and back of waist, on skirt tunic and outlining the round neck is most effective. Flared sleeves have fold of satin messaline, forming cuff effect, and the satin messaline girdle is finished with loop and streamers trimmed with ball shaped satin messaline buttons. Dress is seco (silk and cotton) lined throughout and has skirt SWEEP of about 53 inches. Moderately priced and splendid value. Women's sizcs only. **Give measurements.** Average shipping weight, 1¾ pounds.

Newest Styles in Winter Coats
17T2191
Lustone Velour
$26.75
17T2200
Beaver Fur Cloth
$15.98
17T2186
Velour Plush
$22.95
For Descriptions and Other Colors See Opposite Page
17T2196
All Wool Velour
$26.95

Women's Marmot and Opossum Sets

	Price
41T7400—Kolinsky Brown Set	**$34.50**
41T7405—Taupe Gray Set	**37.75**
41T7401—Kolinsky Brown Scarf	**19.25**
41T7406—Taupe Gray Scarf	**21.25**
41T7402—Kolinsky Brown Muff	**15.25**
41T7407—Taupe Gray Muff	**16.50**

Women's Marmot Fur Set in Kolinsky (dark) brown shade or taupe gray. Large fancy animal style scarf with silk lining. Ball style muff, silk lined, silk ruching. Average shipping weight of set, 3½ pounds; scarf, 1¾ pounds; muff, 2 pounds.

	Price
41T7390—Kolinsky Brown Set	**$47.75**
41T7395—Taupe Gray Set	**52.50**
41T7391—Kolinsky Brown Scarf	**28.00**
41T7396—Taupe Gray Scarf	**30.75**
41T7392—Kolinsky Brown Muff	**19.75**
41T7397—Taupe Gray Muff	**21.75**

Women's Marmot Fur Set, generally sold as Russian Mink, in Kolinsky (dark) brown shade or taupe gray. A glossy haired serviceable fur. Long stole with pockets. Can be worn as in illustration or as a throw. Stole silk lined. Canteen style muff, tail trimmings, silk lining with fancy ends. Average shipping weight of set, 3½ pounds; scarf, 1¾ pounds; muff, 2¼ pounds.

	Price
41T7410—Natural Opossum Set	**$66.00**
41T7415—Black Opossum Set	**66.00**
41T7411—Natural Opossum Scarf	**42.00**
41T7416—Black Opossum Scarf	**42.00**
41T7412—Natural Opossum Muff	**24.00**
41T7417—Black Opossum Muff	**24.00**

Women's High Grade Opossum Fur Set in natural or black shade. Long stole with silk lining and two pockets. Can be worn as in illustration or as a throw. Melon style muff with silk lining and silk ruching. Average shipping weight of set, 3½ pounds; scarf, 2 pounds; muff, 2 pounds.

Charming New Models

31T8660—Navy blue.
31T8661—Black.
EACH **$26.95**

A PLEASING MODEL DESIGNED IN ATTRACTIVE STYLE AND FASHIONED ON THE BECOMING STRAIGHT LINES that form one of the most distinctive features of the Fall and Winter suits. Made of ALL WOOL POPLIN, a good wearing and favorite suit material. The coat, in the season's new length, is lined with good quality silk and cotton TUSSAH. A dressy style touch is given by the overcollar of silk paon velvet. This suit is further enriched by fashionable tailor braid, which is used on large collar of self material, belt, sleeves and pockets. See small view for the pretty back this coat displays with rows of braid and buttons. Skirt is modeled on fashionable straight lines, has slash pockets and is shirred in back under belt of self material. Average SWEEP, 66 inches. For sizes furnished see size paragraph on this page. **When ordering state measurements required.**

31T8670—Navy blue.
31T8671—Taupe gray.
31T8672—Black.
EACH **$57.50**

TRULY A HANDSOME AND DISTINGUISHED SUIT. The "choker" collar of Australian opossum and the elaborate embroidery on sleeves and lower sides of coat show this suit of ALL WOOL VELOUR to be one of the most approved styles of the season. This material is soft napped, dressy in appearance and of splendid wearing quality. The coat, with buckle trimmed belt, is lined with an excellent quality fancy figured SILK TAFFETA. Collar is richly faced and can be turned down and the coat fronts thrown back in lapel effect. Back has knife plait at each side below belt. Skirt has inverted pockets with pointed tabs. Shirred in back under detachable belt. Has a fashionable button trimmed slit extending a few inches above hem at left side. Average SWEEP, 60 inches. See size paragraph on this page. **State measurements.**

31T8665—Navy blue.
31T8666—Black.
EACH **$24.75**

GOOD GRADE MATERIAL AND LATE STYLE FEATURES make this suit a remarkable value at our price of $24.75. Serviceability is assured by the ALL WOOL DOUBLE TWISTED WARP SERGE we have used, a material which is always fashionable and wears well. Coat, in the proper Fall length, is lined with VENETIAN, a satin faced cotton fabric which will give good service. This suit has a vestee of fancy material in contrasting color, giving distinctive style, and is trimmed at bottom with rows of satin faced material. Collar of self material can be worn up to neck if desired. Further attractiveness is added by the rows of satin faced material in clever arrangement at sides of coat on pockets and on sleeves. Belt is in crossover style. See small view for trimming of buttons and satin faced material in back below belt. Neat tailored skirt is shirred at waist in back and finished with a loose button trimmed belt. Average SWEEP, 66 inches. For sizes furnished see size paragraph on this page. **When ordering be sure to state measurements required.**

31T8675—Navy blue.
31T8676—Gray.
31T8677—Brown.
EACH **$29.95**

A SKILLFULLY DESIGNED SUIT SHOWING NEW AND SMART STYLE IDEAS. The material, ALL WOOL BURELLA CLOTH, is an excellent weight suiting with slightly napped surface and will give splendid service. Notice the fashionable and becoming lines displayed in the coat in graduating length, with smart front points and becoming flare. Lined with silk and cotton TUSSAH. Collar and lapels are in one and can be buttoned up to neck if desired. Splendid tailoring shows to excellent advantage in the fine pin tucks at sides above belt and the slot seam effect below, forming hand opening to inverted pockets. The sleeves are also trimmed with slot seam effect and buttons. See small view for back with button trimmed slot seam above belt and soft folds below. The pretty skirt is shirred in the back under a detachable belt. Average SWEEP, 66 inches. You could hardly choose a suit that would give you better service. For sizes furnished see size paragraph on this page. **When ordering be sure to state measurements required.**

SIZES The Suits shown on this page can be furnished in **women's regular sizes only,** from 32 to 44 inches bust measure, proportionate waist measure and from 36 to 42 inches front length of skirt. **When ordering be sure to state chest, bust, waist and hip measures, also front length of skirt.** For simple measuring instructions see order blanks in back of catalog. Average shipping weight, 4 pounds.

Stylish Intermediate Dresses
31T6990
Peggy Cloth
$5.29
31T6970
Wool Serge
$15.48
31T6980
Silk Taffeta
$15.95
31T6965
Cotton Suiting
$3.98
31T6975
Cotton Poplin
$5.98
31T6985
Wool Mixed Serge
$5.98
31T6970—Navy blue. **31T6971**—Dark wine. EACH $15.48
A SERVICEABLE AND MOST ATTRACTIVE DRESS made of good quality ALL WOOL SERGE. The collar, cuffs, sash girdle and skirt pockets are trimmed with military braid and the waist front with row of select quality buttons. The yoke is of plaid silk and small pocket on right side of waist front is piped with same. The skirt, plaited both front and back, has extra full sweep. Closes invisibly in front. Intermediate sizes only, 12½, 14½ and 16½. **When ordering give size.** Average shipping weight, 2 pounds.
31T6975—Navy blue. **31T6976**—Copenhagen blue. **31T6977**—Wine. EACH $5.98
FOR THE GROWING GIRL this little one-piece frock of medium weight MERCERIZED COTTON POPLIN is unusually becoming. Collar and turnback cuffs are stitched with contrasting color thread and the waist front at each side below shoulders is smocked to match. The wide belt with metal buckle is of imitation patent leather. Attractive small slash pockets on tunic. The plaited skirt has wide sweep. Closes invisibly in front. Intermediate sizes, 12½, 14½ and 16½. **When ordering give size.** Average shipping weight, 1¾ pounds.
31T6985—Navy blue. **31T6986**—Wine. EACH $5.98
THIS SLIPOVER MIDDY STYLE DRESS is made of good wearing quality SERGE, about 50 per cent each of wool and cotton. The collar, cuffs and the girdle with sash are all of wool mixed broadcloth; collar, cuffs and sash ends trimmed with rows of narrow white braid, making a most pleasing effect. The shield in waist is ornamented with artificial silk eagle and waist closes at neck with artificial silk lacing. The small broadcloth piped pocket on left side of waist is an added feature. Skirt is full box plaited. Intermediate sizes, 12½, 14½ and 16½. **When ordering give size.** Average shipping weight, 2 pounds.
31T6980—Copenhagen blue. **31T6981**—Navy blue. EACH $15.95
Made of lustrous ALL SILK TAFFETA in a style appropriate for young girls. Rows of pin tucking on waist, sleeves and skirt are a charming feature. Collar in cowl effect in front and pointed in back is set off in front with a neat two-color ornament. Waist and skirt in front trimmed with row of small taffeta covered buttons as are the sleeves; wide belt set off with loop and sash in back. Fastens in back. Intermediate sizes, 12½, 14½ and 16½. **Give size.** Av. shpg. wt., 1½ lbs.
31T6990—Dark blue. EACH $5.29
SAILOR STYLE DRESS of good quality WASHABLE COTTON SUITING called peggy cloth. Collar and cuffs trimmed with rows of white braid, tie is of contrasting color mercerized cotton poplin. Plaits from yoke on each side of waist front extending below belt on skirt are trimmed with select quality pearl buttons and the belt with large buttons of the same kind. Plaited skirt trimmed with large pocket on each side has good full sweep. Fastens in front. Intermediate sizes, 12½, 14½ and 16½. **Give size.** Average shipping weight, 1¾ pounds.
31T6965—Tan, brown trimming. **31T6966**—Navy blue, Copenhagen trimming. EACH $3.98
WASH DRESS made of good quality COTTON SUITING resembling a heavy weight cotton linene. The collar and trimming on cuffs, belt and divided peplum effect are of cotton gabardine in harmonizing color; collar and cuffs set off with rows of white stitching. Fastens with pearl buttons on left shoulder, and belt buttons with same. Intermediate sizes, 12½, 14½ and 16½ only. **When ordering give size.** Average shipping weight, 1½ pounds.

This Season's Most Dainty Waists
27T4175
Silk Georgette Crepe
$10.50
27T4185
Silk Crepe de Chine
$6.50
27T4180
Silk Georgette Crepe
$8.50
27T4190
Silk Georgette Crepe
$6.95
27T4205
Silk Georgette Crepe
$5.95
27T4215
Silk Georgette Crepe
$7.50
27T4195
Silk Georgette Crepe
$7.95
For Descriptions and Other Colors see Opposite Page
27T4220
Silk Georgette Crepe
$10.95
27T4210
Silk Georgette Crepe
$6.95

31T3120
Beacon
$6.98
31T3100
Beacon.
$8.98
31T3140
Crepe de Chine
$14.98
31T3115
Beacon
$7.48
31T3130
Crepe
$3.98
31T3135
Fleeced Flannel
$3.68
31T3110
Beacon
Regular sizes
$4.98
Stout sizes
$6.98
For
Descriptions
and
Other Colors see
Opposite Page
31T3125
Beacon
$2.89
31T3105
Beacon
$9.98

Girls' Fur Sets for Ages 8 to 12 Years

41T7555 — Gray and White Tipped Set Price **$36.00**
41T7560 — Lucille (Medium Brown) Set **45.00**

Girls' Extra High Grade Fur Set made from natural gray and white tipped kit fox skins or from Lucille (medium brown) shade skins. Double furred scarf and animal canteen style muff. Muff silk lined. Average shipping weight of set, 2¼ pounds.

41T7570 — Blue Goat Set.......... Price **$10.50**
41T7575 — Brown Goat Set.......... **10.50**

Girls' Imported China Goat Set, the blue gray imitates wolf, the brown imitates bear. Long haired serviceable fur. Animal style scarf, pillow style muff. Set satin lined. Average shipping weight of set, 2¾ pounds.

41T7520 — Gray Genet Cat Set...... Price **$20.00**
41T7525— Black Spotted Genet Cat Set **20.00**

Girls' High Grade Fur Set in gray or black spotted Genet Cat. A short haired soft fur. Animal style scarf with silk lining and silk ruching. A ball style muff with silk lining. Average shipping weight of set, 2½ lbs.

41T7580—Taupe Nutria Fur Set..... Price **$43.00**

High Grade Taupe Nutria Fur Set (South American beaver). A short haired very soft fur, also very serviceable. Collarette style scarf and melon muff with ruching. Set silk lined. Average shipping weight of set, 2¼ pounds.

41T7510—Tan and Black Set.......... Price **$14.00**
41T7515 — Taupe Gray Set........... **14.00**

Girls' Imported Coney Fur Set with animal style scarf and melon muff. Set silk lined. Average shipping weight of set, 2½ pounds.

41T7545—White Set................ Price **$20.00**

Girls' White Iceland Fox Fur Set made from the long haired Thibet fur in imitation of white fox. Animal style scarf and ball style muff. Satin lined. Average shipping weight of set, 2 pounds.

41T7550—Natural Raccoon Set........ Price **$33.00**

Similar style to 41T7545, only made from the natural grayish brown raccoon skins. Silk lining. Average shipping weight of set, 2¼ pounds.

41T7530—Natural Gray Fox Set....... Price **$19.50**
41T7535 — Taupe Gray Fox Set....... **23.50**

Imported Fox Set in natural gray or taupe gray shade. Animal style scarf with silk lining and animal melon style muff. Muff has velveteen pocket and silk ruching. Average shipping weight of set, 2¾ pounds.

40T9254 **$14.75**
Boys' Knickerbocker Suit of extra fine weave all wool worsted navy blue serge. Guaranteed fast color. Made in the attractive waist seam style illustrated above, so popular this season. Back is made with two welt seams from shoulder to bottom of coat. Half belt with buttons in back. Lined with alpaca. **Full lined** pants cut over roomy patterns are made with button bottoms. **SIZES—10 to 18 years. State size.** Average shipping weight, 3½ pounds.

40T9946—Cap. **$1.45**
Cap to match Suit 40T9254. Made of all wool worsted blue serge in the popular one-piece top golf style. Full twill lined. Cloth lined inside pulldown band. **SIZES—6½, 6⅝, 6¾, 6⅞ and 7. State size.** Average shipping weight, 9 ounces.

40T9250 **Heavy Weight** **$12.75**
Boys' Knickerbocker Suit of extra heavy **all wool worsted** 13-ounce fast color navy blue serge. Made in the handsome convertible style illustrated at the right. Quickly changed from belted model to stylish waist seam effect by simply removing the belt. Back has two curved welt seams from shoulder to waistline. Extra long vent in back. Coat lined with cotton twill. **Full lined** knicker pants are well made, with button bottoms. This is an especially stylish suit and will look well on any boy. **SIZES — 9 to 17 years. State size.** Average shipping weight, 3½ pounds.

40T9944—Cap. **$1.25**
Boys' Eight Quarter Top Golf Style Cap to match Suit 40T9250. All wool worsted navy blue serge. Full twill lined. Cloth lined inside pulldown band. **SIZES—6½, 6⅝, 6¾, 6⅞ and 7. State size.** Average shipping weight, 9 ounces.

A Heavy Weight Serge Suit. 40T9250

40T9252 **$15.35**
Boys' Knickerbocker Suit. Made of extra fine weave all wool worsted navy blue serge. Guaranteed fast color. Style as illustrated above. Two-style double breasted coat may be changed from belted style to waist seam model by simply removing the belt. Yoke in back with two plaits which extend from yoke to bottom of coat. Coat lined with alpaca. **Full lined** pants are made with button bottoms. **SIZES—10 to 18 years. State size.** Average shipping weight, 3½ pounds.

40T9946—Cap. **$1.45**
One-Piece Top Golf Style Cap to match Suit 40T9252. Made of all wool worsted blue serge. Full twill lined. Cloth lined inside pulldown band. **SIZES—6½, 6⅝, 6¾, 6⅞ and 7. State size.** Average shipping weight, 9 ounces.

40T9248 **$11.50**
Boys' Knickerbocker Suit. Made of good quality all wool navy blue fast color serge in the popular style shown at the left. Removable belt. Coat lined with cotton twill. **Full lined** pants, cut over roomy patterns, have button bottoms. **SIZES—9 to 17 years. State size.** Average shipping weight, 3½ pounds.

40T9942—Cap. **98c**
Eight Quarter Top Golf Style Cap to match Suit 40T9248. Made of all wool blue serge. Full twill lined. Cloth lined inside pulldown band. **SIZES—6½, 6⅝, 6¾, 6⅞ and 7. State size.** Average shipping weight, 9 ounces.

Smart Spring Styles
31V9150
Misses All Wool
Poplin
31V9155
All Wool Serge
31V9160
Silk Taffeta
31V9165
All Wool Tricotine
For Prices,
Descriptions and
Other Colors
See Opposite Page

31V5070
Linene
31V5060
Voile
31V5055
Voile
For Prices, Descriptions and Other Colors See Opposite Page
31V5065
Silk Taffeta
31V5075
Gingham

Stylish Dresses
for Misses
and
Small Women
31V5320
Toile
Du Nord
Gingham
31V5325
Taffeta
31V5330
Organdy
31V5335
Linene
31V5340
Voile
31V5345
Voile
For Prices,
Descriptions and
Other Colors See
Opposite Page.

31V5485—Black.
31V5486—Navy blue.
31V5487—Brown.
EACH **$29.95**

ONE OF THE PARTICULAR FEATURES OF THIS MATERNITY DRESS, made of ALL SILK MESSALINE, is the fact that it can be used for all occasions, formal or general. The Russian blouse style hanging loose from shoulders, has soft plaited lace collar which is very becoming. Artificial silk cord girdle with handsome ornaments at ends finishes waistline. Bias folds trim bottom of sleeves and blouse. Top of underskirt is of lawn and is attached to lawn underwaist, as are the sleeves. Fastens at left side. Has adjustable elastic waistband and skirt SWEEP of about 60 inches. Sizes, 34 to 44 inches bust measure. **Give measurements.** Average shipping weight, 1¾ pounds.

31V5490—Copenhagen blue.
31V5491—Reseda green.
EACH **$11.78**

VOILES ARE VERY POPULAR THIS SEASON and this maternity dress of COTTON VOILE is very trim looking. Front of waist is made with yoke on each side with fullness below, and is set off with small pearl buttons. Picot edged collar and turnback cuffs are of white organdy, and the wide belt can be tied in back or brought forward as shown in illustration. Overskirt is full and gives the lower skirt a narrow effect. Waist is lined with lawn and dress fastens at left side. Adjustable elastic waistband and skirt SWEEP of about 70 inches. Sizes, 34 to 44 inches bust measure. **Give measurements.** Average shipping weight, 1¾ pounds.

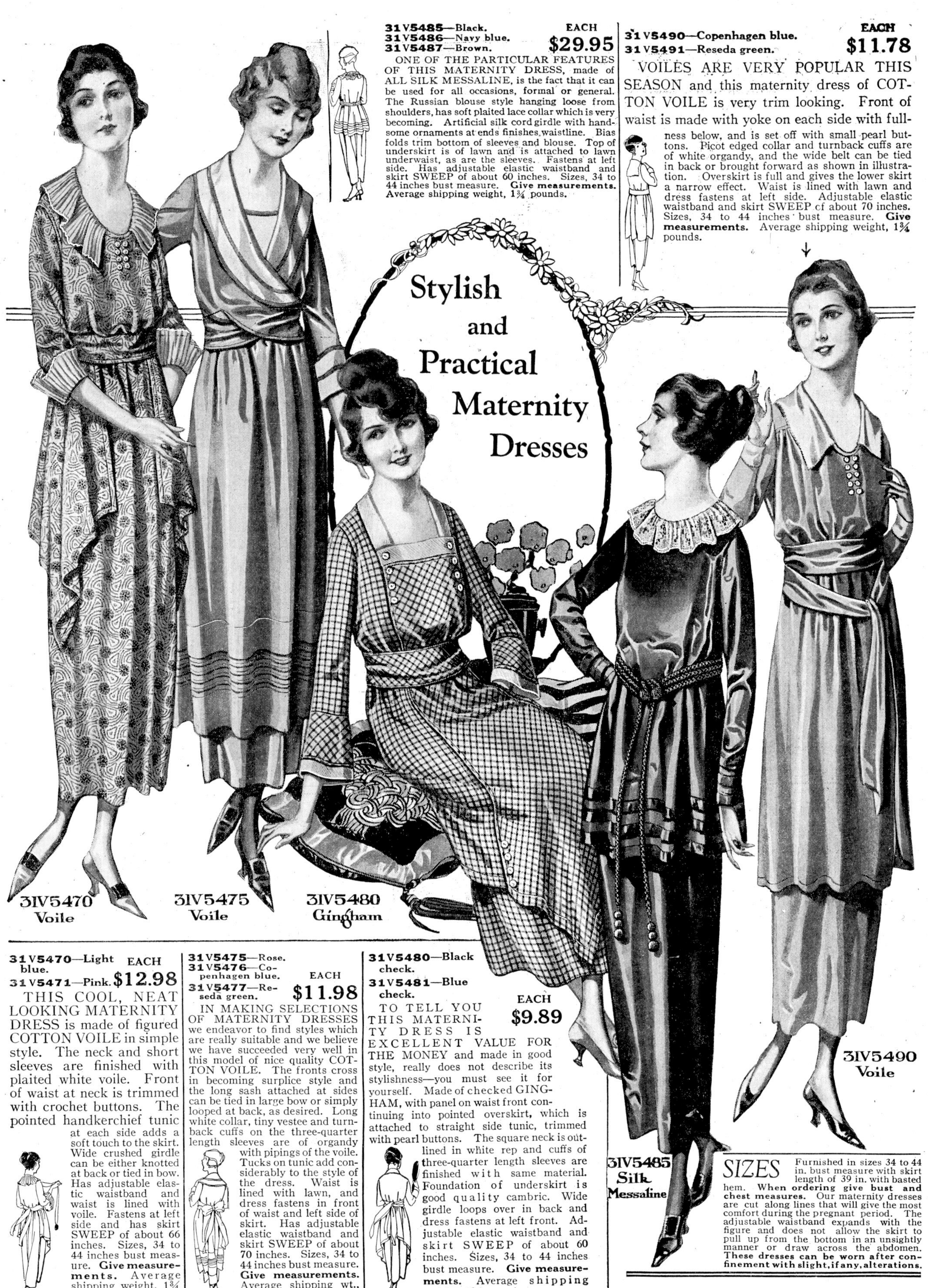

31V5470—Light blue.
31V5471—Pink.
EACH **$12.98**

THIS COOL, NEAT LOOKING MATERNITY DRESS is made of figured COTTON VOILE in simple style. The neck and short sleeves are finished with plaited white voile. Front of waist at neck is trimmed with crochet buttons. The pointed handkerchief tunic at each side adds a soft touch to the skirt. Wide crushed girdle can be either knotted at back or tied in bow. Has adjustable elastic waistband and waist is lined with voile. Fastens at left side and has skirt SWEEP of about 66 inches. Sizes, 34 to 44 inches bust measure. **Give measurements.** Average shipping weight, 1¾ pounds.

31V5475—Rose.
31V5476—Copenhagen blue.
31V5477—Reseda green.
EACH **$11.98**

IN MAKING SELECTIONS OF MATERNITY DRESSES we endeavor to find styles which are really suitable and we believe we have succeeded very well in this model of nice quality COTTON VOILE. The fronts cross in becoming surplice style and the long sash attached at sides can be tied in large bow or simply looped at back, as desired. Long white collar, tiny vestee and turnback cuffs on the three-quarter length sleeves are of organdy with pipings of the voile. Tucks on tunic add considerably to the style of the dress. Waist is lined with lawn, and dress fastens in front of waist and left side of skirt. Has adjustable elastic waistband and skirt SWEEP of about 70 inches. Sizes, 34 to 44 inches bust measure. **Give measurements.** Average shipping wt., 1¾ pounds.

31V5480—Black check.
31V5481—Blue check.
EACH **$9.89**

TO TELL YOU THIS MATERNITY DRESS IS EXCELLENT VALUE FOR THE MONEY and made in good style, really does not describe its stylishness—you must see it for yourself. Made of checked GINGHAM, with panel on waist front continuing into pointed overskirt, which is attached to straight side tunic, trimmed with pearl buttons. The square neck is outlined in white rep and cuffs of three-quarter length sleeves are finished with same material. Foundation of underskirt is good quality cambric. Wide girdle loops over in back and dress fastens at left front. Adjustable elastic waistband and skirt SWEEP of about 60 inches. Sizes, 34 to 44 inches bust measure. **Give measurements.** Average shipping weight, 1¾ pounds.

SIZES Furnished in sizes 34 to 44 in. bust measure with skirt length of 39 in. with basted hem. **When ordering give bust and chest measures.** Our maternity dresses are cut along lines that will give the most comfort during the pregnant period. The adjustable waistband expands with the figure and does not allow the skirt to pull up from the bottom in an unsightly manner or draw across the abdomen. **These dresses can be worn after confinement with slight, if any, alterations.**

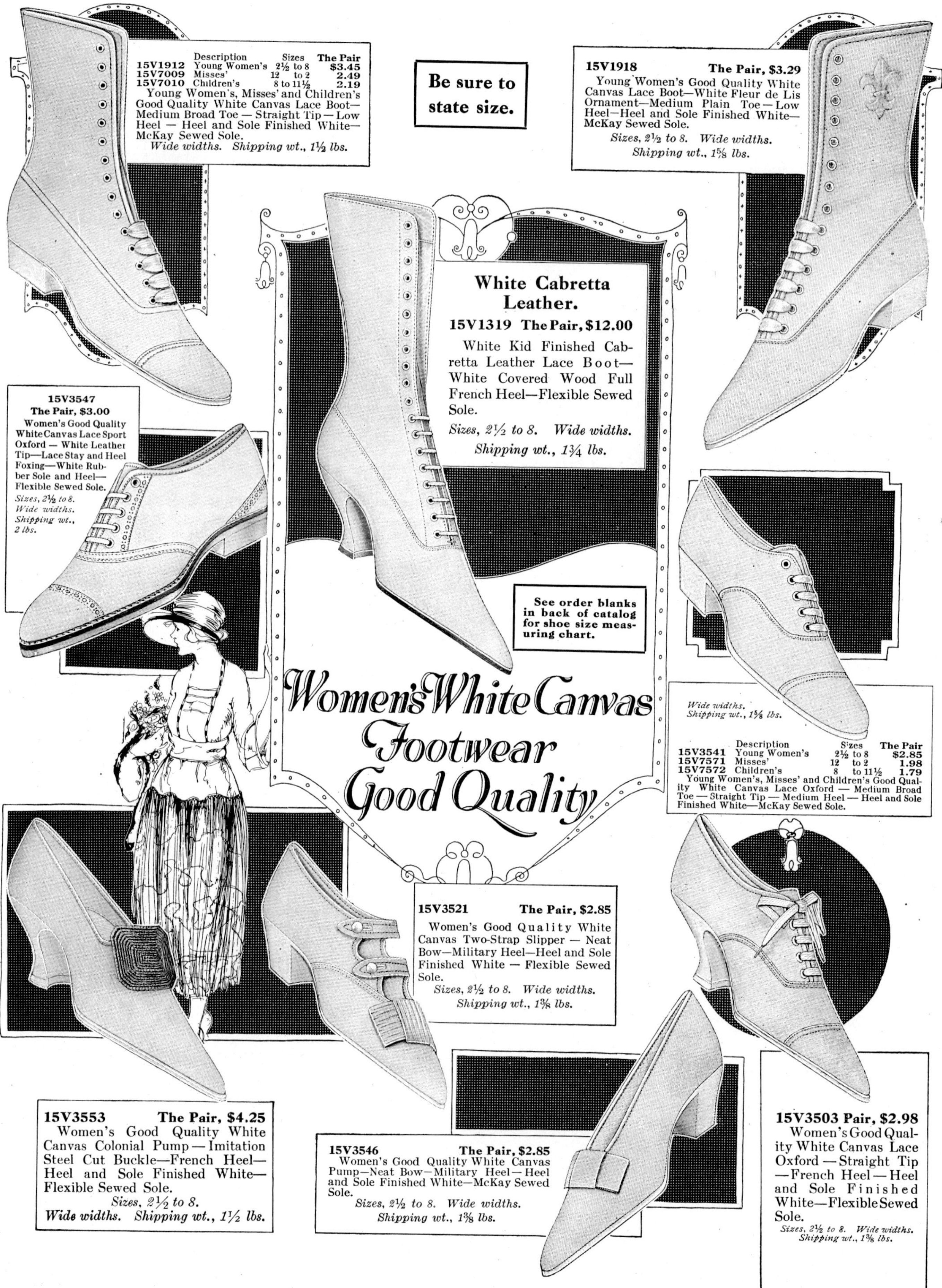
Description Sizes The Pair
15V1912 Young Women's 2½ to 8 $3.45
15V7009 Misses' 12 to 2 2.49
15V7010 Children's 8 to 11½ 2.19
Young Women's, Misses' and Children's Good Quality White Canvas Lace Boot—Medium Broad Toe — Straight Tip — Low Heel — Heel and Sole Finished White—McKay Sewed Sole.
Wide widths. Shipping wt., 1½ lbs.
Be sure to state size.
15V1918 The Pair, $3.29
Young Women's Good Quality White Canvas Lace Boot—White Fleur de Lis Ornament—Medium Plain Toe—Low Heel—Heel and Sole Finished White—McKay Sewed Sole.
Sizes, 2½ to 8. Wide widths.
Shipping wt., 1⅝ lbs.
White Cabretta Leather.
15V1319 The Pair, $12.00
White Kid Finished Cabretta Leather Lace Boot—White Covered Wood Full French Heel—Flexible Sewed Sole.
Sizes, 2½ to 8. Wide widths.
Shipping wt., 1¾ lbs.
15V3547
The Pair, $3.00
Women's Good Quality White Canvas Lace Sport Oxford — White Leather Tip—Lace Stay and Heel Foxing—White Rubber Sole and Heel—Flexible Sewed Sole.
Sizes, 2½ to 8.
Wide widths.
Shipping wt., 2 lbs.
See order blanks in back of catalog for shoe size measuring chart.
Women's White Canvas Footwear Good Quality
Wide widths.
Shipping wt., 1⅜ lbs.
Description Sizes The Pair
15V3541 Young Women's 2½ to 8 $2.85
15V7571 Misses' 12 to 2 1.98
15V7572 Children's 8 to 11½ 1.79
Young Women's, Misses' and Children's Good Quality White Canvas Lace Oxford — Medium Broad Toe — Straight Tip — Medium Heel — Heel and Sole Finished White—McKay Sewed Sole.
15V3521 The Pair, $2.85
Women's Good Quality White Canvas Two-Strap Slipper — Neat Bow—Military Heel—Heel and Sole Finished White — Flexible Sewed Sole.
Sizes, 2½ to 8. Wide widths.
Shipping wt., 1⅜ lbs.
15V3553 The Pair, $4.25
Women's Good Quality White Canvas Colonial Pump—Imitation Steel Cut Buckle—French Heel—Heel and Sole Finished White—Flexible Sewed Sole.
Sizes, 2½ to 8.
Wide widths. Shipping wt., 1½ lbs.
15V3546 The Pair, $2.85
Women's Good Quality White Canvas Pump—Neat Bow—Military Heel—Heel and Sole Finished White—McKay Sewed Sole.
Sizes, 2½ to 8. Wide widths.
Shipping wt., 1⅜ lbs.
15V3503 Pair, $2.98
Women's Good Quality White Canvas Lace Oxford —Straight Tip —French Heel—Heel and Sole Finished White—Flexible Sewed Sole.
Sizes, 2½ to 8. Wide widths.
Shipping wt., 1⅜ lbs.

Distinctive Millinery
Style Square Hats
78V9031
$6 95
78V9037
$6 75
78V9042
$6 98
78V9047
$5 75
78V9052
$4 75
78V9057
$5 85
78V9062
$4 95
78V9067
$4 95
78V9072
$5 48
These hats also furnished in other beautiful color combinations. Complete descriptions on opposite page.

Price, $1.48 Each
38V6107
Women's Fine Quality Nainsook Envelope Chemise. Front shirred and embroidered in dainty colors. Neck and arm openings have pink picot edge. Bottom neatly hemstitched. Sizes, 34 to 44 inches bust measure. State size. Shipping wt., 8 ounces.
Price, $1.98 Each
38V6106
Women's Fine Quality Nainsook Envelope Chemise. Camisole style. Yoke, front and back hemstitched. Has dainty colored embroidered designs in front. Trimmed with neat pattern lace edge. Sizes, 34 to 44 inches bust measure. State size. Shipping weight, 8 ounces.
Price, $1.48 Each
38V6104
Women's Nainsook Envelope Chemise. Front trimmed with embroidery and lace insertion. Neck, arm openings and bottom finished with neat lace edge. Has ribbon draw. Sizes, 34 to 44 inches bust measure. State size. Shipping weight, 8 ounces.
Price, $1.78 Each
38V6130
Women's Fine Quality Nainsook Envelope Chemise. Camisole style. Front neatly shirred and set in with dainty pattern lace insertion. Shoulder straps to match. Bottom neatly hemstitched. Has ribbon draw. Sizes, 34 to 44 inches bust measure. State size. Shipping weight, 8 ounces.
CHEMISES
See pages 306 and 307 for Extra Large Sizes in Undermuslins.
Price, $1.28 Each
38V6105
Women's Nainsook Envelope Chemise. Front trimmed with embroidery. Neck, arm openings and bottom finished with lace edge. Ribbon draw. Sizes, 34 to 44 inches bust measure. State size. Shipping weight, 8 oz.
Price, $1.98 Each
38V6123
Women's One-Piece Chemise and Bloomer Combination. Made of good quality nainsook and trimmed in front with embroidered panel set in with Valenciennes lace. Neck, arm openings and bottoms finished with Valenciennes lace. Has silk ribbon draw. Open crotch. Elastic at knees. Sizes, 34 to 44 inches bust measure. State size. Shipping weight, 8 ounces.
Price, $1.48 Each
38V6125—Pink.
38V6126—White.
Women's Good Quality Nainsook Envelope Chemise. Front hemstitched and embroidered in dainty colors. Neck, arm openings and bottom trimmed with neat lace edging. Ribbon draw. Sizes, 34 to 44 inches bust measure. State size. Shipping weight, 8 ounces.
Price, 98c Each
38V6124
Women's Nainsook Envelope Chemise. Front neatly shirred. Neck, arm openings and bottom trimmed with lace edge. Has ribbon draw. Sizes, 34 to 44 inches bust measure. State size. Shipping wt., 8 ounces.
Price, $1.89 Each
38V6108
Women's Good Quality Nainsook Envelope Chemise. Yoke, front and back trimmed with filet lace and insertion. Neatly shirred in front. Neck, arm openings and bottom finished with filet edge. Has ribbon draw. Sizes, 34 to 44 inches bust measure. State size. Shpg. wt., 8 oz.

We use only standard quality materials in our muslin underwear. See pages 306 and 307 for extra large sizes.

Price, 98c Each
38V6512
Schoolgirls' Good Quality Cambric Underwaist. Reinforced over shoulders and around waist. Neck and arm openings finished with a neat embroidery edge. Closes in back. Taped buttons. Has supporters. Ages, 7 to 14 years. **State age.** Shipping weight, 7 ounces.

Price, 78c Each
38V6513
Schoolgirls' Good Quality Cambric Underwaist, with Supporters. Taped buttons. Closes in back. A very serviceable garment. Ages, 7 to 14 years. **State age.** Shipping weight, 7 ounces.

Price, $1.68 Each
38V6538
Schoolgirls' Nainsook Combination Suit. Neck and bottoms trimmed with good quality embroidery. Buttons in back. Has drop seat. Ages, 7 to 16 years. **State age.** Shipping weight, 8 ounces.

Price, $1.79 Each
38V6539
Schoolgirls' Good Quality Nainsook Combination Suit. Buttons in back. Drop seat. Neck and arm openings finished with a lace edge. Bottoms have lace edged ruffle. Ribbon draw. Ages, 7 to 16 years. **State age.** Shipping weight, 10 oz.

Price, $1.79 Each
38V6520
Schoolgirls' Good Quality Nainsook Skirt on Waist. Has dainty flounce of lawn with Valenciennes lace insertion and edge. Buttons in back. Ages, 7 to 16 years. **State age.** Shipping weight, 10 ounces.

Price, $1.98 Each
38V6524
Schoolgirls' Nainsook Combination Waist and Bloomers. Opens in back. Drop seat. Trimmed at neck and bottoms with ribbon run embroidery insertion and edge. Ages, 7 to 16 years. **State age.** Shipping weight, 10 ounces.

Price, 98c Each
38V6566 Black.
38V6567 White.
Schoolgirls' Better Quality Sateen Bloomers. Elastic at knees. Ages, 7 to 16 years. **State age.** Shipping weight, 9 ounces.

GOOD QUALITY ALWAYS

Price, $1.98 Each
38V6514
Schoolgirls' Attractive Sleeping Garment. Made of good quality nainsook. Collar and cuffs of cross bar nainsook, trimmed with light blue binding. Buttons down front to crotch. Has drop seat. Ages, 7 to 16 years. **State age.** Average shipping weight, 14 oz.

Price, $1.85 Each
38V6521
Schoolgirls' Good Quality Nainsook Underskirt on Waist. Has flounce of pretty design embroidery. Waist buttons down back. Neck and arm openings neatly finished. Ages, 7 to 16 years. **State age.** Shipping weight, 8 ounces.

Price, 75c Each
38V6543—White.
Schoolgirls' Good Quality Cambric Bloomers. Have elastic at knees. Ages, 7 to 16 years. **State age.** Shipping weight, 6 ounces.

Price, 58c Each
38V6507
Schoolgirls' Cambric Underwaist. Reinforced over shoulders and at waist. Taped buttons. Buttons in back. Ages, 7 to 14 years. **State age.** Shipping weight, 4 ounces.

Price, 63c Each
38V6508
Schoolgirls' Good Quality Cambric Underwaist. Buttons in back. Taped buttons. Ages, 7 to 14 years. **State age.** Shipping weight, 4 ounces.

Price, 69c Each
38V6509
Schoolgirls' Good Quality Cambric Underwaist. Double shoulder pieces and sides. Reinforced around waist. Buttons in back. Taped buttons. Ages, 7 to 14 years. **State age.** Shipping weight, 4 ounces.

Price, 89c Each
38V6510
Schoolgirls' Embroidery Trimmed Underwaist. Made of good quality cambric. Buttons in back. Reinforced over shoulders and around waist. Taped buttons. Ages, 7 to 14 years. **State age.** Shipping weight, 4 ounces.

Price, 87c Each
38V6565—Black.
Schoolgirls' Sateen Bloomers. Elastic at knees. Ages, 7 to 16 years. **State age.** Shipping weight, 8 ounces.

Price, 89c Each
38V6561
Blue chambray.
Schoolgirls' Chambray Bloomers. Elastic at knees. Ages, 7 to 16 years. **State age.** Shipping weight, 8 oz.

Attractive Wash Dresses for the 2 to 6-Year Old Tots

Note size specification on pages 275 and 276.

29V7643—White.
Price, each......... **$2.25**
This is a Most Becoming Dress, yet the style is very simple. It is made of closely woven white cotton linene with a white lawn plaited frill on collar and turnback cuffs. This plaited frill is trimmed with gold color picot edge. Dress has short sleeves and looped belt. Ages, 2, 3, 4, 5 and 6 years. **State age.** Average shipping weight, 5 oz.

29V7650—White.
Price, each......... **$3.25**
Little Girls' Dress of dainty white dotted swiss. Valenciennes lace trimmed square collar and turnback cuffs. Attractively trimmed with combination blue and pink hand smocking at high waistline; wide sash can be tied in large bow at back. Short sleeves. A very sensible little garment for Spring and Summer "dress up" days. Comes in ages, 2, 3, 4, 5 and 6 years. **State age.** Average shipping weight, 5 ounces.

29V7648—White.
Price, each........ **$2.65**
A Very Attractive Party Dress of organdy. The waist is neatly trimmed with stitched down embroidery tabs which are edged with Valenciennes lace and caught with satin ribbon rosebud decorations. Tucked waist. The skirt is smartly trimmed with rows of lace. Satin ribbon girdle. Ages, 2, 3, 4, 5 and 6 years. **State age.** Average shipping weight, 6 ounces.

29V7651
White. Price.. **$3.68**
Dainty Dress of fine quality white lawn with machine embroidered organdy medallions on waist, belt and at bottom of skirt. Waist and skirt trimmed with neat Valenciennes lace and insertions. A "best" dress you will be proud to have your little girl wear and a big value at our price. Ages, 2, 3, 4, 5 and 6 years. **State age.** Average shipping weight, 5 ounces.

29V7640—White.
29V7641—Pink.
Price, each....... **$1.98**
Slip-Over Dress for warm days. Made of good weight cotton linene. The white dress has pink stitching on yoke, sleeves, belt and pockets. The pink dress has black stitching. Yokes are embroidered in harmonizing colors. Ages, 2, 3, 4, 5 and 6 years. **State age.** Av. shpg. wt., 5 oz.

29V7638—White.
Price, each............. **$1.68**
We offer here a Very Clever Tailored Dress for boys or girls. Made of fine quality white cotton linene in a belted Russian style. Neatly trimmed with blue gingham collar and cuffs and with all around detachable belt. Dress buttons down front. Long sleeves. You will be highly pleased with the value this dress represents. Ages, 1, 2 and 3 years. **State age.** Average shipping weight, 4 ounces.

29V7644—White, blue trim.
29V7645—Blue, pink trim.
Price, each........................ **$2.75**
A Smart Dress for your little girl. Made of good quality cotton poplin. Front of waist below button trimmed yoke is handsomely hand smocked with colored mercerized twist. Pocket trimmed skirt has plenty of fullness. Long sleeves with turnback cuffs. A garment that will prove a very satisfactory purchase. Ages, 2, 3, 4, 5 and 6 years. **State age.** Average shipping weight, 5 ounces.

29V7647—White.
Price, each........ **$2.35**
A Short-Sleeved, Valenciennes Lace Trimmed Organdy Party Dress. Waist trimmed with two clusters of tucks, embroidery revering and lace insertions. The dainty girdle is of satin ribbon with three silk rosebud decorations. Skirt also trimmed with two clusters of tucks and lace edge. A very attractive and sensible dress for the little miss. Ages, 2, 3, 4, 5 and 6 years. **State age.** Average shipping weight, 5 oz.

29V7642
White. Price.. **$2.45**
Here is a Neat Sailor Style Outdoor Dress. It is made of good quality closely woven cotton linene and is trimmed with blue gingham sailor collar and cuffs, with rows of white strapping. Embroidered design on white dickey. Mercerized cotton lacing. A very attractive dress. Ages, 2, 3, 4, 5 and 6 years. **State age.** Average shpg. weight, 6 ounces.

29V7649
White. Price.. **$2.98**
This simple, but stylish Dress is made of fine quality lawn. Front of waist smartly trimmed with graduated pin tucks, lace and embroidery insertions with lace edge. Bottom of skirt neatly trimmed with tucked embroidery revering, lace insertion and edge. Square neck and short sleeves are lace trimmed. Satin ribbon girdle trimmed with loops and ribbon rosebud. Ages, 2, 3, 4, 5 and 6 yrs. **State age.** Average shipping weight, 4 oz.

29V7639—White.
Price, each........ **$2.28**
One of our best sellers. A Very Reasonably Priced Dress that will prove a very attractive addition to your little girl's wardrobe. Made of white rep. Beautiful white embroidered design on front of waist looks like hand work. Dress buttons at shoulders and along top of sleeves. Machine embroidered scalloped neck and sleeves. Detachable belt. Ages, 2, 3, 4, 5 and 6 years. **State age.** Average shipping wt., 5 oz.

29V7646—White.
Price, each..................... **$1.79**
A Neat Dress for your little girl. Made of nice quality white lawn. Sleeves and square neck daintily edged with Valenciennes lace insertion and edge. Embroidery panel and clusters of pin tucks on front of waist. The dress is finished with an attractive satin ribbon rosette at machine hemstitched belt. Ages, 2, 3, 4, 5 and 6 years. **State age.** Average shipping weight, 5 ounces.

For Larger Girls' Dresses See Pages 54 to 59.

Leather and Corduroy Clothing

41V551—Men's Reversible Leather Coat. **$39.50**

Made of good quality tan sheep grain leather on one side and a heavy rubberized army khaki on the other. Double breasted style, with two slash pockets and all around belt. Can be worn either side out. Length, 34 in. **SIZES—34 to 46 inches chest measure. State chest measurement.** Average shpg. wt., 6½ lbs.

41V556—Men's Reversible Tan Leather and Golden Brown Corduroy Coat. **$35.00**

Otherwise same as above except corduroy side is not rubberized.

41V356—Coat.	**$15.75**
41V357—Riding Breeches.	**9.25**
41V358—Long Pants.	**7.25**

Material, good quality heavy weight olive drab narrow wale thickset corduroy. Norfolk style coat lined with moleskin cloth. Long pants have cuff bottoms, six pockets and welt seams. Riding breeches are shown on figure 486 and have double seat with lacing at calves. **SIZES—Coat, 34 to 46 inches chest measure; riding breeches, 30 to 42 inches waist measure; pants, 30 to 42 inches waist measure and 30 to 36 inches inseam. Give measurements.** See order blank between pages 390 and 391 for measuring instructions. Average shipping weight of coat, 4⅞ pounds; riding breeches, 2⅝ pounds; long pants, 2⅝ pounds.

41V470—Men's High Grade Leather Vest. **$15.75**

Outside material is a dark drab corduroy. Body lining and sleeves of tan leather. Has three front pockets faced with leather piping, yoke effect back with sewed on half belt. Length, 26 inches. **SIZES—34 to 46 inches chest measure. State chest measure.** Average shipping weight, 3¼ pounds.

41V486—Men's Glove Tan Leather Vest. **$22.50**

Made of a good quality sheep grain leather with sleeves of same material. Has a chamois cloth body lining, knit standing collar, knit sleeve wristlets and four set-in pockets. Average length, 27½ inches. **SIZES—34 to 46 inches chest measure. State chest measure.** Average shipping weight, 3⅛ pounds.

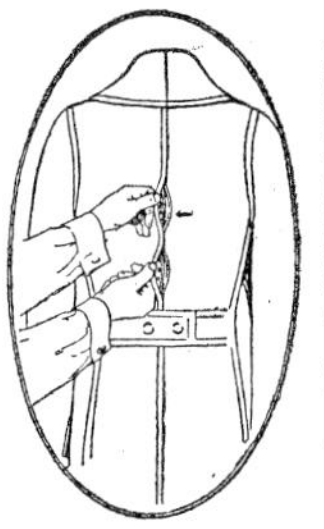

This small illustration shows how the ← center back seam is ventilated and also how the patented rubber rain guard assures double rain security.

Made Doubly Rainproof
Our Strict Manufacturing Standards assure Your Satisfaction. For Instance: All Seams are full Strapped and Cemented, Double Rain Security

SIZES—From 34 to 48 inches chest measure. **State actual chest and sleeve measures,** for coats are made several inches larger to allow for clothing worn underneath. You'll find a special clothing order blank on page 390B, also other order blanks in back of this catalog.

45V3320—Gray.
45V3321—Brown.
45V3322—Dark olive. **$11.75**

An excellent combination of Raincoat and Top Coat. Cloth is a cotton tweed with printed plaid cotton lining and rubber interlining. Four-button, single breasted model, illustrated above, has convertible collar, vegetable ivory buttons, double stitched edges, ventilated center back seam and large ventilation eyelets under arms. Piped pockets and facings. Length, 50 inches. All these features mean a great deal to you in service and comfort. Excellent value. **State chest and sleeve measures.** Average shipping weight, 4¼ lbs.

45V3323—Blue heather.
45V3324—Brown.
45V3325—Oxford gray. **$15.50**

A very dressy Top Coat and Raincoat combined. Made of wool mixed tweed, about one-third wool and two-thirds cotton, with printed plaid cotton back and an interlining of rubber. Single breasted style, illustrated at right, with convertible collar, all around belt, inside patch pockets with flap; closing with three buttons, ventilated center back seam, large ventilation eyelets under arms, vegetable ivory buttons, piped pockets and facings, double stitched edges. Length, 46 inches. **State chest and sleeve measures.** A very substantial value. Average shipping weight, 4½ pounds.

45V3326—Oxford gray.
45V3327—Gray green.
45V3328—Blue and brown heather. **$18.50**

A very stylish and serviceable Raincoat and Top Coat. Material is a fancy wool mixed tweed, about two-thirds wool and one-third cotton, with woven plaid cotton lining and rubber interlining. Stylish single breasted model, illustrated above, has a half belted back. A very popular style. Three buttons, two inside patch pockets with flaps, split sleeve effect, double stitched edges. piped facings and pockets. Length, 46 inches. **State chest and sleeve measures.** Average shipping weight, 5⅛ pounds.

45V3329—Gray.
45V3330—Tan. **$16**

This Fine Wool and Cotton Mixed Cassimere Raincoat can be furnished in ei'
or gray. Material is about 55 per cent wool and 45 per cent cotton. Coat h'
plaid cotton lining and an interlining of rubber. Single breasted model, illı
right, with convertible collar, two slash pockets, sleeve tabs, vegetable ivo
piped pockets and facings, double stitched edges, ventilated center back sea
ventilation eyelets under arms. This represents a fine raincoat value. L
ches. **State chest and sleeve measures.** Average shipping weight,

The original catalog page was torn here.

$1.89 EACH
93V4800—Green Mixture.
93V4801—Blue Mixture.
Men's One-Piece Top Golf Style Cap. Made of good quality wool and cotton mixed cloth in this season's popular shades. Lustrous cloth lining. Leather shield protector in front. Sizes, 6¾ to 7¾. State size desired. Shipping weight, 1 pound.
For Waterproof and Hunting Caps, See Pages 420 and 421.
$1.89 EACH
93V4810—Gray and Black Check.
Men's One-Piece Top Golf Style Cap. Made of a fine quality wool and cotton mixed shepherd cloth. Extremely stylish. Cloth lining and leatherette sweatband. Sizes, 6¾ to 7¾. State size desired. Shpg. wt., 1 pound.
Men's Cloth Hats and Caps
$1.25 EACH
93V4802 Blue.
93V4803—Brown.
Men's Eight-Quarter Top Golf Style Cap. Made of strong wearing rubberized waterproof cotton poplin cloth. Taped seams. Leather sweatband. Sizes, 6¾ to 7¾. State size desired. Shipping wt., 1 lb.
$1.39 EACH
93V4865—Olive Brown.
93V4866—Navy Blue.
Men's Crusher Style Hat. A durable rubberized waterproof cotton poplin cloth is used in making this hat. Has taped seams. Good quality cloth sweatband. Sizes, 6¾ to 7½. State size desired. Shipping weight, 1 pound.
$1.50 EACH
93V4853—Gray Mixture.
93V4854—Brown Mixture.
Men's Fedora or Alpine Style.
The hat is made of good quality cotton cloth. Stitched brim. Cloth lining. Leather sweatband. A bargain at our low price. Sizes, 6¾ to 7½. State size. Shipping weight, 1⅛ pounds.
$2.19 EACH
93V4825
Men's Four-Quarter Top Golf Style Cap. Made of an assortment of lustrous artificial silk and mercerized cotton cloths in a variety of patterns and shades. Cloth sweatband protected in front with leather shield. Good quality cloth lining. An ideal cap for Summer wear. Sizes, 6¾ to 7¾. State size desired. Shipping wt., 1 lb.
$2.00 EACH
93V4823—Assorted Mixtures.
93V4824—Navy Blue Serge.
Men's Eight-Quarter Top Golf Style Cap. A fancy wool and cotton mixed suiting and serge cloths used in making these caps. Taped seams. Leather sweatband. Sizes, 6¾ to 7¾. State size desired. Shipping weight, 1 pound.
$2.50 EACH
93V4828
Men's One-Piece Top Golf Style Cap. Made of a fine quality wool and cotton mixed suiting tweed in various shades. Silk faced cap lining. Leather shield protector in front. You surely will appreciate the style and quality of our best cap. Sizes, 6¾ to 7¾. State size desired. Shipping weight, 1 pound.
$1.50 EACH
93V4808—Gray Mixture.
93V4809—Brown Mixture.
Men's One-Piece Top Golf Style Cap. Made of splendid assortment of cotton cloths in a variety of patterns. Cloth lining. Sizes, 6¾ to 7¾. State size desired. Shipping weight, 1 pound.
$1.50 EACH
93V4857 Gray.
93V4858—Tan.
Men's Crusher Style.
Light Weight Silk and Cotton Poplin Crusher Hat. Has taped seams. Fine quality cloth sweatband. Just the thing for warm weather wear. Sizes, 6¾ to 7½. State size desired. Shpg. wt., 1 lb.
98c EACH
93V4862—White Duck.
Same style as above, unlined.
$2.00 EACH
93V4816
Men's Brassie Style Golf Cap. One of this season's latest models. Made of an assortment of fine quality cloths of various shades. Twill lining. Sizes, 6¾ to 7¾. State size desired. Shipping weight, 1 pound.
$1.75 EACH
93V4813—Plain Tan.
93V4814—Fancy Brown.
93V4815—Fancy Tan.
Men's Eight-Quarter Top Golf Style Cap. Made of a fine quality Palm Beach cloth. Very fashionable this season. Taped seams. Leatherette sweatband. Sizes, 6¾ to 7¾. State size desired. Shipping weight, 1 pound.
$2.50 EACH
93V4840
Men's Fedora or Alpine Style.
Fashionable and Stylish Stitched Cloth Hat. Made of exceptionally fine quality wool and cotton mixed suiting cloth of the latest shades and patterns. Good quality twill lining and sweatband, protected with leather shield in front. Sizes, 6¾ to 7½. State size desired. Shipping weight, 1¼ pounds.
$1.89 EACH
93V4812—Navy Blue.
Men's One-Piece Top Golf Style Cap. Made of a fine quality wool and cotton mixed serge. Good quality cloth lining. Leatherette sweatband. Sizes, 6¾ to 7¾. State size desired. Shipping weight, 1 pound.

For Men

$1.39 EACH **33V334—White background with colored stripe.** Sizes, 14½ to 18. **State size wanted.**

Men's Soft Shirt. Made of good quality percale shirting. White background with fancy colored stripes. Made coat style. Single cuffs. Has attached Hi-Band collar and one pocket. Trimmed with ocean shell pearl buttons. Shipping weight, 10 ounces.

$2.50 EACH **33V351** **Fancy stripe.** Sizes, 14 to 17. **State size.**

Men's Negligee Shirt. Made of good quality cotton poplin shirting with colored stripes, collarband style. Has new detachable double cuffs. Cuffs are attached with three small buttons and are readily detachable for work or for play. On or off in a jiffy. Cuffs are exactly alike on both sides; if soiled, can be folded over into another perfect French cuff, insuring longer life for the shirt and a saving on laundry bills. Shipping weight, 13 ounces.

$2.25 EACH **33V350** **Fancy white.** Sizes, 14 to 17. **State size.**

Men's Negligee Shirt. Made of good grade fancy white madras, collarband style. Has new detachable double cuffs. Cuffs are attached with three small buttons and are readily detachable for work or for play. On or off in a jiffy. Cuffs are exactly alike on both sides; if soiled, can be folded over into another perfect French cuff, insuring longer life for the shirt and a saving on laundry bills. Shipping weight, 13 ounces.

$1.59 EACH **33V387** **Cream-white.** Sizes, 14 to 18. **State size.**

Men's Negligee Shirt. Made of good quality percale shirting. Collarband style, with one detached collar and imitation soft double cuffs. Coat style. Trimmed with pearl buttons. Shipping weight, 10 ounces.

$2.50 EACH **33V352—Fancy stripes.** Sizes, 14 to 17. **State size.**

Men's Negligee Shirt. Made of good quality corded madras, colored stripes on white background. Collarband style. Has new detachable double cuffs. Cuffs are attached with three small buttons and are readily detachable for work or for play. On or off in a jiffy. Cuffs are exactly alike on both sides; if soiled, can be folded over into another perfect French cuff, insuring longer life for the shirt and a saving on laundry bills. Shipping weight, 13 oz.

$1.75 EACH **33V7—White with colored stripe.** Sizes, 14 to 17. **State size.**

Men's Outing Shirt. Made of very good quality percale shirting, white background with fancy colored stripes. Made with convertible or sport collar, coat style. Elbow length sleeves. Trimmed with first quality ocean shell pearl buttons. Shipping weight, 10 ounces.

$1.89 EACH **33V480—Cream-white.** Sizes, 14½ to 18. **State size.**

Men's Soft Shirt. Material in this shirt is cotton pongee, soft and closely woven and will give excellent service. Made with attached soft collar and cuffs. One pocket. Trimmed with pearl buttons. Shipping weight, 10 ounces.

$1.59 EACH **33V286—White with fancy colored stripe.** Sizes, 14 to 17. **State size.**

Men's Outing Shirt. Made of good grade percale. White background with colored stripes. Made with convertible or sport collar, coat style and one pocket. Full length sleeves with single soft cuffs. Pearl buttons. Shipping weight, 11 ounces.

$1.55 EACH **33V3—Plain white.** Sizes, 14 to 17 **State size.**

Men's Outing Shirt. Goo grade percale shirting in pla white. Convertible or spc collar. Coat style, with c pointed faced pocket. Elb length sleeves. Pearl butto Shipping weight, 10 ounces

The original catalog page was torn here.

All Wool Tricotine Full Silk Lined Coat. This is one of our very best styles and is sure to please the woman or miss desiring an extremely stylish and exclusive garment for Spring and Fall wear. The fabric is one of the very best materials used this season and will give remarkable wear and satisfaction. Fastens with large smoked pearl buttons and is attractively trimmed with black ivory buttons. The throw collar is one of the new features this season and is finished with artificial silk tassels. Slash pockets. Coat is 48 inches long and comes in sizes 34 to 46 inches bust measure, is full lined with a beautiful flowered silk lining. **State size when ordering.** Average shipping weight, 3¼ pounds.

17V5085—Navy blue.
17V5086—Black.
17V5087—Tan.
Price, each **$57.50**

Sport Coat for Spring and Fall Wear. The material used in this garment is called Polo cloth, one of the new fabrics for this season. It is all wool and has a soft, woolly surface. The cloth comes in the new Spring shades as listed below. Coat is 36 inches long with deep yoke lining of self material, belt all around and is attractively trimmed with large smoked pearl buttons. Comes in women's and misses' sizes, 34 to 46 inches bust measure. **Be sure to state size when ordering.** Average shipping weight, 3 pounds.

17V5088—Pekin blue.
17V5089—Tan.
Price, each **$27.50**

Women's and Misses' Spring and Fall Coat. One of the new and attractive models for this season's wear. Made of our best quality all wool poplin. Garment is 48 inches long and is half lined, including sleeves, with a durable wearing silk mixed fabric in a becoming pattern. Collar beautifully trimmed with rows of tailored pin tucks to match tucks on back. Large patch pockets, all around belt fastening at side front with large fancy buttons matching those trimming collar and back. Bust measure, 34 to 46 inches. **Be sure to state size.** Average shipping weight, 3¼ pounds.

17V5093—Navy blue.
17V5094—Black.
17V5095—Liberty blue.
Price, each **$35.95**

Attractive Model for Spring and Fall Wear. Made in the popular loose back style of our best quality all wool velour, an ideal fabric, soft and velvety in finish. Back has wide plait at each side trimmed with cloth covered buttons and artificial silk stitching at center. Belted fronts, fancy patch pockets trimmed with pin tucks and cloth covered buttons. Garment is 48 inches long and comes in sizes 34 to 46 inches bust measure and is half lined, including sleeves, with a silk mixed fabric in harmonizing color. **State size when ordering.** Average shipping weight, 3½ lbs.

17V5090—Golden brown.
17V5091—Pekin blue.
17V5092—Light tan.
Price, each **$29.95**

The original catalog page was torn here.